Examinations of Criminal Responsibility

Foundations in Mental Health Case Law

Richard I. Frederick

David F. Mrad

Richart L. DeMier

Professional Resource Press
Sarasota, FL

Published by
Professional Resource Press
(An Imprint of the Professional Resource Exchange, Inc.)
Post Office Box 15560
Sarasota, FL 34277-1560

Printed in the United States of America

Copyright © 2007
Professional Resource Exchange, Inc.

The copy editor for this book was Patricia Rockwood, the managing editor was Debbie Fink, the production coordinator was Laurie Girsch, and the cover designer was Stacey Sanders.

Library of Congress Cataloging-in-Publication Data

Frederick, Richard I., 1958-
    Examinations of criminal responsibility : foundations in mental health case law /
Richard I. Frederick, David F. Mrad, Richart L. DeMier.
        p. cm.
    Includes bibliographical references.
    ISBN-13: 978-1-56887-102-8
    ISBN-10: 1-56887-102-3
        1. Insanity--Jurisprudence--United States. 2. Criminal liability--United States. I.
Mrad, David F. II. DeMier, Richart L., 1962- III. Title.

KF9242.Z9.F74 2007
345.73'04--dc22

                                                                        2007061000

Table of Contents

Introduction to the Volume v

Section 1 – State and Federal Statutes in the United States Pertaining to Insanity 1

Introduction to Section 1 3

Section 2 – Roots of the Insanity Defense in the United States 7

Introduction to Section 2 9
Cases
    Rex v. Arnold 11
    Rex v. Hadfield 21
    Queen v. M'Naghten 35
    State v. Pike 41
    Parsons v. State 55
Summary 71

Section 3 – Insanity and the U.S. Constitution 73

Introduction to Section 3 75
Cases
    Powell v. Texas 79
    Davis v. United States 93
    Leland v. Oregon 99
    Finger v. Nevada 107
    Clark v. Arizona 125
Summary 147

Section 4 – The D.C. Experiment   149

Introduction to Section 4   151
Cases
   Durham v. United States   153
   McDonald v. United States   167
   United States v. Brawner   171
Summary   187

Section 5 – What Is "Wrongfulness"?   189

Introduction to Section 5   191
Cases
   United States v. Sullivan   193
   United States v. Segna   199
   United States v. Dubray   205
Summary   209

Section 6 – What to Do With
Insanity Acquittees?   211

Introduction to Section 6   213
Cases
   Lyles v. United States   215
   Jones v. United States   221
   Foucha v. Louisiana   231
Summary   259

Section 7 – Prosecuting the Mentally Ill   261

Introduction to Section 7   263
Cases
   Whalem v. United States   265
   Marble v. United States   269
   United States v. Edwards   277
Summary   283

Appendices   285

Appendix A: Legal Citations   287
Appendix B: Relevant Clauses and Amendments of
         the United States Constitution   291

Introduction to the Volume

This book concerns how courts in the United States have articulated issues related to the determination of criminal responsibility. More specifically, this book reviews how courts have struggled to articulate a process by which individuals should be considered not criminally responsible for their actions; this condition is commonly referred to as "insanity." The entire body of court opinions about criminal responsibility constitutes "insanity case law." In a previous book,[1] we examined competency to stand trial. The U.S. Supreme Court has ruled that *competency* is a constitutionally protected status, but the Supreme Court has resisted delineating constitutional protection for pleading *insanity*. Consequently, there exist a variety of standards to determine when a person is insane (and, thus, not criminally responsible), and some states now reject an insanity defense altogether. In our first section, we review the current construction of the determination of insanity in federal jurisdictions and identify some meaningful differences in some state jurisdictions.

Mental health professionals must marry clinical judgments with the legal standards that define insanity. In order to develop conclusions that are useful and understandable to the courts, clinicians must discern what courts consider to be the core issues of insanity. In essence, judicial guidelines concerning the nature and scope of insanity determine how the evaluation proceeds. As its *primary* focus, this book examines how the courts construe criminal responsibility. By exploring the thinking of courts in resolving procedural and substantive issues related to criminal responsibility, we intend to help clinicians identify those areas meriting

---

[1] Frederick, R. I., DeMier, R. L., & Towers, K. (2004). *Examinations of Competency to Stand Trial: Foundations in Mental Health Case Law.* Sarasota, FL: Professional Resource Press.

special attention when completing an examination of criminal responsibility. We will not discuss at length any particular procedures for clinical assessment of psychological characteristics associated with criminal responsibility.

The Supreme Court and all other appellate courts generally render opinions based on an analysis of the facts at hand and by searching for foundations in previous appellate decisions (i.e., finding precedents in case law). In determining whether to address an issue on appeal, the courts generally determine whether the issue is one of settled law (previously heard and decided) or whether a new application of law is required to address an inequity.

In this book, we will review case law pertaining to many facets of criminal responsibility. Section 1 provides an overview of current federal standards and representative state standards for criminal responsibility. Section 2 explores the roots of the insanity defense in ancient British law and early American law. Section 3 includes five cases addressing constitutional rights to an insanity defense. Section 4 reports three cases that reflect the struggles of the D.C. appellate courts in the 1950s and 1960s to capture the essence of insanity. In Section 5, we present cases that articulate thinking about what constitutes the "wrongfulness" that some insane individuals cannot appreciate. Section 6 reviews dispositional issues for insanity acquittees. Section 7 concerns the prosecution of the mentally ill and whether they should have the right to refuse an insanity defense.

For all but the early British cases, we present a *brief*, which is a concise summary of the case. A brief encapsulates the essential facts of the case, the issue before the court, the court's analysis, and the holding. Following the brief, we present Edited Excerpts of discussion by the court as an amplification of the reasons it has reached its holding.

Edited Excerpts

Edited Excerpts are intended to communicate the essentially important views of the court with respect to the issue of criminal responsibility. Many cases are appealed on more than one issue. We have removed the text of the case that is not directly relevant to the issue of criminal responsibility. Additionally, legal decisions often contain content and format that make them difficult to read. In our Edited Excerpts, we have liberally changed format and have excised text to improve readability. These changes are not generally evident. As an example, consider the following passage from *United States v. Brawner*:

> The landmark opinion was written by Judge [**9] Bazelon in Durham v.
> United States, 94 U.S. App. D.C. 228, 214 F.2d 862 (1954). Prior to Durham
> the law of the District of Columbia was established by United States v. Lee,
> 15 D.C. (4 Mackey) 489, 496 (1886) and Smith v. United States, 59 App.
> D.C. 144, 36 F.2d 548 (1929), which, taken together, stated a traditional test
> of insanity, in terms of right and wrong n2 and irresistible impulse. n3 Durham
> adopted the "product rule," pioneered in State v. Pike, 49 N.H. 399, 402 (1869-
> 1870), and exculpated from criminal responsibility those whose forbidden
> acts were the product of a mental disease or defect.

We modified this text to read:

> The landmark opinion was written by Judge Bazelon in *Durham v. United
> States*. Prior to *Durham* the law of the District of Columbia was established
> by *United States v. Lee* and *Smith v. United States*, which, taken together,
> stated a traditional test of insanity, in terms of right and wrong and irresistible
> impulse. *Durham* adopted the "product rule," pioneered in *State v. Pike* (1870),
> and exculpated from criminal responsibility those whose forbidden acts were
> the product of a mental disease or defect.

We often excise many pages of the original case law. Sometimes we
will change the text or insert words to improve readability. Additions and
changes to the text to improve readability are noted by brackets. Because
changes might not be evident, it is extremely important that the reader
understand that our Edited Excerpts cannot be cited to accurately reflect
what is in the original text of the decision. Readers who wish to cite the
original text of a case must obtain the text. Within our treatment of each
case, we have provided the proper citation to obtain the original text. A
list of full case citations is provided in Appendix A (pp. 287-290).

Jurisdictional Scope

In the United States, there are two types of controlling law: statutory
law and case law. Statutory law comprises laws enacted by state or federal
legislatures. For example, federal criminal law is codified in the U.S.
Code, Section 18. Other types of law (e.g., real estate law and bankruptcy
law) are also written into statute and enacted by legislatures. Statutory
law also includes rules of evidence and defines procedures to be followed
by the judiciary in the resolution of disputes.

Case law refers to the body of law promulgated by state and federal
judicial systems. When the meaning or appropriate application of law is
in dispute, individuals or groups appeal to higher courts for resolution.
The party who raises an issue is generally known as the petitioner or
appellant, and the party who counters is the respondent or appellee.

Most cases in this book originated at a state or federal trial court, and most cases involved issues appealed to higher courts. States and the federal government have sets of appellate courts which culminate in the highest court in the state or, in the federal system, in the United States Supreme Court. The names of appellate courts vary among jurisdictions. For example, most state systems culminate in a state Supreme Court. In contrast, New York's highest court is the Court of Appeals; lower New York courts are called Supreme Courts.

In the federal government, trial courts are called district courts. The United States and its territories are currently divided into 13 circuits. Decisions of a district court can be appealed to the appropriate Circuit Court of Appeals. Decisions of circuit courts can be appealed to the United States Supreme Court.

Most cases begin at the trial court level, and, as the result of appeals, the case is heard by courts of higher authority in ascending order. When there is an allegation that a state law conflicts with federal law, or when a party contends that a right bestowed by the United States Constitution has been violated, state cases can be appealed within the federal judiciary.

The resulting body of case law provides guidance regarding the interpretation and application of law. Decisions from case law may have either jurisdictional authority or persuasive authority. Jurisdictional authority means that the holding of the appellate court becomes law in the jurisdiction controlled by that court. For example, *United States v. Dubray* is a federal appellate decision issued by the Court of Appeals for the Eighth Circuit. Unless subsequently overturned by the United States Supreme Court, the ruling is controlling law in the Eighth Circuit.

In some cases, a court is presented with an issue or question that has not previously arisen in that jurisdiction. In such cases, a court might look to the opinion of another court for analysis or guidance. Arguments and decisions from another jurisdiction may establish persuasive authority for a particular position, but they are not binding. The United States Supreme Court has jurisdictional authority in all states and federal circuits. Many cases heard by the United States Supreme Court concern alleged violations of constitutional rights. Decisions of that court often serve to establish the minimum degree of rights afforded by the United States Constitution. No state can offer fewer rights than those specified by the Constitution (as interpreted by the United States Supreme Court). By establishing this minimum, however, the United States Supreme Court in no way bars states from offering *more* protection than that minimally required by the Constitution. In other words, when the United States Supreme Court establishes a minimum level of a constitutional right, states are free to offer more rights than required, but never less.

Most appellate decisions are made by panels of judges. In some cases, opinions are shared by all judges hearing the case, and the resulting opinion is a unanimous one. At other times, judges view aspects of the case differently, and the opinion is offered by the majority of judges who heard the case. The majority opinion is controlling law. In some cases, judges who agree with the majority decision offer a separate concurring opinion to more clearly voice their own views. Those who disagree with the majority sometimes write dissenting opinions that explain why they would have reached a different ruling. We have included excerpts from majority, concurring, and dissenting opinions. We believe that both the prevailing and dissenting opinions provide insight for the clinician about how courts think about psycholegal issues.

Most of the decisions presented in this book were heard in federal courts. District court decisions have standing only in the trial court, and circuit appellate decisions are controlling only in that circuit, although either may be cited for their persuasive authority. Decisions of the United States Supreme Court are binding in all jurisdictions, although states may offer more protections than those determined to be minimally required by the Constitution.

Section 1

State and Federal Statutes in the United States Pertaining to Insanity

Introduction to Section 1

Introduction to Section 1

When the insanity defense is raised, judges and juries are charged to consider the defendant's mental state at the time of a charged criminal act. Individuals often assume uniformity among laws concerning the insanity defense, but jurisdictions vary widely about what insanity is. What is recognized as law in one state may well be the subject of fierce debate in another. Historically, insanity has been conceptualized in a number of different and sometimes contradictory ways. Cases that helped shape the current status of insanity defenses are the subject of this work. This chapter provides a brief overview of current thinking regarding the insanity defense, as well as an introduction to some of the ideas that were the focus of the cases discussed herein. Language from some specific statutes will be offered for illustrative purposes. Although current statutes regarding the insanity defense vary, a brief discussion of the more common elements of those laws will provide a context for these landmark cases.

Statutes are often guided by case law. "Settled case law" refers to an area of law that has been well established. For example, in the area of mental health law, the issue of trial competency is settled. The U.S. Supreme Court has determined that the competency to proceed is a constitutional right; cases from that court and others have provided explicit guidance regarding competency doctrine. In contrast, the U.S. Supreme Court has not directly addressed the constitutionality of the insanity doctrine. Although some cases may be read to suggest that the Supreme Court endorses the defense, other cases (e.g., *Powell*) deliberately avoid recognizing the issue as a constitutional one. Consequently, statutory laws relating to insanity are "unsettled"; some states continue to modify their statutes regarding insanity. For example, in the case we present,

Finger v. Nevada, the State Supreme Court required the legislature to undo its elimination of the insanity defense.

Some elements of insanity standards are common. Most jurisdictions employ a "cognitive" test of insanity (one that relates only to whether defendants knew they were doing wrong); some jurisdictions add a "volitional" test (one that relates to whether defendants could stop themselves from doing what they knew was wrong). These cognitive and volitional "prongs" have long been established in case law, and key judicial thinking about these issues is reflected in the cases we review. States vary in their definition of the insanity defense. Although most states offer a formal insanity defense, typically called not guilty by reason of insanity, some states have abolished the defense; others have substituted a verdict of "guilty but mentally ill."

Insanity standards are concerned with mental state at the time of the offense conduct, and they obviously require that defendants have exhibited some type of mental impairment. For example, federal law (18 USC 17) dictates, "It is an affirmative defense to a prosecution under any Federal statute that, *at the time of the commission of the acts* constituting the offense, the defendant, *as a result of a severe mental disease or defect*, was unable to appreciate the nature and quality or the wrongfulness of his acts" [emphases added]. Note that federal law requires that the mental condition be "serious" in nature; many jurisdictions specifically preclude examiners from construing repetitive criminal activity as a form of mental illness.

Historically, the issue of the insanity defense is an emotional one. Public outcry in *M'Naghten's* case may have prompted Queen Victoria to demand English judges to establish a more stringent insanity test. Similarly, in the wake of John Hinckley's attempted assassination of President Reagan in 1981, Congress passed the Insanity Defense Reform Act (IDRA) in 1984. That legislation established, for the first time, a federal statutory insanity defense. The IDRA tightened the federal definition of insanity, limiting the issue to the cognitive prong. As will be observed in *Finger*, emotionally driven legislative changes in the insanity defense may nevertheless be unconstitutional, and the courts often serve as a moderating element in establishing what insanity is and how it is to be identified.

Despite the federal definition of insanity, states remain free to endorse or reject the insanity defense, unless, as in Nevada, the State Supreme Court finds that the modification or elimination of an insanity defense is unconstitutional. During the mid-1980s, many states revised their positions regarding the insanity defense. The most drastic changes involved some states which rejected the insanity defense outright. For example, Utah law provides for a determination that a criminal defendant has a mental illness, but that determination does not equate with insanity. In most states with such a scheme, the finding that a defendant is guilty but mentally ill mandates mental health treatment, but there is no abdication of responsibility for the offense conduct.

What struck us as we searched through cases was how consistent thinking has been about insanity for hundreds of years. There is a basic idea in all these cases that people ought not to be punished if their behavior results from mental disorder. The difficult problems have been to find a way to articulate this concept so that it does not lead to inconsistency, keeps up with current thinking about what mental disorder is, and, in American cases, conforms itself to understanding of constitutional protections for defendants.

Section 2

Roots of the Insanity Defense in the United States

Introduction to Section 2

Cases

    Rex v. Arnold

    Rex v. Hadfield

    Queen v. M'Naghten

    State v. Pike

    Parsons v. State

Summary

Introduction to Section 2

For centuries societies have struggled with how to be fair when holding individuals accountable for their behavior. Distinctions in "intent" became integrated into the law[1]; mental impairments that prevent intent became exculpatory. As understanding about mental impairment improved, courts were able to better articulate what was necessary to acquit behavior that would otherwise be considered criminal. In 17th century England, Sirs Edward Coke and Matthew Hale emphasized loss of memory and inability to understand as key elements of mental impairment, with a *total* loss of memory or understanding necessary to acquit defendants. Since the 18th century, English and American common law has been struggling with recurring issues of: whether the lack of understanding had to be complete or partial, permanent or temporary; which mental disorders constitute

---

[1] Consider, for example, this excerpt from *State v. Pike*: "Prior to the statute of 23, Henry 8th, all felonious homicides were of one sort. That statute made a distinction between homicides committed wilfully, 'of malice prepensed,' and those not so committed. The former are now designated by the term, 'murder,' the latter by 'manslaughter.' The practice has been in charging manslaughter to allege the act to have been done 'feloniously,' or 'wilfully and feloniously'; in charging murder to allege it to have been done 'feloniously, wilfully, and of his malice aforethought.'" The words "malice aforethought" long ago acquired in law a settled meaning somewhat different from their popular signification. In their legal sense, these words do not import an actual intention to kill the deceased. "Malice, although in its popular sense, it means hatred, ill-will, or hostility to another, yet, in its legal sense, has a very different meaning, perhaps well expressed by the words—'a wrong motive of any kind;' it signifies 'the wilful doing of an injurious act, without lawful excuse.' So 'malice aforethought' 'is not so properly spite or malevolence to the deceased in particular, as any evil design in general; the dictate of a wicked depraved and malignant heart; *un disposition a faire un male chose*; and it may be either *express* or *implied* in law.' Blackstone. It does not mean premeditated personal hatred or revenge against the person killed; but it means that kind of unlawful purpose, which, if persevered in, must produce mischief, such as if accompanied with those circumstances that show the heart to be perversely wicked, is adjudged to be proof of malice prepense."

mental impairment sufficient to acquit; who is capable of testifying about a defendant's mental state; when "delusions" constitute an excuse; and what role volition and control play in criminal responsibility.

To present examples of how judicial reasoning began to evolve, we present five cases from the 18th and 19th centuries. For the first two cases, *Rex v. Arnold* (1724) and *Rex v. Hadfield* (1800), we present excerpts from the trial transcripts. *Arnold* emphasizes the severity of impairment that was required to be excused from one's actions. Justice Tracy ruled that to be found insane the defendant had to suffer from more than "a frantic or idle humour" but needed to have a total absence of understanding like a "wild beast." Arnold, who shot at a member of the House of Lords, was required to stand alone "in the box" and depended primarily on the court to conduct his defense. Arnold was convicted because it was easily demonstrated that he was not a "wild beast" in his actions, which included planning and resolve. Hadfield, on the other hand, shot at the king, and his trial was before the House of Lords, where he was afforded active representation. *Hadfield* emphasizes the importance of delusions when a defendant could not possibly be considered a "wild beast." Although the same legal precedents and standards applied as in *Arnold*, Hadfield was acquitted primarily because of the eloquence and argument of his skilled defense attorney, Lord Erskine.

Most readers will be familiar with the next case, *Queen v. M'Naghten* (1843). We do not present the actual case, but the subsequent panel of inquiry before the House of Lords. We present the questions asked by Parliament of the most distinguished judges in England at the time. Their responses established the most famous and lasting standard of insanity, the *M'Naghten* "right-wrong" test, which is practically indistinguishable from the standards currently used in federal jurisdictions and many state courts in the United States.

Lastly, we present two state supreme court decisions: *State v. Pike*, an 1870 New Hampshire case, and *Parsons v. State*, an 1886 Alabama case. These cases both summarize the previous English and American common law and conclude that the *M'Naghten* rule is insufficient to determine whose behavior should be excused. *Pike* broadens the class of defendants who should be excused by emphasizing the causal link between their disorder and their criminal behavior. Finally, toward the end of the century, when the maturing field of medicine spoke more scientifically about mental disorder, *Parsons* introduced the importance of behavioral control (not just understanding) in determining who is responsible for their acts, establishing the "irresistible impulse" test.

Rex v. Arnold

16 How.St.Tr. 695 (1724)[1]

Rex v. Arnold is often referred to in discussions of insanity as the "wild beast case." Such references greatly gloss over the well-developed thinking regarding insanity which had been articulated well before this case was tried. Indeed, this case reflects careful distinctions between "ideocy" and "lunacy." The former denotes some permanent condition present since birth, and the latter refers to mental disorders that have different levels of manifestation at different times. This case, which has been here heavily redacted to reduce length, reveals a strict adherence to procedure, a careful analysis of evidence, and, ultimately, some sort of mitigation for the defendant, who, as voluminous evidence reveals, is obviously mentally ill, but not obviously insane. Even in face of powerful evidence of mental disorder, it is interesting to note persistent prosecutorial concern that the defendant may be feigning insanity.

Edited Excerpts[2]

The Trial of Edward Arnold, for Felony (in maliciously and wilfully shooting at, and wounding, the Right Hon. The Lord Onslow), at the Assizes held at Kingston upon Thames, in Surrey, March 20, 1724, before the Hon. Robert Tracy, esq., one of his Majesty's Justices of the Court of Common-Pleas.

Serj. Cheshire [Prosecutor]: Gentlemen, the fact this person hath been guilty of, was committed in this manner. On the 28th day of August last, [lord Onslow] had been out with gentlemen a hunting a fox-chase. Upon his returning down a lane in the king's highway, as will appear by the evidence, one Mr. Flutter was on my lord's left hand, and Mr. Fawks almost on his right, my lord in the middle; Mr. Flutter was then observing the prisoner at the bar coming up with his gun cock'd, and the muzzle towards him, asked him, what was the meaning of his coming that manner, with his muzzle of his gun, and the gun cock'd? The man makes no answer, goes on a pace or two, turns back, and takes aim, and shoots at this noble lord. The blast being so near, it struck him off his horse, wounded him in

---

[1] *Rex v. Arnold*, as reported in *A Complete Collection of State Trials and Proceedings for High Treason and Other Crimes and Misdemeanors From the Earliest Period to the Year 1783 With Notes and Other Illustrations*, compiled by T. B. Howell, Vol XVI (1816), p. 695.

[2] Readers are advised to quote only from the original published cases. See pages vi and vii.

a cruel manner; it proved (it pleased God) not mortal, and that because he could not buy such shot as he designed. My lord, it must naturally strike horror to those about him, who had no apprehension of this kind, to find the noble person thus shot. You will easily believe, they alighted to his assistance, they got him to the bank; he cry'd, The villain hath killed me; as well he might. Some of the company observing the fellow, he went on his way thirty or forty paces. They overtook him, and he resisted at first, but being brought to the noble lord, whom he had thus wounded, he makes no excuse; he seemed to struggle, according to the account I have in my brief; he seemed to be pale and livid, and to have great rancour, and aimed, with the musket, to do that that the shot had not done; but that, you might easily imagine, was prevented.

Gentlemen, one would wonder how a thing of this kind could enter into his head; but upon enquiry, this cruel, barbarous man hath meditated on this in his thought for some time; and now, after the facts are done, people are apt to make discoveries, and they knew further than they knew before. One would be apt to enquire, what could be the occasion of this? One would think that this noble lord had abused and injured this man to the last degree; so far from that, that this noble lord was unknown to the man; the man did not know him, but was forced to seek opportunities to know this noble lord, that he might seek this revenge. It is not properly revenge, because revenge is a return to an injury, but here was no injury done this man by my lord; my lord did not know him, nor, for aught I know, the man did not know my lord. But how then came this about? According to the tenor of his confession, it arose from the most wicked things. The noble lord is known to you all, he hath always appeared in the service of his country, an assertor of the liberties thereof, always endeavored to support the present government, in the House of Hanover, and is for the Protestant religion, against rebels, and for suppressing clubs, and places of meeting for people's wicked enterprizes; and, if that is a fault, I hope it is a fault most of you are guilty of, and will be guilty of; that you are for asserting liberties of your country and your religion, and for supporting the crown; and if this man is to be believed, the people had inspired him, brought him to a pitch of enthusiasm, I don't know what to call it, that my lord was an enemy to his country, and he thought he should do God and his country good service, by destroying him. Hence it is necessary to shew what evidence we have in open to you, and tell you what preparation (it comes out) that this fellow made; and it is very proper, because that perfectly throws aside any of the pretences whereby to throw a dust in your eyes, to extenuate the crime, that he had acted like a madman; he had a steady and resolute design, and used all proper means to effect it.

Gentlemen, though he acted like a wicked man, void of reason, you will have little reason to think he acted like a madman. Every man that so departs from reason, every wicked man may be said to be a madman, but I hope that shall not skreen all that so act, and free and exempt them from punishment.

My lord, the morning this happened he went to the house of one Smith, and had a quarter of a pound of powder, and a pound of shot; and the person directed them to No. 2 [not having No. 1, the larger shot he asked for], and gave him that shot which was a larger shot than he used to have [to shoot rabbits]. And it seems he is a marksman, as you will hear. It was always his business to aim at the head.

He had the powder and the shot; and that morning he was met by one, who hearing him discharge his gun, asked what he had been doing, what he had killed, as you will hear from one of the witnesses. Says he, I only did it to discharge my gun. Gentlemen, this is to show that the purpose was steady in him, and he would meet with no disappointment, but that his purposes might take effect. You know, a gun that hath been charged some time, and laid by, some wet or damp may happen to it to prevent its going off; in order to hinder that, he first discharges his gun, and then loads again, that he might be secure of its going off. And after he had thus prepared himself, the next thing was to be apprized which way my lord was gone, which way his dogs went. He was asked the question, "Are you going hunting?" He falls out into a rage, that my lord Onslow was an enemy to his country; and if he could meet him, he would shoot him. Within a few minutes afterwards, this noble lord with his company, as I have mentioned, came by. The man being thus prepared, discharged his gun, and executed his wicked design.

Excerpts From Testimony

Serj. Cheshire: Pray, will you tell my lord and the jury, whether you saw the prisoner at the bar that day my lord Onslow was shot?

Sturt: Before he shot my lord Onslow, he called at my house, and asked, if my lord's hounds were out a hunting? I told him I did not know; with that he stood humming and talking to himself, swearing and cursing, and damned my lord Onslow several times; and stood so for near a quarter of an hour. He swore and cursed. Says he, "God damn him, if I see him, I will shoot my lord Onslow."

Mr. Marsh: At this time, or any time before, did you take him for a madman.

Sturt: I did not take him for a sober man; I thought he was not right in his senses, he took to swearing so much. I have heard him swear; he would talk inwardly to himself, that I could not distinguish. We did not take him to be in his right senses. He was very often so, a great many of the neighbours know it.

Serj. Cheshire: I think, Sir, you have the honour of acting in the commission of the peace?

Allen: I have the trouble of it, I don't think it any honour.

Serj. Cheshire: Pray tell my lord and the jury what you know of the matter.

Allen: My lord, I live at Guilford, and hearing of this sad accident I went down to the house of correction, and examined him, and I found him in a very sullen mood, and I could get nothing out of him for a long time, and he could not look at me in the face. With a great deal of difficulty and persuasion, at last he expressed himself thus: "I don't trouble my lord Onslow, why do you trouble me?" And he had been pretty much teized and baited by the people, exclaiming against him, and coming into the prison to see such a monster. I thought the next day, after he had slept on it, he might be in a better temper, so I left him then, and went again the next day, but I did not find him so, for he run on with abundance of vehemence against my lord Onslow, and that he was the author of all the tumults, disturbances, and confusions, and wicked devices, that had happened in the country. He was very fond of those words, "wicked devices." I remember, some days after I had examined him, I met with two of his sisters, gentlewomen of very good reputation. They knew me first, and told me who they were. I being short-sighted could not recollect them, and in the night-time; and they represented to me, how miserably affected they were with this sad accident; and I said, "To be sure, it is very deplorable." They replied, "To be sure, my brother is mad; without he had been mad he would not have done so." "Why," says I, "that is the best turn you can give to it." His behavior is very extravagant, that I did say; so it was to be sure; what could I have said? Would you have had me tell the ladies what a rogue they had for their brother?

W. Arnold: The prisoner at the bar is my brother; I believe him to be a madman. In my father's time I have heard him curse him, and call him wicked and abominable names, without any provocation. I have heard him talk to himself, sometimes catch at his words, sometimes break out into passions of cursing and swearing, without any provocation. After this I have heard him to burst out into foolish laughter, and grin like any madman.

The 10th of July last he came to my house in Cannon-street; I finding of him there, I asked him what brought him to town? he said he could not tell. What business have you in town? It is not a proper place for you; you have not much money to spend. Besides, you may fall into bad company. Says he, I come to see you, I think; what else have I to do? says he, I can't be easy; my lord Onslow hath bewitched me; he plagues me day and night; I can't eat or drink; if I eat anything, it comes up. I am, says he, as if they pumped the breath out of my body.

Mary Arnold: I have seen the prisoner several times under great disorders, insomuch, that I took him for a man out of his sense at sundry times. I have been in the family eleven years; and to the best of my knowledge, I never heard him speak six sensible words together. And after the death of my father, he left the house. Before the death of my father, I went down every summer. I have seen him in great disorder. One fine day in the summer-time, his sister, his own sister, went into the garden; they kept a dairy, and the pots and the milk-pans were out, and he threw a stick and she reproved him. Pray don't says she, you'll break the milk-pans. He catches it up and threw it at my sister, and struck her with it about the temples; with that, she fell into a passion of tears, had like to have fainted away; we got water, and recovered her; but we were afraid that he had prejudiced her eyes, and that she would lose the sight of one of her eyes.

After the hurry and the suprize I went to him, and reproved him severely, and asked him, how he could do such a wicked thing to his own sister? He laughed at me, and I drew back, for fear he should do me a mischief. Then I did declare, that I believed he was at times, a madman. When he sat at the table, he would not sit like other people; he would put his fingers out, and had strange, surprising, antic ways, which I never did see in any person in my life before. And after the death of my father, he laid at an old woman's house that used to weed in the garden, and when she and I have talked about Edward, the old woman would say, Depend on it, Mr. Edward is a madman.

Serj. Cheshire: If you apprehended it to be so, would not every body be amazed, that nobody took care of this brother?

M. Arnold: It was hard to confine a poor creature; his father did not think it fit to do it. The last time I saw the prisoner, he came to my house; it was about a month before he committed this fact; and as I was sitting, he come in at the back-door, and in a great confusion. I had a niece with me, that had never seen him before; says I, Don't be frightened at him, he won't hurt you; but he talked very much, and look'd extremely wild, and he sat in a strange manner, and my maid reprimanded him for sitting so. Says I, Will you have a dish of tea? No, he would have some beer. I ordered them to mix it with the small-beer, for fear of making him worse. He talk'd extremely inwardly; says I, Speak out like a man, if I can answer you, I will. He told me he was bewitch'd; he talk'd to himself, and I heard him several times. Says I, who has bewitch'd you? He told me, The imps. I asked him what he meant by imps? He told me, they danced in his room all night, and he could not lie in his bed for them, and the devil did tempt him, and the imps stood by his bed. After some time, he would have another mug of drink, but I would not give it to him.

> *Says I, who has bewitch'd you? He told me, The imps danced in his room all night, and he could not lie in his bed for them, and the devil did tempt him, and the imps stood by his bed.*

Eleanor Arnold: I have seen him for nine hours together, talk nonsense, sometimes curse and swear without the least provocation. My lord, sometimes when we have gone out, he hath got the fuel, swept it up together, and made it up into a great fire, as if he would fire the house. I have seen him take live coals out of the wood fire, and throw them into his father's plate. He would often talk to himself several hours. Sometimes he would be in the most tormenting agonies. And I do declare that I have been in terrible frights, for fear he would do some murder.

Serj. Cheshire: If you apprehended your brother in these melancholy circumstances, why did you not take care of him?

E. Arnold: We applied to the minister of the parish, who was a very good man, Mr. Woodward, and desired that he would endeavour to reclaim him. He talked to him, but at last, he declared, he ought to be put into some mad-house.

Serj. Darnell: You did not think him so mad, as that it was necessary to confine him?

E. Arnold: I did, in my conscience, think so.

Serj. Darnell: And you did not confine him?

E. Arnold: It was not in my power.

Mary Martin: Mr. Edward Arnold was in my house, which people said was mad. Ned Arnold, mad Ned Arnold. People would give him that report; or crazy Ned Arnold. Ned Arnold was in my house, and accordingly called for a mug of beer. And please you, I keep a public house. When I fetched him a mug of beer, he sat himself down by the fire; he fell a swearing and cursing, and swore that my lord Onslow was in his belly. Says I, Ned, what makes you swear, and curse my lord Onslow so? It is pity, Ned, but my lord should know it. If he knew he was in your belly, he would quickly come out of it. Says I, If you will have, Ned, a chariot, you and I will go to him. Then we concluded what time to go, which was about eight or nine o'clock the next morning, to go to my lord Onslow's, and tell him he was in his belly. I only talked in a jokerly way. And it please you, my lord, he was there looking in his bosom. Says my daughter, about 18 or 19, not 20 years old, Can't you shit? Because he said he could not eat or drink. If I shit, says he, it won't stink like another man's turd. My lord, it is true.

Swetman: I took him to be a crazy sort of fellow, not to be in his senses at all times. He would say he was plagued with the bugs and bollies, that he could not rest a night; he was fain to stop his ears with the rug, or he could not sleep. In the morning sometimes he hath asked me whether I could rest? I told him, very well. I asked him, how he rested? Says he, I am

> *He would say he was plagued with the bugs and bollies, that he could not rest a night; he was fain to stop his ears with the rug, or he could not sleep.*

plagued with the bugs and bollies. He lodged at my house 15 months.

Solicitor for the Prisoner: My lord, I desire he may be asked, whether he did not hear him say any thing of my lord Onslow?

Swetman: He said, My lord Onslow had brought a hamper of wine into the kitchen, and sat it on the dresser over night, and when he rose in the morning, the wine was drank out of the hamper, and the empty bottles were upon the dresser. When I have come home, it is true, says he, my lord hath been frigetting here, and my lord keeps company with your wife, and your house is disturbed, they keep dancing above stairs, that I cannot rest. I have opened the kitchen door, to show him that it was not so; that there was no hamper nor bottles there.

Serj. Cheshire: My lord, I beg take leave to take notice of the evidence that has been offered, and the defence that hath been made on the behalf of the prisoner; and I think there can be nothing plainer, than that the defendant is guilty of this wilful and malicious shooting, as it is laid in the indictment. Gentlemen, now I may say the fact hath been proved to you in the proper way. The act, the manner of the act, and the behaviour after the act: he did behave himself like a lunatic; but I must submit it to you, whether there is any appearance in his behavior like a distracted man, so as to have the protection of the law. Gentlemen, that he designed this act, you have evidence of his coming to the witness asking for the biggest shot; he never used to call for any but that sort to kill rabbits; but now he calls for the biggest sort; he had a different use for it than he used to have. The preparation is very suitable to the design; at that time his behaviour is as usual; that he calls for the powder and shot, and pays for it, in the same proportion that he used to do. There does not appear at that time any great disorder in his behavior. As to the fact, they that were present could find he was sullen; he went on, he took aim as well as any body could; and his behaviour afterwards, his countenance was pale and livid, which shews guilt, and thoughts of remorse, anger, and revenge. As to the man's case, upon their evidence, they have made the point very material, what condition of understanding and sanity of mind this man had at the time. I must agree that a man that is a madman, a lunatic at the time, he cannot in the law be said to be guilty of felony. When I have so far consented as this, that the other side should see it is all of a piece with the usage the prisoner hath met with; but I must submit it to my lord's direction, whether they have given any proof that the man was at the time, or before, a disordered, lunatic man, deprived of his senses by the visitation of God Almighty. And as to the rule of judging, it is not, that a man acts like a madman, and doth an act that a person in his right reason ought not to do. No man that kills another voluntarily, acts like a man in the use of his reason. No man that commits a sin, a wilful sin, can say that he acts with reason. He parts with his reason. But consider what the law says, that the man that commits such an act, is moved by an instigation of the devil; which is brought in there to shew the horror of the fact. And if the man doth act as if the devil moved him, and that no man in his senses and right mind would do so, you must not interpret it, that every man that acts thus is a madman; then your lives and fortunes are all at stake, and at the mercy of a wicked man. Every wicked man acts by a malicious wilful will. Therefore consider the evidence given is of this kind, and you cannot blame them. I don't blame them; here are five of the relations, two brothers, two sisters, and one sister-in-law; that they should come and do all they can to save their brother from hanging. It will be a trouble to them and a disgrace.

Notwithstanding, now they swear that they have always looked upon him to be a lunatic, and deprived of his senses; it is impossible to believe them in earnest. He was always left to himself, never confined, or any commission of lunacy taken out. The law is now for any justice of peace to have power to confine such a person. It is dangerous for all men; it would be to have the lives of all persons in their power. It is very remarkable, that this man had the use of a gun, most of them speak for a great many years last past; he had it in his father's time. Don't you think these were wise people to let him do so, if they thought him a madman; they would not have trusted these arms for him to have access to, when they were told that morning the man was gone to buy powder and ball, if they looked upon him as a frantic man; sure they ought to remove those instruments and mischief out of his way, so that it should not have been in his power to do what he did do.

Serj. Comyns: If a person have no mind, he can be capable of no malicious design. Therefore we humbly submit that must be the evidence to excuse the person, that he had no malice or design in the attempt made on this noble lord. But if upon the evidence it appears, that he acted with design, with deliberation, with sedulity, and a long, fixed, designed malice, and there is no evidence of insanity that can shew he had no malice to excuse him; then he is guilty.

Serj. Darnell: My lord, I am very unwilling to take up any more of your lord's time. I apprehend, the insanity of the man must be reckoned at the time he doth the fact; if he hath intervals, and kills a man in those intervals, he is as much subject to the law as any other man; therefore taking it all to be true, that the man is sometimes out of his senses, it will then fall under the consideration, whether at the time that he

> *If a man be deprived of his reason, and consequently of his intention, he cannot be guilty; and if that be the case, though he had actually killed my lord Onslow, he is exempted from punishment.*

did this fact, it was not in his intervals? And if so, he must suffer the law.

Mr. Marsh: I only beg leave to take notice, that I think it is very extraordinary in these relations, that they should not take care, when they apprehended him to be mad, to secure him. I don't apprehend that he was at a distance from any of them; but as to two of his sisters, that lived in the town, where this man every day came, in the neighbourhood of Guilford, they say, they lived there three years, and give several instances of his insanity. It don't appear they ever sent any person to him to let him blood, or to give him any advice or physic; that doth not only make them blame-worthy, but, I apprehend, makes the evidence they have given of his insanity incred-ible, as coming from them,

> *It is not every frantic and idle humour of a man that will exempt him from justice, and the punishment of the law.*

because it is hardly credible he should be so, and that they not take care of him as they ought.

Just. Tracy: This is the evidence on both sides. Now I have laid it before you; and you must consider of it. And the shooting my lord Onslow, which is the fact for which the prisoner is indicted, is proved beyond all manner of contradiction; but whether this shooting was malicious, that depends upon the sanity of the man. That he shot, and that wilfully is proved. But whether maliciously, that is the thing. That is the question, whether this man hath the use of his reason and sense? If he was under the visitation of God, and could not distinguish between good and evil, and did not know what he did, though he committed the greater offence, yet he could not be guilty of any offence against the law whatsoever; for guilt arises from the mind, and the wicked will and intention of the man. If a man be deprived of his reason, and consequently of his intention, he cannot be guilty; and if that be the case, though he had actually killed my lord Onslow, he is exempted from punishment. Punishment is intended for example, and to deter other persons from wicked designs; but the punishment of a madman, a person that hath no design, can have no example. This is on one side. On the other side, we must be very cautious; it is not every frantic and idle humour of a man that will exempt him from justice, and the punishment of the law. When a man is guilty of a great offence, it must be very plain and clear, before a man is allowed such an exemption; therefore it is not every kind of frantic humour or something unaccountable in a man's actions, that points him out to be such a madman as is to be exempted from punishment. It must be a man that is totally deprived of his understanding and memory, and doth not know what he is doing, no more than an infant, than a brute, or a wild beast, such a one is never the object of punishment; therefore I must have it to your consideration, whether the condition this man was in, as it is represented to you on one side, or the other, doth shew a man, who knew what he was doing, and was able to distinguish whether he was doing good or evil, and understood what he did. And it is to be observed, they admit he was a lunatic, and not an ideot. A man that is an ideot, that is born so, never recovers, but a lunatic may, and hath his intervals; and they admit he was a lunatic. You are to consider what he was at this day, when he committed this fact. There you have a great many circumstances about the buying of powder and the shot; his going backward and forward. And if you believe he was sensible and had the use of his reason, and understood what he did, then he is not within the exemptions of the law, but is as subject to punishment as any other person. Gentlemen, I must leave it to you.

Then the Jury withdrew to consider of their verdict, and in a short time returned again.

[The jury returned a verdict of guilty.]

Whereupon, he received sentence of death; but at the intercession of the right honourable the lord Onslow, his execution was respited. And he continued a prisoner in the new gaol, Southwark, upwards of thirty years, and there died.

Rex v. Hadfield

27 How.St.Tr. 1282 (1800)[1]

The case of James Hadfield does not reflect any significant change in English law, but it introduces a new aspect of judicial reasoning about criminal responsibility. It highlights the significance of having an active defense attorney working on behalf of the defendant rather than depending on the court to conduct a defense on behalf of the defendant. Here, Lord Erskine conducts a vigorous defense for Hadfield. The case was before Parliament—owing to the severity of the charge: treason in the form of attempted assassination of the King. Lord Erskine successfully argued from the application of decisions about mental capacity in civil law that the literal application of a "wild beast" or "total deprivation" in criminal law was flawed. As in *Arnold*, the prosecution's case depended for the most part on showing that Arnold's immediate actions, when broken down into their constituent elements, were rational, goal-directed, and driven by purpose. Lord Erskine successfully argued that if the purpose could be demonstrated to be "insane," such an analysis was specious and led to incorrect conclusions about mental state at the time of the offense.

It was also helpful to Lord Erskine to be able to physically demonstrate Hadfield's injuries in war that led to his mental disorder, and to glory in Hadfield's valor during which he received the injuries that precipitated his delusions. So effective was Erskine's defense that the trial was summarily ended and a verdict delivered instantaneously. *Hadfield* is also noteworthy for the introduction of the expert witness. Erskine, who actually called no such witnesses, referred to them in two ways. The first was to explain how mental disease can be explained physiologically. The second way was to hold up the expert as better able than even he, a formidable questioner, to delineate the nature of delusional thought. That is, Erskine showed that "lunacy" was not always detectable by the untrained individual and that experts could illuminate that which was unseen. Finally, *Hadfield* is noteworthy for its influence on Parliament to establish procedures for those acquitted by reason of insanity. Hadfield himself remained in confinement until his death, but his confinement was not, like Arnold's, in prison.

[1] From Howell, T. J. (1800). *A Complete Collection of State Trials and Proceedings for High Treason and Other Crimes and Misdemeanors Fom the Earliest Period to the Year 1783 With Notes and Illustrations,* compiled by T. B. Howell and continued from the year 1783 to the present time.

Edited Excerpts[2]

Proceedings on the Trial of James Hadfield, at the Bar of the Court of King's Bench for High Treason, June 26, 1800.

Mr. Attorney General: Gentlemen, the facts, I think, will be proven distinctly and plainly; namely, that on the 15th of May last, when his majesty went to the Theatre Royal in Drury Lane, at the moment of his entering into the theatre and advancing to the front of that box in which his majesty sits, the prisoner at the bar, who was then in the pit, a little removed from the centre of the pit, farther from the box where his majesty stood (in a position, therefore, which enabled him to take a very direct view of that box which you will recollect is a little elevated), got upon the bench upon which he had been sitting, drew a pistol which he had before concealed, and discharged it at the person of the king: Providence warded off the blow, and it so happened that the slugs with which it will appear the pistol was loaded struck different parts of the box very near the person of his majesty, but happily hurt no one.

Gentlemen, the fact of his firing of the pistol at the king will be so clearly distinctly and so manifestly proved, that there can be no doubt of his guilt, if some excuse cannot be offered. From circumstances, I must presume, that the excuse which will be offered is, that the prisoner at the bar labours under the misfortune of insanity. Gentlemen, it will be my duty to explain to you, under the correction of the Court, what I conceive to be the law of this country upon this subject. I apprehend that according to the law of this country, if a man is completely deranged, so that he knows not what he does, if a man is so lost to all sense, in consequence of the infirmity of disease, that he is incapable of distinguishing between good and evil—that he is incapable of forming a judgment upon the consequences of the act which he is about to do, that *then* the mercy of our law says, he cannot be guilty of a crime. If a man does an act ignorantly—that is, if in doing of that which is perfectly lawful, without knowing it, he does that which is unlawful; for instance, if discharging a pistol for a lawful purpose, by mere accident, that pistol should have destroyed a man, he could not be deemed guilty of murder, because he had no intent whatever of doing that which was the result of his act. But it would be a grievous thing for the safety of all persons in this country, if men who occasionally labour under insanity should therefore be held excused, whatever crimes they may commit.

---

[2] Readers are advised to quote only from the original published cases. See pages vi and vii.

Gentlemen, in the case of idiots—of those who are so afflicted by the absolute privation of reason, so that the person knows not what he does and never has known—a man of that description stands excused, because heaven has not blessed him with that use of the faculty of reason which enables him to distinguish between right and wrong. An infant, a child who has not attained the maturity of reason which enables him to exert the faculty as it ought to be exerted, is also excused, because he is not able to distinguish between right and wrong. A madman, labouring under the extreme of the disorder when in a phrenzy, or a person who is suffering the severity, for instance, of a violent fever, may do an act of which he is perfectly unconscious, and for which, therefore, he cannot be deemed to be responsible. But when it is to be considered in a court of criminal justice what is the result of the act that has been done, the jury who are to try the person accused for that act are to weigh *the degree of discretion* which the person accused possessed.

If it were alleged that a person was an idiot, you would try what is the ordinary degree of faculty of his mind; you would see whether, in the ordinary intercourse of life, he had the capacity to distinguish so far as would enable him to see whether that which he had done was right or wrong; persons of extremely weak understanding have committed crimes, and have suffered for those crimes, though their understanding was below the ordinary level of the understandings of mankind; but the juries have found that they possessed that competent understanding which enabled them to discern good from evil; and if they had that degree of understanding, the peace of the world requires that they should be criminally responsible for the acts that they do.

In the case of a child, you measure his capacity in the same manner; it is not the *age* of the child, but the *capacity* of the child, and you judge it principally from that which he stands charged; for instance, if a child having done a criminal act, shows a consciousness that he has done wrong; if he endeavours to conceal it; if he does that which demonstrates that although he had not a complete view of the subject—he did not understand the enormity of his guilt—he did not see it in all its consequences as a person possessed of a complete mature understanding would do—yet if he possessed that degree of sense which enabled him to judge whether the act which he was committing was right or wrong, that has constantly been held sufficient to induce a jury to find infants of very tender years guilty of offences. Gentlemen, I conceive that the law of this country states it to be so in the case of persons labouring under that disorder which is commonly called lunacy, that is, a person who is occasionally insane but has lucid intervals. The law I take to be clearly and distinctly laid down by those authorities for whom we have professionally the greatest respect—by those for whom in the succession of ages all that have stood in the place in which we stand have had respect.

My lord chief justice Coke, in laying down the law upon the subject, is very clear and very precise; he states, in his Pleas of the Crown, that "he that is *non compos mentis*, and totally deprived of all compassings and imaginations, cannot commit high treason by compassing or imagining the death of the king, but it must be an absolute madness, and a total deprivation of memory." My lord chief justice Hale, in commenting upon

> *He that is* non compos mentis*, and totally deprived of all compassings and imaginations, cannot commit high treason by compassing or imagining the death of the king, but it must be an absolute madness, and a total deprivation of memory.*

the passage, observe, that the true rule is, to judge in the same way in which you would judge with respect to an infant, whether there was that competent degree of reason which enabled the person accused to judge whether he was doing right or wrong; he says that the passage in my lord Coke is general; the qualification he conceives to be that which I have stated; and in cases which have come before the Court at different times such have been the decisions.

Gentlemen, [a] case to which I shall call your attention, is one which probably has already occurred to your minds, I mean the case of my lord Ferrers. That my lord Ferrers occasionally laboured under the misfortune of insanity, there can be no doubt. He had murdered a person of the name of Johnson, his steward—he had done it deliberately, shooting him in a room in his own house; the situation of the man after he was shot, and till the time of his death—the fact of his being alone in the room with my lord Ferrers, and other facts which were sufficient demonstration of the guilt of murder, supposing my lord Ferrers to be an object of punishment, were clearly and distinctly proved. It was alleged, that the consequence of that fact; namely, that it was murder, did not follow; because my lord Ferrers was incapable of knowing what he did, that he laboured under the misfortune of insanity, and therefore was not capable of forming a proper judgment upon the act which he did.

The law as laid down by my lord Coke—as laid down by my lord Hale, and as I have taken the liberty of stating it to you, was stated, was urged, was commented upon with infinite ability by the learned gentlemen who then stood as counsel for the crown upon that prosecution; and it was insisted, that it was not necessary that a person committing a crime should have the full and complete use of his reason, but, as my lord Hale emphatically expresses himself, A COMPETENT USE OF IT. Whether he had that use of it which was sufficient to have restrained those passions which produced the crime; and that if there be thought, design, and faculty to distinguish the nature of actions, to discover the difference between moral good and evil, then, upon the fact of the offence proved, the judgment of the law must take place.

The Lords, with one voice, found my lord Ferrers guilty of the offence wherewith he was charged, judging of his capacity *at the moment*, not whether at any former times he had been deranged in his mind; not whether he was one of those unfortunate persons who labour under the affliction of insanity, that is, of occasional insanity with lucid intervals—if there is a total and absolute insanity and deprivation of the mind, there can be no doubt the sufferer cannot be guilty of the offence—but whether at the time had that capacity of mind which was capable of forming intention, whether he weighed the motives, proceeded deliberately, and knew the consequences of what he did. Gentlemen, I think you will find, that the prisoner at the bar, whatever may have been at times the situation of his mind, was, at the time he committed this act, at least so far possessed of it as to have that competent degree of reason which my lord Hale says is necessary to make a man guilty of the offence.

Gentlemen, when the evidence will detail to you the conduct of the prisoner, you will find him acting as other men would do upon similar occasions; you will find that he cautiously left one of his pistols behind him, *for a reason which he himself assigned*; he was capable, therefore, of assigning a reason for the act which he was then doing, you will find him going to the place where he purchased the gunpowder which he made use of—you will find that he conducted himself there like any other man— that he was capable of a contract to that extent, which indeed no man would have an idea that he was not capable of; that is capable of discerning what was the article he wanted, and what was the price that he was to pay for it.

Gentlemen, you will find him, in conversation with different people, stating his intention to go to the play; stating afterwards that he was going to the play; so that he had clearly conceived in his mind the deliberate purpose of going to the play. You will find him conversing with those persons upon the subject, representing himself as unable to stay with them, being obliged to go upon the business which he then had in hand. When he came to the theatre, he had that use of his understanding, which enabled him to procure the admission; he had that use of his understanding, which enabled him to place himself in that part of the theatre most fit for his purpose, namely, the pit, at a small distance from the orchestra, a little removed from the centre; where he had the most complete view of, and the most complete aim at that box in which his majesty was to be. The faculties of the mind were used for all these purposes, and must have been used. He had a competent degree of reason to distinguish upon all these particulars, and he did distinguish. After persons came about him in the theatre, he had that degree of reason which prompted him to conceal the pistol—which prompted him to conduct himself quietly, orderly, and with all that sobriety which a person patiently waiting for the representation of a piece upon the stage ordinarily uses.

Gentlemen, when his majesty entered the box, and the prisoner's dreadful purpose was to be put in execution, you will find him taking the utmost advantage for that purpose, by raising himself upon the seat, which, elevating him above every other person, enabled him to accomplish his purpose undisturbed. If he had stayed below, his arm might have been struck down the moment he raised it; when he stood upon the seat, he was above every body near him, and therefore could the more readily effect his purpose. There is thought, design, and contrivance in this; and he had a mind equal to that thought, equal to that design, equal to that contrivance; he knew whether or not it was advantageous to place himself in that situation; can you believe that he did not know the consequence of the act which he was about to do? He fired in that direction; the slugs struck against parts of the box; but such was the interposition of Providence, that they did no mischief; they were directly aimed at the spot in which his majesty was, but one struck upon the side, and the other, I believe, over that box. After he had done the act, he dropped the pistol; that might have been involuntary; at the same time, it has somewhat the appearance of design. He was hurried over the partition between the pit and the orchestra, and he was then in the kind of heat and agitation which naturally prevails on such occasions. He was asked what could prompt him to do what he did. Gentlemen, those who saw him at that moment will describe, how far he appeared to them to be in the possession of his understanding, and conscious of the act that he had done, and of the consequence of that act—that he knew that, by the law, his life was forfeit.

Defence – The Honourable Thomas Erskine

The law, as it regards this most unfortunate infirmity of the human mind, like the law in all its branches, aims at the utmost degree of precision; but there are some subjects, and the present is one of them, upon which it is extremely difficult to be precise. The general principle is clear, but the application is most difficult.

It is agreed by all jurists, and is established by the law of this and every other country, that it is the REASON OF MAN which makes him accountable for his actions; and that the deprivation of reason acquits him of crime. This principle is indisputable; yet so fearfully and wonderfully are we made, so infinitely subtle is the spiritual part of our being, so difficult is it to trace with accuracy the effect of diseased intellect upon human action, that I may appeal to all who hear me, whether there are any causes more difficult, or, which, indeed, so often confound the learning of the judges themselves, as when insanity, or the effects and consequences of insanity, become the subjects of legal consideration and judgment.

I agree with Mr. Justice Tracy, that it is not every man of an idle, frantic appearance and behaviour, who is to be considered as a lunatic, either as it regards obligations or crimes; but that he must appear to the jury to be *non compos mentis*, in the legal acceptation of the term; and that, not at any *anterior period*, which can have no bearing on the case whatsoever, but *at the moment* when the contract was entered into, or the crime committed.

The attorney-general, standing undoubtedly upon the most revered authorities of the law, has laid it down, that to protect a man from *criminal responsibility*, there must be a TOTAL *deprivation of memory and understanding*. I admit that this is the very expression used both by lord Coke and by lord Hale; but the true interpretation of it deserves the utmost attention and consideration of the Court. If a TOTAL *deprivation of memory* was intended by these great lawyers to be taken in the *literal* sense of the words; if it was meant, that, to protect a man from punishment, he must be in such a state of prostrated intellect, as not to know his name, nor his condition, nor his relation toward others—that if a husband, he should not know he was married; or if a father, could not remember that he had children; nor know the road to his house, nor his property in it—then no such madness ever existed in the world. It is IDIOCY alone which places a man in this helpless condition, where, from an *original* mal-organization,

> **If a TOTAL deprivation of memory was intended to protect a man from punishment, he must be in such a state of prostrated intellect, as not to know his name, nor his condition, nor his relation toward others—then no such madness ever existed in the world.**

there is the human frame alone, without the human capacity; and which, indeed, meets the very definition of lord Hale himself, "Idiocy of fatuity *a nativitate, vel dementia naturalis,* is such a one who knows not to tell twenty shillings, nor knows his own age, or who was his father." But in all the cases which have filled Westminster-hall with the most complicated considerations—the lunatics and other insane persons who have been the subjects of them, have not only had memory, *in my sense of the expression*—they have not only had the most perfect knowledge and recollection of all the relations they stood in towards others, and of the acts and circumstances of their lives, but have, in general, been remarkable for subtlety and acuteness. Defects in their reasonings have seldom been traceable—the disease consisting in the delusive sources of thought; all their deductions within the scope of the malady, being founded upon the *immovable* assumption of matters as *realities*, either without any foundation whatsoever, or so distorted and disfigured by fancy, as to be almost nearly the same thing as their creation. It is true, indeed, that in some, perhaps in many cases, the human mind is stormed in its citadel, and laid prostrate under the stroke of frenzy; these unhappy sufferers, however, are not so much considered by physicians as maniacs to be in a state of delirium from fever. There, indeed, all the ideas are overwhelmed—for reason is not merely disturbed, *but driven wholly from her seat.* Such unhappy patients are unconscious, therefore, except at short intervals, even of external objects; or, at least, are wholly incapable of considering their relations. Such persons *and such persons alone* (except idiots) *are wholly deprived of their* UNDERSTANDINGS, in the attorney-general's seeming sense of that expression. But these cases are not only extremely rare, but never can become the subjects of judicial difficulty. There can be but one judgment concerning them. In other cases, reason is not driven from her seat, but distraction sits down upon it along with her, holds her, trembling, upon it, and frightens her from her propriety. Such patients are victims to delusions of the most alarming description, which so overpower the faculties, and usurp so firmly the place of realities, as not to be dislodged and shaken by the organs of perception and sense. In such cases the images frequently vary, but in the same subject are generally of the same terrific character. Here, too, no judicial difficulties can present themselves, for who could balance upon the judgment to be pronounced in cases of such extreme disease? Another class, branching out into almost infinite subdivisions, under which, indeed, the former, and every case of insanity, may be classed, is, where the delusions are not of that frightful character, but infinitely various, and often extremely *circumscribed*; yet where imagination (*within the bounds of the malady*) still holds the most uncontrollable dominion over reality and fact; *and these are the cases which frequently mock the wisdom of the wisest in judicial trials*; because such persons often reason with a subtlety which puts in the shade the ordinary conceptions of mankind. Their conclusions are just, and frequently profound; but the *premises from which they reason*, WHEN WITHIN THE RANGE OF THE MALADY, are uniformly false—not false from any defect of knowledge or judgment, but, because a delusive image, the inseparable companion of real insanity, is thrust upon the subjugated understanding, incapable of resistance, because unconscious of attack.

Delusion, therefore, where there is no frenzy or raving madness, is the true character of insanity; and where it cannot be predicated of a man standing for life or death for a crime, he ought not, in my opinion, to be acquitted; and if courts of law were to be governed by any other principle, every departure from sober, rational conduct, would be an emancipation from criminal justice. I shall place my claim to your verdict upon no such dangerous foundation. I must convince you, not only that the unhappy prisoner was a lunatic, within my own definition of lunacy, but that the act in question was the IMMEDIATE, UNQUALIFIED OFFSPRING OF THE DISEASE. In *civil* cases, as I have already said, the law avoids every act of the lunatic during the period of the lunacy; although the delusion may be extremely circumscribed; although the mind may be quite sound in all that is not within the shades of the very partial eclipse; and although the act to be avoided can in no way be connected with the influence of the insanity. But to deliver a lunatic from the responsibility to *criminal*

> **Gentlemen, it has pleased God so to visit the unhappy man before you; to shake his reason to its citadel; to cause him to build up as realities, the most impossible phantoms of the mind, and to be impelled by them as motives irresistible.**

justice, above all, in a case of such atrocity as the present, the relation between the disease and the act should be apparent.

Gentlemen, it has pleased God so to visit the unhappy man before you; to shake his reason to its citadel; to cause him to build up as realities, the most impossible phantoms of the mind, and to be impelled by them as motives *irresistible*; the whole fabric being nothing but the unhappy vision of his disease—existing no where else—having no foundation whatsoever in the nature of things.

[A long description of two cases of mentally disordered offenders.]

Now, gentlemen, let us look to the application of these cases. I am not examining, *for the present*, whether either of these persons ought to have been acquitted, *if they had stood in the place of the prisoner now before you*; that is quite a distinct consideration, which we shall come to hereafter. The direct application is *only this*; that if I bring before you such evidence of the prisoner's insanity as, *if believed to have really existed*, shall, in the opinion of the Court, as the rule for your verdict in point of law, be sufficient for his deliverance, then that you ought not to be shaken in giving full credit to such evidence, notwithstanding the report of those who were present at his apprehension, *who describe him as discovering no symptom whatsoever of mental incapacity or disorder*; because I have shown you that insane persons frequently appear in the utmost state of ability and composure, even in the highest paroxysms of insanity, except when frenzy is the characteristic of the disease. In this respect, the cases I have cited to you, have the most *decided application*; because they apply to the overthrow of the whole of the evidence (admitting at the same time the truth of it), by which the prisoner's case can alone be encountered.

But it is said, that whatever delusions may overshadow the mind, every person ought to be responsible for crimes, *who has the knowledge of good and evil*. I think I can presently convince you, that there is something too general in this mode of considering the subject; and you do not, therefore, find any such proposition in the language of the celebrated writer alluded to by the attorney general in his speech. Let me suppose that the character of an insane delusion consisted in the belief that some given person was any brute animal, or an inanimate being (and such cases have existed), and that upon the trial of such a lunatic for murder, you firmly, upon your oaths, were convinced, upon the uncontradicted evidence of an hundred persons, that he believed the man he had destroyed to have been a potter's vessel; that it was quite impossible to doubt that fact, *although to all other intents and purposes he was sane*; conversing, reasoning, and acting, as men not in any manner tainted with insanity, converse, and reason, and conduct themselves. Suppose farther, that he believed the man whom he destroyed, but whom he destroyed as a potter's vessel, to be the property of another; and that he had malice against such supposed person, and that he meant to injure him, knowing the act he was doing was to be malicious and injurious, and that, in short, he had full knowledge of all the principles of good and evil; yet would it be possible to convict such a person of murder, if, from the influence of his disease, he was ignorant of the relation he stood in to the man he had destroyed, and was utterly *unconscious* that he had struck at the life of a human being? I only put this case that the knowledge of good and evil is too general a description.

Gentlemen, the facts of this melancholy case lie within a narrow compass. The unfortunate person before you was a soldier. He became so, I believe in the year 1793—and is now about 29 years of age. He served in Flanders under the duke of York, as appears by his Royal Highness's evidence; and being a most approved soldier, he was one of those singled out as an orderly man to attend upon the person of the commander in chief. You have been witnesses, gentlemen, to the calmness with which the prisoner has sitten in his place during the trial. There was but one exception to it. You saw the emotion which overpowered him when the illustrious person now in court, took his seat upon the bench. (As soon as his royal highness entered, the prisoner said, "God Almighty bless his good soul, I love him dearly.") The king himself whom he was supposed to have so malignantly attacked, never had a more gallant, loyal, or suffering soldier. His gallantry and loyalty will be proved; his sufferings speak for themselves.

About five miles from Lisle, upon the attack made on the British army, this unfortunate soldier was in the fifteenth light dragoons, in the thickest of the ranks, exposing his life for his prince, whom he is supposed today to have sought to murder. The first wound he received is most materially connected with the subject we are considering; you may see the effect of it now. (Mr. Erskine put his hand to the prisoner's head, who stood by him at the bar of the Court.) The point of a sword was impelled against him with all the force of a man urging his horse in battle. Either, that by the immediate operation of surgery the displaced part of the skull must have been taken away, or been forced inward on the brain. The second stroke, also speaks for itself. You may now see its effects. (Here Mr. Erskine touched the head of the prisoner.) He was cut across all the nerves which give sensibility and animation to the body, and his head hung down almost dissevered, until by the act of surgery it was placed in the position in which you now see it; but thus, almost destroyed, he still recollected his duty, and continued to maintain the glory of his country, when a sword divided the membrane of his neck where it terminate with his head; yet he still kept his place though his helmet had been thrown off by the blow which I secondly described, when by another sword, he was cut into the very brain—you may now see its membrane uncovered.

It may be said that many soldiers receive grievous wounds without their producing insanity. So they may undoubtedly; but we are here upon *the fact*. There was a discussion the other day, on whether a man, who had seemingly been hurt by a fall beyond remedy, could get up and walk.

The people around said it was impossible, but he did get up and walk, and so there was an end to the impossibility. The effects of the prisoner's wound were known by the *immediate* effects of insanity, and it would have been strange indeed if any other event had followed. We are not here upon a case of insanity arising from the spiritual part of man, as it may be affected by hereditary trait—by intemperance, or by violent passions, the operations of which are various and uncertain; but we have to deal with a species of insanity more resembling what has been described as idiocy, proceeding from original mal-organization. *There* the disease is, from its very nature, *incurable*; and so where a man (*like the prisoner*) has become insane from *violence to the brain, which permanently affects its structure*, however such a man may appear occasionally to others, his disease is *immovable*; and if the prisoner, therefore, were to live a thousand years, he *never* could recover from the consequences of that day.

But that is not all. Another blow was still aimed at him, which he held up his arm to avoid, when his hand was cut to the bone. It is an afflicting subject, gentlemen, and better to be spoken of by those who understand it; and, to end all farther description, he was then thrust almost through and through the body with a bayonet, and left in a ditch amongst the slain. He was afterwards carried to a hospital, where he was known by his tongue to one of his countrymen, who will be examined as a witness, who found him, not merely as a wounded soldier deprived of the powers of his body, but bereft of his senses for ever.

He was affected, from the very beginning, with that species of madness, which from violent agitation, fills the mind with the most inconceivable imaginations, wholly unfitting it for all dealing with human affairs according to the sober estimate and standard of reason. He imagined that he had constant intercourse with the Almighty Author of all things; that the world was coming to a conclusion; and that, like our blessed Saviour, he was to sacrifice himself for its salvation; and so obstinately did this morbid image continue, that you will be convinced he went to the theatre to perform, as he imagined, that blessed sacrifice; and, because he would not be guilty of suicide, though called upon by the imperious voice of Heaven, he wished that by the appearance of crime his life might be taken away from him by others. This bewildered, extravagant species of madness appeared immediately after his wounds on his first entering the hospital, and on the very same account he was discharged from the army on his return to England.

To proceed with proofs of his insanity *down to the very period of his supposed guilt.* This unfortunate man before you is the father of an infant of eight months; and I have no doubt, that if the boy had been brought into court (*but this is a grave place for the consideration of justice, and not a theatre for stage effect*)—I say, I have no doubt whatever, that if this poor infant had been brought into court, you would have seen the unhappy father wrung with all the emotions of parental affection; yet, upon the Tuesday preceding the Thursday when he went to the playhouse, you will find his disease still urging him forward with the impression *that the time was come*, when he must be destroyed for the benefit of mankind; and in the confusion, or rather *delirium* of this wild conception, he came to the bed of the mother, who had this infant in her arms, and endeavored her to dash its brains against the wall. The family was alarmed; and the neighbours being called in, the child was, with difficulty, rescued from the unhappy parent, who, in his madness, would have destroyed it.

Now let me, for a moment, suppose that he had succeeded in the accomplishment of his insane purpose; and the question had been, whether he was guilty of murder. Surely the affection for this infant, up to the very moment of his distracted violence, would have been conclusive in his favour; but not more so than his loyalty to the king, and his attachment to the duke of York, as applicable to the case before us; yet at that very period, even of extreme distraction, he conversed as rationally on all other subjects, as he did to the duke of York at the theatre. The prisoner knew perfectly that he was the husband of the woman, and the father of the child. The tears of affection ran down his face at the very moment that he was about to accomplish its destruction, but during the whole of this scene of horror, he was not at all deprived of memory, in the attorney-general's sense of the expression. He could have communicated, at that moment, every circumstance of his past life, and every thing connected with his present condition, *except only the quality of the act he was meditating*. In *that*, he was under the over-ruling dominion of a morbid imagination, and conceived that he was acting against the dictates of nature, in obedience to the superior commands of Heaven, which had told him, that the moment he was dead, and the infant with him, all nature was to be changed, and all mankind were to be redeemed by his dissolution. There was not an idea in his mind, from the beginning to the end, of the destruction of the king; on the contrary, he always maintained his loyalty, lamented that he could not go again to fight his battles in the field.

You have a man before you, who will appear, upon the evidence, to have received those almost deadly wounds which I described to you, producing the immediate and immoveable effects which the eminent surgeon will prove that they could not but have produced; it will appear, that from that period he was visited with the severest paroxysms of madness, and was repeatedly confined with all the coercion which it is necessary to practise upon lunatics; yet what is quite decisive against the imputation of treason against the person of the king, his loyalty never forsook him. Sane or insane, it was his very characteristic to love his sovereign and his country, although the delusions which distracted him were some times *in other respects*, as contradictory as they were violent.

The charge against the prisoner is the overt act of compassing the death of the king, in firing a pistol at his majesty. You will have to decide, whether you attribute it wholly to mischief and malice, or wholly to insanity, or the one mixing itself with the other. If you find it attributable to mischief and malice *only*, LET THE MAN DIE. The law demands his death for public safety. If you consider it as conscious malice and mischief combining itself with insanity, I leave him in the hands of the court, to say how he is to be dealt with; it is a question too difficult for me. I do not stand here to disturb the order of society; or to bring confusion upon my country; but, if you find that the act was committed wholly under the dominion of insanity; if you are satisfied that he went to the theatre, contemplating his own destruction only; and that, when he fired the pistol, he did not *maliciously* aim at the person of the king—you will then be bound, even upon the principle of which the attorney-general himself humanely and honourably stated to you, to acquit this most unhappy prisoner.

There is, however, another consideration which I ought distinctly to present to you; because I think that more turns upon it than any other view of the subject; namely, whether the prisoner's defence can be impeached for artifice or fraud; because I admit, that if at the moment when he was apprehended, there can be fairly imputed to him any pretence or counterfeit of insanity, it would taint the whole case, and leave him without protection; but for such a suspicion there is not even a shadow of foundation.

Foreman of the Jury: We find the prisoner is Not Guilty; he being under the influence of Insanity at the time the act was committed.

Note: This case gave rise to the two statutes of 40 Geo. 3rd, chapters 93 and 94, by virtue of the latter of which (for the safe custody of insane persons charged with offences) Hadfield was continued in custody.

Queen v. M'Naghten

10 Clark & F.200, 2 Eng. Rep. 718 (H.L. 1843)

Facts

Daniel M'Naghten believed he was persecuted by Tories, and he sought to assassinate Prime Minister Robert Peel. Failing to accurately identify Peel from behind, he inadvertently shot the Prime Minister's secretary, Edward Drummond, who died several weeks later. M'Naghten pleaded not guilty. Witnesses testified regarding M'Naghten's mental state at trial, and he was found not guilty, on the grounds of insanity. This verdict created a public outcry regarding the insanity defense, and the issue was debated in the House of Lords. As a result, several questions were posed by the House of Lords to the British judiciary. The responses were crafted into the M'Naghten Rules in Britain, and remain in force.

Issue

Specific questions to be addressed by the judiciary included the following: What is the proper standard for insanity? What questions should be posed to the jury, and how should the jury be instructed? What is the proper role of the medical professional?

Holding

The most important result of this case is the wording of the "M'Naghten standard" for insanity. The case held:

> to establish a defense on the ground of insanity, it must be clearly proved that, at the time of the committing of the act, the party accused was laboring under such a defect of reason, from disease of the mind, as not to know the nature and quality of the act he was doing; or, if he did know it, that he did not know he was doing what was wrong.

Analysis

Although over 160 years old, this case remains among the most widely cited in mental health law. The resultant "M'Naghten standard" is the most prevalent standard of insanity in the United States.

Edited Excerpts[1]

The prisoner had been indicted for that he, on the 20th day of January 1843, did kill and murder Edward Drummond. The prisoner pleaded Not guilty.

Witnesses were called on the part of the prisoner, to prove that he was not, at the time of committing this act, in a sound state of mind. The medical evidence was in substance this: That persons of otherwise sound mind, might be affected by morbid delusions: that the prisoner was in that condition: that a person so labouring under a morbid delusion, might have a moral perception of right and wrong, but that in the case of the prisoner it was a delusion which carried him away beyond the power of his own control, and left him no such perception; and that he was not capable of exercising any control over acts which had connection with his delusion: that it was the nature of the disease with which the prisoner was affected, to go on gradually until it had reached a climax, when it burst forth with irresistible insanity: that a man might go on for years quietly, though at the same time under its influence, but would all at once break out into the most extravagant and violent paroxysms.

Some of the witnesses who gave this evidence, had previously examined the prisoner: others had never seen him till he appeared in Court, and they formed their opinions on hearing the evidence given by the other witnesses.

Lord Chief Justice Tindal: The question to be determined is, whether at the time the act in question was committed, the prisoner had or had not the use of his understanding, so as to know that what he was doing was a wrong or wicked act. If the jurors should be of the opinion that the prisoner was not sensible, at the time he committed it, that he was violating the laws both of God and man, then he would be entitled to a verdict in his favor; but, if on the contrary, they were of the opinion that when he committed the act he was in a sound state of mind, then their verdict must be against him.

Verdict, Not guilty, on the ground of insanity.

This verdict and the question of the nature and extent of the unsoundness of mind which would excuse the commission of a felony of this sort, [was] made the subject of debate in the House of Lords. Accordingly, all the Judges attended their Lordships, [and] the following questions of law were propounded to them:

---

[1] Readers are advised to quote only from the original published cases. See pages vi and vii.

1st. What is the law respecting alleged crimes committed by persons afflicted with insane delusion, in respect of one or more particular subjects or persons: as, for instance, where at the time of the commission of the alleged crime, the accused knew he was acting contrary to law but did the act complained of with a view, under the influence of insane delusion, of redressing or revenging some supposed grievance or injury, or of producing some supposed public benefit?

2nd. What are the proper questions to be submitted to the jury, when a person alleged to be afflicted with insane delusions respecting one or more particular subjects or persons, is charged with the commission of a crime (murder, for example), and insanity is set up as a defense?

3rd. In what terms ought the question to be left to the jury, as to the prisoner's state of mind at the time when the act was committed?

4th. If a person under an insane delusion as to existing facts, commits an offense in consequence thereof, is he thereby excused?

5th. Can a medical man conversant with the disease of insanity, who never saw the prisoner previously to trial, but who was present during the whole trial and the examination of all the witnesses, be asked his opinion as to the state of the prisoner's mind at the time of the commission of the alleged crime, or his opinion whether the prisoner was conscious at the time of doing the act, that he was acting contrary to law, or whether he was laboring under any and what delusion at the time?

[Various replies among the Judges]

What is the law respecting the alleged crime, when at the time of the commission of it, the accused knew he was acting contrary to the law, but did the act with a view, under the influence of insane delusion, of redressing or revenging some supposed grievance or injury, or of producing some supposed public benefit? If I were to understand this question according to the strict meaning of its terms, it would require, in order to answer it, a solution of all questions of law which could arise on the circumstances stated in the question, either by explicitly stating and answering such questions, or by stating some principles or rules which would suffice for their solution. I am quite unable to do so, and, indeed, doubt whether it be possible to be done; and therefore request to be permitted to answer the question only so far as it comprehends the question, whether a person, circumstanced as stated in the question, is, for that reason only, to be found not guilty of a crime respecting which the question of his guilt has been duly raised in a criminal proceeding and I am of the opinion that he is not. There is no law, that I am aware of, that makes persons in the state described in the question not responsible for their criminal acts. To render a person irresponsible for crime on account of unsoundness of mind, the unsoundness should, according to the law as it has long been understood and held, be such as rendered him incapable of knowing right from wrong. The terms used in the question cannot be said (with reference only to the use of language) to be equivalent to a description of this kind and degree of unsoundness of mind. If the state described in the question be one which involves or is necessarily connected with such an unsoundness, this is not a matter of law but of physiology, and not of that obvious and familiar kind as to be inferred without proof.

The questions necessarily to be submitted to the jury, are those questions of fact which are raised on the record. In a criminal trial, the question commonly is, whether the accused be guilty or not guilty; but, in order to assist the jury in coming to a right conclusion on this necessary and ultimate question, it is usual and proper to submit such subordinate or intermediate questions, as the course which the trial has taken may have made it convenient to direct their attention to. What those questions are, and the manner of submitting them, is a matter of discretion for the Judge: a discretion to be guided by a consideration of all the circumstances attending the inquiry. In performing this duty, it is sometimes necessary or convenient to inform the jury as to the law; and if, on a trial such as is suggested in the question, he should have occasion to state what kind and degree of insanity would amount to a defense, it should be stated conformably to what I have mentioned in my answer to the first question, as being, in my opinion, the law on this subject.

In answer to [the first] question, assuming that your Lordships' inquiries are confined to those persons who labor under such partial delusions only, and are not in other respects insane, we are of the opinion that, notwithstanding the party accused did the act complained of with a view, under the influence of insane delusion, or redressing or revenging some supposed grievance or injury, or of producing some public benefit, he is nevertheless

> **He is nevertheless punishable according to the nature of the crime committed if he knew at the time of committing such crime that he was acting contrary to law.**

punishable according to the nature of the crime committed if he knew at the time of committing such crime that he was acting contrary to law; by which expression we understand your Lordships to mean the law of the land.

[The second and third] questions appear to us to be more conveniently answered together, we have to submit our opinion to be, that the jurors ought to be told in all cases that every man is to be presumed to be sane, and to possess a sufficient degree of reason to be responsible for his crimes, until the contrary be proved to their satisfaction; and that to establish a defense on the ground of insanity, it must be clearly proved that, at the time of the committing of the act, the party accused was laboring under such a defect of reason, from disease of the mind, as not to know the nature and quality of the act he was doing; or, if he did

> *The mode putting the latter part of the question to the jury on these occasions has generally been, whether the accused at the time of doing the act knew the difference between right and wrong.*

know it, that he did not know he was doing what was wrong. The mode putting the latter part of the question to the jury on these occasions has generally been, whether the accused at the time of doing the act knew the difference between right and wrong: which mode, though rarely, if ever, leading to any mistake with the jury, is not, as we conceive, so accurate when put generally and in the abstract, as when put with reference to the party's knowledge of right and wrong in respect to the very act with which he is charged. If the question were to be put as to the knowledge of the accused solely and exclusively to the law of the land, it might tend to confound the jury, by inducing them to believe that an actual knowledge of the law of the land was essential in order to lead to a conviction; whereas the law is administered upon the principle that every one must be taken conclusively to know it, without proof that he does know it. If the accused was conscious that the act was one which he ought not to do, and if that act was at the same time contrary to the law of the land, he is punishable; and the usual course thereof has been to leave the question to the jury, whether the party accused had a sufficient degree of reason to know that he was doing an act that was wrong: and this course we think is correct, accompanied by such observations and explanations as the circumstances of each particular case may require.

[The answer to the fourth question] must of course depend on the nature of the delusion: but, making the same assumption as we did before, namely, that he labors under such partial delusion only, and is not in other respects insane, we think he must be considered in the same situation as to responsibility as if the facts with respect to the delusion were real. For example, if under the influence of his delusion he supposes another man to be in the act of attempting to take away his life, and he kills that man, as he supposes, in self-defense, he would be exempt from punishment. If his delusion was that the deceased had inflicted a serious injury to his character and fortune, and he killed him in revenge for such supposed injury, he would be liable to punishment.

In answer [to the last question] we state to your Lordships, that we think the medical man, under the circumstances supposed, cannot in strictness be asked his opinion in the terms above stated, because each of those questions involves the determination of the truth of the facts deposed to, which it is for the jury to decide, and the questions are not mere questions upon a matter of science, in which case such evidence is admissible. But where the facts are admitted or not disputed, and the question becomes substantially one of science only, it may be convenient to allow the question to be put in that general form, though the same cannot be insisted on as a matter of right.

State v. Pike

49 N.H. 399 (1870)

Facts

The facts of this case are not provided in great detail. Pike was an alcoholic, and he killed a man during a robbery attempt by striking him with an ax. At trial, he claimed he was insane because of alcoholism. The trial court ruled that the question of whether alcoholism was a disease is a question of fact for the jury, as was the question of whether he was insane as a result of alcoholism. The court instructed the jury that the defendant was presumed to be sane, but where there was evidence casting doubt on this presumption, the state must prove beyond reasonable doubt that the defendant was sane. The court accepted testimony from nonexperts that the defendant was an alcoholic, but rejected testimony from nonexperts that the defendant was insane. Pike objected to the instructions regarding presumption of sanity, to the presumption of sanity, and to the exclusion of lay witnesses testifying regarding his "insanity."

Issue

Is "dipsomania" in a class of disorders which can be assumed to produce insanity? Can witnesses, not experts, testify as to whether they believed the defendant to be insane? Should defendants be presumed to be insane, or should the prosecution be required to prove the sanity of every defendant when intent is an element of the crime?

Holding

Whether dipsomania is a disease is a question of science and fact, not law. The court was correct in rejecting it as a basis for insanity without testimony by experts, as it is commonly known that dipsomania is not a form of insanity. Intoxication is "a fact open to the observation of every man," and nonexperts can testify to its occurrence. But insanity is not such a fact, so nonexperts cannot testify that a defendant appeared "insane." Every defendant is presumed to be sane until there is evidence to dispute the presumption.

Analysis

If there are any diseases whose existence is so much a matter of history and general knowledge that the court may properly assume the disease exists when charging a jury, dipsomania certainly does not fall with that class. Whether there is such a disease as dipsomania is a question of science and fact, not of law. Intoxication, however, is a fact open to the observation of everyone and "no special skill or learning" is requisite to discern it. Therefore, nonexperts can testify about intoxication, but not insanity, which requires special skill or learning. Nonexperts were allowed to describe Pike's appearance and his conduct. It was for the jury to say what inferences should be drawn from the facts described. It is a long-standing principle that "every person of mature age is presumed to be sane, until there is evidence tending to show insanity."

Pike is most interesting for its dissent by Judge Doe, who questions many of the underlying principles about insanity, including whether nonexperts can testify reliably about it and whether the concept of insanity is not overly restrictive. Although his was the dissenting opinion, Doe's commentary on the insanity defense is really the basis in American law for the "product test," in which insanity is construed to reflect behavior that is a product of mental disorder. Doe's opinion is cited in the majority opinion of *Parsons*, an important case that continued a relaxing of the insanity standard—to include a product test and an irresistible impulse test.

Edited Excerpts[1]

Indictment against Josiah L. Pike for murder. The defendant did strike and beat—giving to the said Thomas Brown then and there, with the axe aforesaid, and by the stroke aforesaid, in the manner aforesaid, in and upon the left side of the head of him, the said Thomas Brown, one mortal wound of the length of four inches and of the depth of one inch. Witnesses, not experts, called by the defendant were not allowed to testify that from their observations of his appearance and conduct before the alleged murder, they formed the opinion that he was insane, and defendant excepted. The court instructed the jury, as requested by the defendant, that, if they found that the defendant killed Brown in a manner that would be criminal and unlawful if the defendant were sane—the verdict should be "not guilty by reason of insanity" if the killing was the offspring or product of mental disease in the defendant; that neither delusion nor

---

[1] Readers are advised to quote only from the original published cases. See pages vi and vii.

knowledge of right and wrong, nor design or cunning in planning and executing the killing and escaping or avoiding detection, nor ability to recognize acquaintances, or to labor or transact business or manage affairs, is, as a matter of law, a test of mental disease; but that all symptoms and all tests of mental disease are purely matters of fact to be determined by the jury.

Dissent by Doe

Witnesses, not experts, called by the defendant, were not allowed to testify that from their observations of his appearance and conduct before the alleged murder, they formed the opinion that he was insane. This testimony should have been received. In England no express decision of the point can be found for the reason that such evidence has always been admitted without objection. It has been universally regarded as so clearly competent that it seems no English lawyer has ever presented to any court, any objection, question or doubt in regard to it.

Thus upon a question of insanity witnesses, not professional men, may be permitted to give their opinion in connection with the facts observed by them. But this evidence is always confined to those who have observed the facts, and is never permitted where the opinion of the witness is derived from the representation of others. Upon a question of insanity, for instance, witnesses who have observed the conduct of the patient, and been acquainted with his conversation, may testify to his acts and sayings, and give the result of their observation; but where mere opinion is required upon a given state of facts, that opinion is to be derived from professional men. If his opinion is formed upon the testimony of other witnesses, the jury have as good an opportunity as the witness to form an opinion; if it is formed upon hearsay, it is mere indirect proof of hearsay; of a hypothetical case, the jury can form an opinion as well as a non-expert witness. But if the opinion of the witness is formed upon his own observations, he had a better opportunity to form an opinion than the jury can have from a description of the acts and words of the person whose sanity is in question; because such a description cannot generally convey any adequate idea of the signs of sanity or insanity as they appear to an observer. It is necessary as far as possible that the impression produced by the acts and words, should be conveyed to the jury, and it cannot generally be conveyed by a mere description or recital of them.

To me it seems a plain proposition that upon enquiries as to mental imbecility, it will be found impracticable in many cases to come to a satisfactory conclusion without receiving to some extent the opinions of witnesses. Mental imbecility is exhibited, in part, by attitude, by gesture, by the tones of the voice and the expression of the eye and the face. Can these be described in language so as to convey to one not an eye-witness an adequate conception of their force? And so it is in regard to questions respecting the temper in which words have been spoken, or acts done. Were they said or done kindly or rudely—in good humor or in anger; in jest or in earnest? What answer can be given to these enquiries if the observer is not permitted to state his impression or belief? Must a *facsimile* be attempted so as to bring before the jury the very tone, look, gestures, and manner, and let them collect thereupon the disposition of the speaker or agent? Unquestionably before a witness can be received to testify as to the fact of capacity, it must appear that he had an adequate opportunity of observing and judging of capacity. But so different are the powers and the habits of observation in different persons, that no general rule can be laid down as to what shall be deemed a sufficient opportunity of observation, other than it has in fact enabled the observer to form a belief or judgment thereupon.

A careful daily observer of a person feigning madness, would witness innumerable acts, motions and expressions of countenance, which, with the attending incidents and circumstances, would conclusively satisfy him of the fictitious character of the pretended malady, but which he could never communicate to a jury or scientific man, so as to give them a fair conception of their real importance. From poverty of language, these facts, should a witness attempt to detail them, would necessarily be mixed up with opinions general or partial, in spite of his best efforts to avoid it. There are things well known to all persons, which our language only enables us to express by words of comparison—such are the peculiar features of the face indicating an excitement of the passions, affections and emotions of the mind, as hope, fear, love, hatred, pleasure, pain, and so on. Testimony affirming the existence or absence of either of these, is but a matter of opinion. So the statement of the fact that a man's whole conduct is natural, is but the opinion of the witness, formed by comparing the particular conduct spoken of, with the acts of the past life of the individual. It would hardly be claimed that such evidence should be excluded, yet it is equivalent to an opinion that the person is sane.

In criminal cases, it is often a question how nearly a footprint in earth or snow, corresponded to the form of a shoe of the prisoner. A witness who has seen the footprint and the shoe, is allowed to give his opinion on the subject, because a mere description of forms would not be the best evidence. If a plaster cast of the track, or the original impression itself preserved by freezing, could be produced, this evidence of its form would be more satisfactory than any verbal description. So it is when an impression has been made upon the mind of a witness by the appearance and conduct of the prisoner, indicating sanity or insanity; that impression is the best evidence the witness can give on the subject. His description of the appearance and conduct, is, in fact, but indirect and imperfect evidence of the impression; when he gives the original impression itself, it is as if a footprint were brought into court.

On the other side, a witness is allowed to say that the defendant did not appear natural, or did appear peculiarly or strangely; that also is a clear opinion; and if it were necessarily understood and taken as a full and explicit opinion that the defendant was insane, there would be no injustice, and the exception excluding opinions would be totally abolished. If "unnatural," by its peculiar use in this connection, should, in evidence, come to be synonymous with "insane," as "natural" is understood to be synonymous with "sane," the legal question now under consideration would dwindle to a point of literary taste. But the effect of the opinion that the defendant did not appear natural, or did appear peculiarly or strangely, falls far short of the effect of an opinion that he appeared to be insane; and the state has this great and unfair advantage over the accused. If he has feigned insanity for the purpose of escaping punishment, a mere narration by the witnesses of their observations of him, would probably appear like very strong evidence of insanity; whereas this evidence might be properly and truthfully rebutted by their opinions; they might have observed evidence of simulation which they could not describe.

One witness testified that he shut up his shop, and started to go away when the defendant was there; and another testified that he left a bed in which the defendant was, and went to sleep in another bed. This evidence was introduced to show that these witnesses were afraid of the defendant; and their fears were proved in this way to show that in their opinions the defendant was insane. If their acts could be proved to show their fears, and their fears be proved as evidence of their opinions, they could testify directly to their opinions, and say that they were afraid of the defendant because they thought him insane. When the testimony of witnesses is offered to prove that they treated the defendant as an insane man, it amounts to an offer to prove by the witnesses, a previous practical expression of their opinions; and the question arises whether their conduct is a species of the best evidence of their opinions. This question concerns not the competency of their opinions, but the method of proving them. Whatever the true method may be in theory, a question of sanity is seldom, if ever, tried without a very effective use being made of evidence showing that the person whose sanity is in controversy, was, or was not, treated as an insane person by his family, neighbors, friends, or acquaintances.

The defendant's exception to the instructions given to the jury in relation to his responsibility raises the general question of the legal tests of insanity. This was the first instance in which such instructions were ever given; but they are an application of ancient and fundamental principles of the common law. A product of mental disease is not a contract, a will, or a crime; and the tests of mental disease are matters of fact. Tried by the standard of legal precedent, the instructions are wrong; tried by the standard of legal principle, they are right. We have come to a point where we can plainly see that the paths of precedent and principle diverge, and where we must choose between them.

Blackstone says, "The king indeed, on behalf of an idiot, may void his grants or other acts. But it hath been said that a *non compos* himself shall not be permitted to allege his own insanity in order to avoid such grant: for that no man shall be allowed to stultify himself, or plead his own disability. The progress of this notion is somewhat curious." Blackstone gives its history, showing that it did not prevail in the time of Edward I; that "under Edward III, a scruple began to arise whether a man should be permitted to *blemish* himself by pleading his own insanity; and afterwards" it was doubted whether a plaintiff who had executed a release since the commencement of his suit, and who was taken to be sane at its commencement and at the time of pleading, should be permitted to plead an intermediate deprivation of reason existing at the execution of the release, "and the question was asked how he came to remember the release if out of his senses when he gave it. Under Henry VI, this way of reasoning was seriously adopted by the judges, and from these loose authorities which Fitzherbert does not scruple to reject as being contrary to reason, the maxim that a man shall not stultify himself, hath been handed down as settled law." In 1767, Lord Mansfield stated the law thus, "It hath been said to be a maxim that no man can plead his being a lunatic to avoid a deed executed, or excuse an act done at that time, because it is said if he was a lunatic he could not remember any action he did during the period of his insanity. And this was doctrine formerly laid down by some judges; but I am glad to find that of late it hath been generally exploded; for the reason assigned for it, is, in my opinion, wholly insufficient to support it; because, though he could not remember what passed during his insanity, yet he might justly say, If he ever executed such a deed, or did such an action, it must have been during his confinement or lunacy; for he did not do it either before or since that time. As to the case in which a man's plea of insanity was actually set aside; it was nothing more than this: It was when they pleaded *ore tenus*[2]; the man pleaded that he was at the time out of his senses. It was replied, How do you know that you was out of your senses? No man that is so, knows himself to be so. And according his plea was, upon this quibble, set aside; not because it was not a valid one if he was out of his senses; but because they concluded he was not out of his senses."

Sir P. Wilde said, "What is to be the proof of disease? What is to be the test, if there be a test, of morbid mental action? The existence of mental "delusions," it would perhaps be answered. But this only postpones the question, in place of answering it. For what is a mental delusion? How is it to be defined so as to constitute a test universally applicable, of mental disorder or disease. The word is not a very fortunate one. In common parlance a man

> **For what is a mental delusion? How is it to be defined so as to constitute a test universally applicable, of mental disorder or disease. The word is not a very fortunate one. In common parlance a man may be said to be under a "delusion" when he only labors under a mistake.**

may be said to be under a "delusion" when he only labors under a mistake. The "delusion" intended, is of course something very different. To say that a "morbid" or an "insane delusion" is to beg the question. For the "delusion" to be sought is to be the test of insanity; and to say that an insane or morbid delusion is the test of insanity or disease, does not advance the enquiry. "A belief of facts which no rational person would have believed" says Sir John Nicholl. "No *rational* person." This too appears open to a like objection, for what are the limits of a rational man's belief? And to say that a belief exceeds them, is only to say that it is irrational or insane. "The belief of things as realities which exist only in the imagination of the patient," says Lord Brougham in *Waring v. Waring*. But surely sane people often imagine things to exist which have no existence in reality both in the physical and moral world. What else gives rise to unfounded fears, unjust suspicions, baseless hopes, or romantic dreams? I turn to another definition. It is by Dr. Willis, a man of great eminence, and is quoted by Sir John Nicholl in *Dew v. Clark*. "A pertinacious adherence to some delusive idea in opposition to plain evidence of its falsity." This seems to offer a surer ground: but then the "evidence" of the falsity is to be "plain," and who shall say if it be so or

---

[2] *ore tenus.* Verbally.

not? In many or most cases it would be easy enough. Those who have entertained the "delusive idea" that their bodies were made of glass or their legs of butter (as it may be found in medical works that some have done), certainly have "plain evidence" at hand—the evidence of their senses—of its falsity.

But what if the delusive idea concerns a subject in which the senses play no part, and the "plain evidence" by which it is to be discharged is matter of reasoning and addressed to the intellectual faculty? Will all sane men agree whether the evidence is plain or not? And if not, shall one man in all cases pronounce another a monomaniac when the evidence is plain, to his reason, of the falsity of the other's ideas? I find no fault with the language of these definitions as fairly and properly describing the mental phenomena they are used to depict. I only assert that the existence of mental delusions thus defined, is not capable of being erected into an universal test of mental disease. It is no doubt true that mental disease is always accompanied by the exhibition of thoughts and ideas that are false and unfounded, and may therefore be properly called "delusive." But what I mean to convey on this head is this, that the question of insanity and the question of "delusions" is really one and the same—that the *only* delusions which prove insanity are insane delusions—and that the broad enquiry into mental health or disease cannot in all cases be either narrowed or determined by any previous or substituted enquiry into the existence of what are called "delusions." I say in all cases, for in some such as those to which I have already alluded, where the delusive idea ought to receive its condemnation and expulsion at once from the simple action of the senses, the contrary is the case; and the same may be said of delusions obviously opposed to the simple, ordinary, and universal action of reason in healthy minds. These are the simple cases about which no one would doubt, and in them the proof of the "delusions" is also the proof of insanity without more.

But what is to be said of the more complicated cases? What if the diseased action of the mind does not exhibit itself on the surface, as it were, opposing its hallucinations to the common senses or reasons of all mankind, but can be tracked only in the recesses of abstract thought or religious speculation—regions in which the mental action of the sane produces no common result—and all is question and conflict? In what form of words could a "delusion" be defined which would be a positive test of insanity in such cases as these? In none, I conceive, but "*insane delusions*," or words of the like import, which carry with them the whole breadth of the general enquiry. How then, is this question of insanity to be approached by a legal tribunal? What tests are to be applied for disease?

What limits assigned within which, extravagance of thought is to be pronounced compatible with mental health? The decided cases offer no light on these heads. I nowhere find any attempt to devise such tests, or assign such limits. Nor do I conceive that any tests, however elaborate, beyond the common and ordinary method of judging in such matters, would be competent to bear the strain of individual cases in the course of experience. The judge held it to be the duty of the court "to inform itself, as far as opportunity permits, of the general results of medical observation," and he quoted Dr. Ray, Dr. Prichard, and Dr. Esquirol. If the American law of insanity is to be that which the English probate court holds, from time to time, to be a matter of fact depending upon "the general results of medical observation," and the progress of medical science, we have no assurance that this branch of our law will be more stable hereafter than it has been heretofore.

The attempt to establish a legal test of mental disease, has been as unsuccessful in criminal, as in testamentary cases. In England, from 1826 to 1867 delusion was applied as the test in the latter; but it was not adopted in the former; and it was not shown how it happened that what was an infallible test of mental disease in a man when he disinherited his child, was no test of mental disease in him when he deprived his child of life. It has been held within one hundred and fifty years that the test in criminal cases is whether the defendant was totally deprived of his understanding and memory and did not know what he was doing any more than a wild beast. *King v. Arnold*. This was the original form of the knowledge test. In 1800 the Attorney General of England declared that this test had never been contradicted, but had always been adopted (*King v. Hadfield*). Erskine, in the same case said: "I will employ no artifices of speech. The attorney-general, standing undoubtedly upon the most revered authorities of the law, has laid it down, that to protect a man from *criminal responsibility*, there must be a total *deprivation of memory and understanding.*" The effort of Erskine was made with such "artifices of speech," that the court seem to have been mystified. When Lord Kenyon, satisfied that the defendant was insane, stopped the trial, and ordered a verdict of acquittal, his remark, that "With regard to the law as it has been laid down, there can be no doubt upon earth," apparently meant as it had been laid down by the Attorney General and by Erskine. He seems not to have understood that the ancient test was questioned; and yet, tried by that test, Hadfield must have been convicted. Hadfield's acquittal was not a judicial adoption of delusion as the test in the place of knowledge of right and wrong; it was probably an instance of the bewildering effect of Erskine's adroitness, rhetoric, and eloquence.

The common instincts of humanity have abandoned the original "wild beast" form of the knowledge test, only to adopt others equally arbitrary, though less shocking to the intelligence and sensibility of the age. Knowledge of right and wrong, in some degree, with more or less of explanation and variation, has always been, in theory, the test of criminal capacity in England, and generally in this country: the English courts have never recognized delusion as the test. They have noticed delusion only so far as it destroyed the knowledge of right and wrong; which is the same as an explicit rejection of it as a test. If knowledge of right and wrong is the test, it is immaterial whether that knowledge be destroyed by disease assuming the form of delusion, or any other form. It is matter of history that insanity has been for the most part, a growth of the modern state of society. Like many other diseases, it is caused, in a great degree, by the habits and incidents of civilized life. In the earlier and ruder ages, it was comparatively rare. Its present extent has been chiefly attained within a few hundred years. Until recently, there were no asylums for the insane, and no experts devoting their lives exclusively to the practical study and treatment of the disease. The necessary opportunities for obtaining a thorough understanding of it, did not exist until they were furnished by the positions of superintendents of asylums and their assistants. Consequently, until recently, there was very little knowledge of the subject.

In old books it is often found under the head of lunacy. Lord Hale was the first writer who undertook to introduce into a law book any considerable statement of the facts of mental disease. Not only was he guided by the best medical authorities of his day, but he carefully used the language of medical men. Among other current medical ideas which he recorded, was this: the insanity "which is interpolated, and by certain periods and vicissitudes," "is that, which is usually called *lunacy*, for the moon hath a great influence in all diseases of the brain, especially in this kind of *dementia*; such persons commonly in the full and change of the moon especially about the equinoxes and summer solstice, are usually in the height of their distemper"; and "such persons as have their lucid intervals (which ordinarily happens between the full and change of the moon) in such intervals, have usually at least a competent use of reason."

He did not imagine that this medical lunar theory was a principle of the common law. Lord Erskine, in delivering judgment in *Cranmer's case*, said, "the moon has no influence"; and the reporter inserted this marginal note, "In cases of lunacy, the notion, that the moon has an influence, erroneous." The reporter may not have distinguished between law and fact; but Erskine did not suppose that he was announcing his disagreement with Hale on a point of law. The other causes, symptoms, and tests of mental disease recorded by Hale, were as clear matters of fact as the lunar theory. The doctrines of insanity and witchcraft stated by Lord Hale, were held by him in common with the most enlightened classes of the most civilized nations. He was not their author, nor was he responsible for them. They were equally doctrines of fact; one was no more a matter of law than the other; and they are equally entitled to oblivion, although the ancient doctrine of insanity outlived the ancient doctrine of witchcraft. When we remember that the universal belief in witchcraft has been overcome within two hundred years, it is easy to understand how the phenomena of insanity were long regarded as supernatural. Witchcraft and demoniacal possession were accepted as truths taught by miraculous inspiration.

Cases of insanity were found, answering the biblical description of cases of demoniacal possession; but the suggestion that any of the latter might be cases of mental or physical disease, was received as an attack upon the infallibility of the scriptures. This state of things discouraged investigation, and encouraged the belief that insanity, at least in some of its forms, was demoniacal possession. The natural causes and operations of cerebral disease were mysterious; the theological clouds that encompassed it, were appalling. In a period of ignorance, credulity, superstition, and religious terrorism, before there was a science of medicine, we should not expect to find any scientific or accurate understanding of such a malady. Well might the boldest shrink from the exploration of a condition believed to be, in its origin, beyond the bounds of nature, and curable only by the power of exorcism. As the ancient theory of diabolism gradually passed away, insanity was still attributed to special providences, and not to the operation of the general laws of health. The sufferers were treated for wickedness rather than sickness. Among men of science, the investigation of the subject is now disencumbered of all theological complications. But this is a modern emancipation not yet realized by the mass of even the most enlightened communities. Very few persons have an adequate conception of the fact that insanity is a disease. The common notion of it, is of something not merely marvellous, but also peculiarly, vaguely, and indescribably connected with a higher or lower world. The insane are generally considered as more than sick; and if they are not spoken of as possessed, their condition, to the popular apprehension, is still enveloped in a supernatural shadow.

The Lord Chancellor of England declared, in the House of Lords, on the 11th day of March, 1862, that "the introduction of medical opinions and medical theories into this subject, has proceeded upon the vicious principle of considering insanity as a disease." This remark indicates how slowly legal superstitions are worn out, and how dogmatically the highest legal authorities of this age maintain, as law, tests of insanity, which are medical theories differing from those rejected by the same authorities, only in being the obsolete theories of a progressive science. It was, for a long time, supposed that men, however insane, if they knew an act to be wrong, could refrain from doing it. But whether that supposition is correct or not, is a pure question of fact. The sup-

> *It was, for a long time, supposed that men, however insane, if they knew an act to be wrong, could refrain from doing it.*

position is a supposition of fact, in other words, a medical supposition, in other words, a medical theory. Whether it originated in the medical or any other profession, or in the general notions of mankind, is immaterial. It is as medical in its nature as the opposite theory. The knowledge test in all its forms, and the delusion test, are medical theories introduced in immature stages of science, in the dim light of earlier times, and subsequently, upon more extensive observations and more critical examinations, repudiated by the medical profession. But legal tribunals have claimed those tests as immutable principles of law.

When the authorities of the common law began to deal with insanity, they adopted the prevailing medical theories. Without any conspicuous or material partition between law and fact, without a plain demarcation between a circumscribed province of the court and an independent province of the jury, the judges gave to juries, on questions of insanity, the best opinions which the times afforded. In this manner, opinions purely medical and pathological in their character, relating entirely to questions of fact, and full of error as medical experts now testify, passed into books of law, and acquired the force of judicial decisions. Defective medical theories usurped the position of common-law principles. The usurpation, when detected, should cease. The law does not change with every advance of science; nor does it maintain a fantastic consistency by adhering to medical mistakes which science has corrected. The legal principle however much it may formerly have been obscured by pathological darkness and confusion of law and fact, is, that a product of mental disease is not a contract, a will, or a crime. It is often difficult to ascertain whether an individual had a mental disease, and whether an act was the product of that disease; but these difficulties arise from the nature of the facts to be investigated, and not from the law; they are practical difficulties to be solved by the jury, and not legal difficulties for the court.

It is the common practice for experts, under the oath of a witness, to inform the jury, in substance, that knowledge is not the test, and for the judge, not under the oath of a witness, to inform the jury that knowledge is the test. And the situation is still more impressive, when the judge is forced by an impulse of humanity, as he often is, to substantially advise the jury to acquit the accused on the testimony of the experts, in violation of the test asserted by himself. The predicament is one which cannot be prolonged after it is realized. If the tests of insanity are matters of law, the practice of allowing experts to testify what they are, should be discontinued; if they are matters of fact, the judge should no longer testify without being sworn as a witness and showing himself qualified to testify as an expert. To say that the expert testifies to the tests of mental disease as a fact, and the judge declares the test of criminal responsibility as a rule of law, is only to state the dilemma in another form.

For, if the alleged act of a defendant, was the act of his mental disease, it was not, in law, his act, and he is no more responsible for it than he would be if it had been the act of his involuntary intoxi-

> *For, if the alleged act of a defendant, was the act of his mental disease, it was not, in law, his act, and he is no more responsible for it than he would be if it had been the act of his involuntary intoxication, or of another person using the defendant's hand against his utmost resistance.*

cation, or of another person using the defendant's hand against his utmost resistance; if the defendant's knowledge is the test of responsibility in one of these cases, it is the test in all of them. If he does know the act to be wrong, he is equally irresponsible whether his will is overcome, and his hand used, by the

> *When disease is the propelling, uncontrollable power, the man is as innocent as the weapon.*

irresistible power of his own mental disease, or by the irresistible power of another person. When disease is the propelling, uncontrollable power, the man is as innocent as the weapon—the mental and moral elements are as guiltless as the material. If his mental, moral, and bodily strength is subjugated and pressed to an involuntary service, it is immaterial whether it is done by his disease, or by another man, or a brute or any physical force of art or nature set in operation without any fault on his part. If a man knowing the difference between right and wrong, but deprived, by either of those agencies, of the power to choose between them, is punished, he is punished for his inability to make the choice—he is punished for incapacity; and that is the very thing for which the law says he shall not be punished. He might as well be punished for an incapacity to distinguish right from wrong, as for an incapacity to resist a mental disease which forces upon him its choice of the wrong.

> *If a man knowing the difference between right and wrong, but deprived, by either of those agencies, of the power to choose between them, is punished, he is punished for his inability to make the choice—he is punished for incapacity; and that is the very thing for which the law says he shall not be punished.*

Parsons v. State

2 So. 854 (1886)

Facts

Bennett Parsons was shot and killed by his wife, Nancy, and daughter, Joe Parsons. Evidence at their trial showed that Joe was an "idiot" and Nancy was a "lunatic," believing "insane delusions" that her husband had supernatural powers to inflict disease on her and was going to use a "supernatural trick" to take her life. The trial court charged the jury with instructions indicating that defendants must be found sane if they knew their acts were unlawful and morally wrong and that delusions are no justification *unless* the delusional beliefs, if true, would excuse homicide under the law for a sane person. The defense objected to the jury instructions and proposed two alternatives. First the defense argued for an instruction that defendants are not guilty if their acts are "offspring or product of mental disease." Second, the defense proposed an instruction that defendants are not guilty if "moved to action by an insane impulse controlling their will or their judgment." The jury convicted the defendants of second-degree murder, and Nancy and Joe Parsons appealed.

Issue

Is the insanity criteria, essentially the *M'Naghten* rule, an adequate test of legal responsibility given the current state of knowledge (in 1886)?

Holding

No. The convictions were reversed and the case remanded.

Analysis

The Alabama Supreme Court reviewed several important English and American cases and the writings of several contemporary renowned psychiatrists. The court criticized the *M'Naghten* rule as a "single test" of insanity, based on 100-year-old medical theories. They pointed out that directors of asylums testify that anyone can easily find insane residents who can distinguish right from wrong, and management of asylums presupposes such a knowledge. They emphasized, "No one can deny that there are two constituent elements of legal responsibility: (1) Capacity of intellectual discrimination; and (2) Freedom of will." Finally, they adopted

new criteria for insanity which stated that even a person who knows right
from wrong may be considered not legally responsible if (a) they had lost
the power to choose between right and wrong and to avoid the act, as that
their "free agency" was destroyed, and (b) the crime was "so connected
with such mental disease" in terms of cause and effect that it was a "product
of it solely."

Edited Excerpts[1]

PARSONS v. STATE

Supreme Court of Alabama

Opinion by Somerville

The indictment in this case charged that the defendants, Nancy J.
Parsons and [daughter] Joe Parsons, unlawfully and with malice
aforethought killed Bennett Parsons by shooting him with a gun. On said
trial the evidence, on behalf of the State, tended to show that the
defendants, Joe Parsons and Nancy J. Parsons, murdered Bennett Parsons
on Jan. 31, 1885, by shooting him with a gun.

The evidence on behalf of defendants tended to show that defendant,
Joe Parsons, was at the time of said killing, and had always been an idiot;
and that defendant, Nancy Parsons, was, at the time of said killing, insane
or lunatic; that the act of
Nancy, assisting in the
killing of deceased, was the
result of an insane delusion
that deceased possessed supernatural power to inflict

> **Joe Parsons was at the time of
> said killing and had always been
> an idiot.**

her with disease, and power by means of a supernatural trick, to take her
life; that deceased by means of such supernatural power had caused said
Nancy to be sick and in bad health for a long time, and that her act at the
time of said killing, in assisting therein, was under the insane delusion
that she was in great danger of the loss of her life from deceased, to be
effected by a supernatural trick. The defendant, Nancy, was the wife of
deceased, and defendant, Joe, was his daughter. The evidence also tended
to show insanity for two generations in the families of said defendants.

---

[1] Readers are advised to quote only from the original published cases. See pages vi and vii.

The court charged the jury that, "When insanity is relied on as a defense to crime, and such insanity consists of a delusion merely, and the defendant is not shown to be otherwise insane, then such delusion is no justification or excuse of homicide unless the perpetrator was insanely deluded into the belief of the existence of a fact or state of facts which, if true, would justify or excuse the homicide under the law applicable to sane persons." The defendants duly excepted to the giving of this charge.

The jury, on their retirement, found the defendants guilty of murder in the second degree, and this appeal is prosecuted from the judgment rendered on such finding.

The capacity to distinguish between right and wrong, either abstractly or as applied to the particular act, as a legal test of responsibility for crime, is repudiated by the modern and more advanced authorities, legal and medical, who lay down the following rules which the court now adopts: (1) where there is no such capacity to distinguish between right and wrong as applied to the particular act, there is no legal responsibility; (2) where there is such capacity, a defendant is nevertheless not legally responsible, if, by reason of the duress of mental disease, he has so far lost the power to choose between right and wrong, as not to avoid doing the act in question, so that his free agency was at the time destroyed; and, at the same time, the alleged crime was so connected with such mental disease, in the relation of cause and effect, as to have been the product or offspring of it solely.

In this case the defendants have been convicted of the murder of Bennett Parsons, by shooting him with a gun, one of the defendants being the wife and the other the daughter of the deceased. The defense set up in the trial was the plea of insanity, the evidence tending to show that the daughter was an idiot, and the mother and wife a lunatic, subject to insane delusions, and that the killing on her part was the offspring and product of those delusions.

It has become of late a matter of comment among intelligent men, including the most advanced thinkers in the medical and legal professions, that the deliverances of the law courts on this branch of our jurisprudence have not heretofore been at all satisfactory, either in the soundness of their theories, or in their practical application. The earliest English decisions, striving to establish rules and tests on the subject, including alike the legal rules of criminal and civil responsibility, and the supposed tests of the existence of the disease of insanity itself, are now admitted to have been deplorably erroneous, and, to say nothing of their vacillating character, have long since been abandoned. The views of the ablest of the old text writers and sages of the law were equally confused and uncertain in the treatment of these subjects, and they are now entirely exploded.

So great a jurist as Lord Coke, in his attempted classification of madmen, laid down the legal rule of criminal responsibility to be that one should "wholly have lost his memory and understanding"; as to which Mr. Erskine, when defending Hadfield for shooting the King, in the year 1800, justly observed: "No such madman ever existed in the world." After this great and historical case, the existence of delusion promised for a while to become the sole test of insanity, and acting under the duress of such delusion was recognized in effect as the legal rule of responsibility. Lord Kenyon, after ordering a verdict of acquittal in that case, declared with emphasis that there was "no doubt on earth" the law was correctly stated in the argument of counsel. But, as it was soon discovered that insanity often existed without delusions, as well as delusions without insanity, this view was also abandoned. Lord Hale had before declared that the rule of responsibility was measured by the mental capacity possessed by a child fourteen years of age, and Mr. Justice Tracy, and other judges, had ventured to decide that, to be non-punishable for alleged acts of crime, "a man must be totally deprived of his understanding and memory, so as not to know what he was doing—no more than an infant, a brute, or a wild beast."

All these rules have necessarily been discarded in modern times in the light of the new scientific knowledge acquired by a more thorough study of the disease of insanity. In *Bellingham's* Case, decided in 1812, by Lord Mansfield at the Old Bailey, the test was held to consist in a knowledge that murder, the crime there committed, was "against the laws of God and nature," thus meaning an ability to distinguish between right and wrong in the abstract. This rule was not adhered to, but seems to have been modified so as to make the test rather a knowledge of right and wrong as applied to the particular act. The great leading case on this subject in England, is *M'Naghten's* Case, decided in 1843 before the English House of Lords. It was decided by the judges in that case, that, in order to entitle the accused to acquittal, it must be clearly proved that, at the time of committing the offense, he was laboring under such a defect of reason, from disease of the mind, as not to know the nature and quality of the act he was doing, or, if he did, not to know that what he was doing was wrong. This rule is commonly supposed to have heretofore been adopted by this court, and has been followed by the general current of American adjudications.

In view of these conflicting decisions, and of the new light thrown on the disease of insanity by the discoveries of modern psychological medicine, the courts of the country may well hesitate before blindly following in the unsteady footsteps found upon the old sandstones of our common law jurisprudence a century ago. We do not hesitate to say that we re-open the discussion of this subject with no little reluctance, having long hesitated to disturb our past decisions on this branch of the law. Nothing could induce us to do so except an imperious sense of duty, which has

> *In view of the new light thrown on the disease of insanity, the courts of the country may well hesitate before blindly following in the unsteady footsteps found upon the old sandstones of our common law jurisprudence a century ago.*

been excited by a protracted investigation and study, impressing our minds with the conviction that the law of insanity as declared by the courts on many points, and especially the rule of criminal accountability, and the assumed tests of disease, to that extent which confers legal irresponsibility, have not kept pace with the progress of thought and discovery, in the present advanced stages of medical science. Though science has led the way, the courts of England have declined to follow, as shown by their adherence to the rulings in *M'Naghten's* Case.

It is not surprising that this state of affairs has elicited from a learned law writer, who treats of this subject, the humiliating declaration, that, under the influence of these ancient theories, "the memorials of our jurisprudence are written all over with cases in which those who are now understood to have been insane, have been executed as criminals." There is good reason, both for this fact, and for the existence of unsatisfactory rules on this subject. In what we say we do not intend to give countenance to acquittals of criminals, frequent examples of which have been witnessed in modern times, based on the doctrine of moral or emotional insanity, unconnected with mental disease, which is not yet sufficiently supported by psychology, or recognized by law as an excuse for crime.

In ancient times, lunatics were not regarded as "unfortunate sufferers from

> *In ancient times, lunatics were not regarded as "unfortunate sufferers from disease, but rather as subjects of demoniacal possession, or as self-made victims of evil passions."*

disease, but rather as subjects of demoniacal possession, or as self-made victims of evil passions." They were not cared for humanely in asylums and hospitals, but were incarcerated in jails, punished with chains and stripes, and often sentenced to death by burning or the gibbet. When put on their trial, the issue before the court then was not as now. If acquitted, they could only be turned loose on the community to repeat their crimes without molestation or restraint. They could not be committed to hospitals, as at the present day, to be kept

> **They were not cared for humanely in asylums and hospitals, but were incarcerated in jails, punished with chains and stripes, and often sentenced to death by burning or the gibbet.**

in custody, cared for by medical attention, and often cured. It was not until the beginning of the present century that the progress of Christian civilization asserted itself by the exposure of the then existing barbarities, and that the outcry of philanthropists succeeded in eliciting an investigation of the British Parliament looking to their suppression. Up to that period the medical treatment of the insane is known to have been conducted upon a basis of ignorance, inhumanity, and empiricism. Being punished for wickedness, rather than treated for disease, this is not surprising. The exposure of these evils not only led to the establishment of that most beneficent of modern civilized charities—the Hospital and Asylum for the Insane—but also furnished hitherto unequalled opportunities to the medical profession of investigating and treating insanity on the pathological basis of its being a disease of the mind.

Under these new and more favorable conditions the medical jurisprudence of insanity has assumed an entirely new phase. The nature and exciting causes of the disease have been thoroughly studied and more fully comprehended. The result is that the "right and wrong test," as it is sometimes called, which, it must be remembered, itself originated with the medical profession, in the mere dawn of the scientific knowledge of insanity, has been condemned by the great current of modern medical authorities, who believe it to be "founded on an ignorant and imperfect view of the disease."

The question then presented seems to be, whether an old rule of legal responsibility shall be adhered to, based on theories of physicians promulgated a hundred years ago, which refuse to recognize any evidence of insanity, except the single test of mental capacity to distinguish right and wrong—or whether the courts will recognize as a possible fact, if capable of proof by clear and satisfactory testimony, the doctrine, now alleged by those of the medical profession who have made insanity a special subject of investigation, that the old test is wrong, and that there is no single test by which the existence of the disease, to that degree which exempts from punishment, can in every case be infallibly detected. There is inherent in it the vital principle of juridical evolution, which preserves itself by a constant struggle for approximation to the highest practical wisdom. It is not like the laws of the Medes and Persians, which could not be changed. In establishing any new rule, we should strive, however, to have proper regard for two opposite aspects of the subject, lest, in the words of Lord Hale, "on one side, there be a kind of inhumanity towards the defects of human nature; or, on the other, too great indulgence to great crimes."

It is everywhere admitted, and as to this there can be no doubt, that an idiot, lunatic, or other person of diseased mind, who is afflicted to such extent as not to know whether he is doing right or wrong, is not punishable for any act which he may do while in that state. Can the courts justly say, however, that the only test or rule of responsibility in criminal cases is the power to distinguish right from wrong, whether in the abstract, or as applied to the particular case? Or may there not be insane persons, of a diseased brain, who, while capable of perceiving the difference between right and wrong, are, as matter of fact, so far under the duress of such disease as to destroy the power to choose between right and wrong? Will the courts assume as a fact, not to be rebutted by any amount of evidence, or any new discoveries of medical science, that there is, and can be no such state of the mind as that described by a writer on psychological medicine, as one "in which the reason has lost its empire over the passions, and the actions by which they are manifested, to such a degree that the individual can neither repress the former, nor abstain from the latter?"

We first consider what is the proper legal rule of responsibility in criminal cases. No one can deny that there must be two constituent elements of legal responsibility in the commission of every crime, and no rule can be just and reasonable which fails to recognize either of them: (1) Capacity of intellectual discrimination; and (2) Freedom of will. Mr. Wharton, after recognizing this fundamental and obvious principle, observes: "If there be either incapacity to distinguish between right and wrong as to the particular act, or delusion as to the act, or inability to refrain from doing the act, there is no responsibility." Says Mr. Bishop, in discussing this subject: "There can not be, and there is not, in any locality, or age, a law punishing men for what they can not avoid."

If therefore, it be true, as matter of fact, that the disease of insanity can, in its action on the human brain through a shattered nervous organization, or in any other mode, so affect the mind as to subvert the freedom of the will, and thereby destroy the power of the victim to choose between the right and wrong, although he perceive it—by which we mean the power of volition to adhere in action to the right and abstain from the wrong—is such a one criminally responsible for an act done under the influence of such controlling disease? We clearly think not, and such, we believe to be the just, reasonable, and humane rule, towards which all the modern authorities in this country, legislation in England, and the laws of other civilized countries of the world, are gradually, but surely tending, as we shall further on attempt more fully to show.

We next consider the question as to the probable existence of such a disease, and the test of its presence in a given case. It will not do for the courts to dogmatically deny the possible existence of such a disease, or its pathological and psychical effects, because this is a matter of evidence, not of law, or judicial cognizance. Its existence, and effect on the mind and conduct of the patient, is a question of fact to be proved, just as much as the possible existence of cholera or yellow fever formerly was before these diseases became the subjects of common knowledge, or the effects of delirium from fever, or intoxication from opium and alcoholic stimulants would be. The courts could, with just as much propriety, years ago, have denied the existence of the Copernican system of the universe, the efficacy of steam and electricity as a motive power, or the possibility of communication in a few moments between the continents of Europe and America by the magnetic telegraph, or that of the instantaneous transmission of the human voice from one distant city to another by the use of the telephone. These are scientific facts, first discovered by experts before becoming matters of common knowledge. So, in like manner, must be every other unknown scientific fact in whatever profession or department of knowledge. The existence of such a cerebral disease, as that which we have described, is earnestly alleged by the superintendents of insane hospitals, and other experts, who constantly have experimental dealings with the insane, and they are permitted every day to so testify before juries. The truth of their testimony—or what is the same thing, the existence or non-existence of such a disease of the mind—in each particular case, is necessarily a matter for the determination of the jury from the evidence.

So it is equally obvious that the courts, can not, upon any sound principle, undertake to say what are the invariable or infallible tests of such disease. The attempt has been repeatedly made, and has proved a confessed failure in practice. "Such a test," says Mr. Bishop, "has never been found, not because those who have searched for it have not been able and diligent, but because it does not exist." In this conclusion, Dr.

Ray, in his learned work on the *Medical Jurisprudence of Insanity*, fully concurs. The symptoms and causes of insanity are so variable, and its pathology so complex, that no two cases may be just alike. "The fact of its existence," says Dr. Ray, "is never established by any single diagnostic symptom, but by the whole body of symptoms, no particular one of which is present in every case." Its exciting causes being moral, psychical, and physical, are the especial subjects of specialists' study. What effect may be exerted on the given patient by age, sex, occupation, the seasons, personal surroundings, hereditary transmission, and other causes, is the subject of evidence based on investigation, diagnosis, observation, and experiment. Peculiar opportunities, never before enjoyed in the history of our race, are offered in the present age for the ascertainment of these facts, by the establishment of asylums for the custody and treatment of the insane, which Christian benevolence and statesmanship have substituted for jails and gibbets. The testimony of these experts—differ as they may in many doubtful cases—would seem to be the best which can be obtained, however unsatisfactory it may be in some respects.

In the present state of our law, under the rule in *M'Naghten's* Case, we are confronted with this practical difficulty, which itself demonstrates the defects of the rule. The courts in effect charge the juries, as matter of law, that no such mental disease exists, as that often testified to by medical writers, superintendents of insane hospitals, and other experts—that there can be as matter of scientific fact no cerebral defect, congenital or acquired, which destroys the patient's power of self-control—his liberty of will and action—provided only he retains a mental consciousness of right and wrong. The experts are immediately put under oath, and tell the juries just the contrary, as matter of evidence; asserting that no one of ordinary intelligence can spend an hour in the wards of an insane asylum without discovering such cases, and in fact that "the whole management of such asylums presupposes a knowledge of right and wrong on the part of their inmates." The result in practice, we repeat, is, that the courts charge one way, and the jury, following an alleged higher law of humanity, find another, in harmony with the evidence.

In Bucknill on *Criminal Lunacy*, it is asserted as "the result of observation and experience, that in all lunatics, and in the most degraded idiots, whenever manifestations of any mental action can be educed, the feeling of right and wrong may be proved to exist." "With regard to this test," says Dr. Russell Reynolds, in his work on *The Scientific Value of the Legal Tests of Insanity*, "I may say, and most emphatically, that it is utterly untrustworthy, because untrue to the obvious facts of Nature."

In the learned treatise of Drs. Bucknill and Tuke on *Psychological Medicine*, the legal tests of responsibility are discussed, and the adherence of the courts to the right and wrong test is deplored as unfortunate, the true principle being stated to be "whether, in consequence of congenital defect or acquired disease, the power of self-control is absent altogether, or is so far wanting as to render the individual irresponsible." It is observed by the authors: "As has again and again been shown, the unconsciousness of right and wrong is one thing, and the powerlessness through cerebral defect or disease to do right is another. To confound them in an asylum would have the effect of transferring a considerable number of the inmates thence to the treadmill or the gallows."

Dr. Peter Bryce, Superintendent of the Alabama Insane Hospital for more than a quarter century past, alluding to the moral and disciplinary treatment to which the insane inmates are subjected, observes: "They are dealt with in this institution, as far as it is practicable to do so, as rational beings; and it seldom happens that we meet with an insane person who can not be made to discern, to some feeble extent, his duties to himself and others, and his true relations to society." Other distinguished writers on the medical jurisprudence of insanity have expressed like views, with comparative unanimity. And no where do we find the rule more emphatically condemned than by those who have the practical care and treatment of the insane in the various lunatic asylums of every civilized country. A notable instance is found in the following resolution unanimously passed at the annual meeting of the British Association of medical officers of Asylums and Hospitals for the Insane, held in London, July 14, 1864, where there were present fifty-four medical officers:

"Resolved, That so much of the legal test of the mental condition of an alleged criminal lunatic as renders him a responsible agent, because he knows the difference between right and wrong, is inconsistent with the fact, well known to every member of this meeting, that the power of distinguishing between right and wrong exists very frequently in those who are undoubtedly insane, and is often associated with dangerous and uncontrollable delusions." These testimonials as to a scientific fact are recognized by intelligent men in the affairs of every day business, and are constantly acted on by juries. They can not be silently ignored by judges. Whether established or not, there is certainly respectable evidence tending to establish it, and this is all the courts can require.

Nor are the modern law writers silent in their disapproval of the alleged test under discussion. It meets with the criticism or condemnation of the most respectable and advanced in thought among them, the tendency being to incorporate in the legal rule of responsibility "not only the knowledge of good and evil, but the power to choose the one, and refrain from the other." The following practicable suggestion is made in the able treatise of Balfour Browne: "In a case of alleged insanity, then," he says, "if the individual suffering from enfeeblement of intellect, delusion, or any other form of mental aberration, was looked upon as, to the extent of this delusion, under the influence of duress (the dire duress of disease), and in so far incapacitated to choose the good and eschew the evil, in so far, it seems to us," he continues, "would the requirements of the law be fulfilled; and in that way it would afford an opening, by the evidence of experts, for the proof of the amount of self-duress in each individual case, and thus alone can the criterion of law and the criterion of the inductive science of medical psychology be made to coincide." This, in our judgment, is the practical solution of the difficulty before us, as it preserves to the courts and the juries, respectively, a harmonious field for the full assertion of their time honored functions.

The case of *United States v. Lawrence*, tried in 1835, presented an instance of delusion, the prisoner supposing himself to be the King of England and of the United States as an appendage of England, and that General Jackson, then President, stood in his way in the enjoyment of the right. Acting under the duress of this delusion, the accused assaulted the President by attempting to shoot him with a pistol. He was, in five minutes, acquitted by the jury on the ground of insanity.

The case of the *United States v. Guiteau*, is still fresh in contemporary recollection, and a mention of it can scarcely be omitted in the discussion of the subject of insanity. The accused was tried, sentenced, and executed for the assassination of James A. Garfield, then President of the United States, which occurred in July, 1881. The accused himself testified that he was impelled to commit the act of killing by inspiration from the Almighty, in order, as he declared, "to unite the two factions of the Republican party, and thereby save the government from going into the hands of the ex-rebels and their Northern allies." There was evidence of various symptoms of mental unsoundness, and some evidence tending to prove such an alleged delusion, but there was also evidence to the contrary, strongly supported by the most distinguished experts, and looking to the conclusion, that the accused entertained no such delusion, but that, being a very eccentric and immoral man, he acted from moral obliquity, the morbid love of notoriety, and with the expressed hope that the faction of the Republican party, in whose interest he professed to act, would intervene to protect him. The case was tried before the United States District Court, for the District of Columbia, before Mr. Justice Cox, whose charge to the jury is replete with interest and learning. While he adopted the right and wrong test of insanity, he yet recognized the principle, that, if the accused in fact entertained an insane delusion, which was the product of the disease of insanity, and not of a malicious heart and vicious nature, and acted solely under the influence of such delusion, he could not be charged with entertaining a criminal intent. An insane delusion was defined to be "an unreasoning and incorrigible belief in the existence of facts, which are either impossible absolutely, or impossible under the circumstances of the individual," and no doubt the case was largely determined by the application of this definition by the jury. It must ever be a mere matter of speculation what influence may have been exerted upon them by the high personal and political significance of the deceased, as the Chief Magistrate of the Government, or other peculiar surroundings of a partisan nature. The case in its facts is so peculiar as scarcely to serve the purpose of a useful precedent in the future.

In *State v. Felter*, the capacity to distinguish between right and wrong was held not to be a safe test of criminal responsibility in all cases, and it was accordingly decided, that, if a person commit a homicide, knowing it to be wrong, but do so under the influence of an uncontrollable and irresistible impulse, arising not from natural passion, but from an insane condition of the mind, he is not criminally responsible. In *Hopps v. People*, which was an indictment for murder, the same rule was recognized in different words. It was there held, that if, at the time of the killing, the defendant was not of sound mind, but affected with insanity, and such disease was the efficient cause of the act, operating to create an uncontrollable impulse so as to deprive the accused of the power of volition in the matter, and he would not have done the act but for the existence of such condition of mind, he ought to be acquitted.

Numerous other cases could be cited bearing on this particular phase of the law, and supporting the above views with more or less clearness of statement. That some of these cases adopt the extreme view, and recognize moral insanity as a defense to crime, and others adopt a measure of proof for the establishment of insanity more liberal to the defendant than our own rule, can neither lessen their weight as authority, nor destroy the force of their logic. Many of them go further on each of these points than this court has done, and are, therefore, stronger authorities than they would otherwise be in support of our views.

The practical trouble is for the courts to determine in what particular cases the party on trial is to be transferred from the category of sane to that of insane criminals—where, in other words, the border line of punishability is adjudged to be passed. But, as has been said in reference to an every day fact of nature, no one can say where twilight ends or begins, but there is ample distinction nevertheless between day and night. We think we can safely rely in this matter upon the intelligence of our juries, guided by the testimony of men who have practically made a study of the disease of insanity; and enlightened by a conscientious desire, on the one hand, to enforce the criminal laws of the land, and on the other, not to deal harshly with any

> **But, as has been said in reference to an every day fact of nature, no one can say where twilight ends or begins, but there is ample distinction nevertheless between day and night.**

unfortunate victim of a diseased mind, acting without the light of reason, or the power of volition.

It is almost needless to add that where one does not act under the duress of a diseased mind, or insane delusion, but from motives of anger, revenge or other passion, he can not claim to be shielded from punishment for crime on the ground of insanity. Insanity proper, is more or less a mental derangement, coexisting often, it is true, with a disturbance of the emotions, affections and other moral powers. A mere moral, or emotional insanity, so-called, unconnected with disease of the mind, or irresistible impulse resulting from mere moral obliquity, or wicked propensities and habits, is not recognized as a defense to crime in our courts.

The charges refused by the court raise the question as to how far one acting under the influence of an insane delusion is to be exempted from criminal accountability. The evidence tended to show that one of the defendants, Mrs. Nancy J. Parsons, acted under the influence of an insane delusion that the deceased, whom she assisted in killing, possessed supernatural power to afflict her with disease and to take her life by some "supernatural trick"; that by means of such power the deceased had caused defendant to be in bad health for a long time, and that she acted under the belief that she was in great danger of the loss of her life from the conduct of deceased operating by means of such supernatural power.

The rule in *M'Naghten's* Case, as decided by the English judges, and supposed to have been adopted by the court, is that the defense of insane delusion can be allowed to prevail in a criminal case only when the imaginary state of facts would, if real, justify or excuse the act; or, in the language of the English judges themselves, the defendant "must be considered in the same situation as to responsibility, as if the facts with respect to which the delusion exists were real." It is apparent, from what we have said, that this rule can not be correct as applied to all cases of this nature, even limiting it as done by the English judges to cases where one "labors under partial delusion, and is not in other respects insane." If the rule declared by the English judges be correct, it necessarily follows that the only possible instance of excusable homicide in cases of delusional insanity would be, where the delusion, if real, would have been such as to create, in the mind of a reasonable man, a just apprehension of imminent peril to life or limb. It would follow also, under this rule, that the partially insane man, afflicted with delusions, would no more be excusable than a sane man would be, if, perchance, it was by his fault the difficulty was provoked, whether by word or deed; or, if he may have been so negligent as not to have declined combat when he could do so safely, without increasing his peril of life or limb. If this has been the law heretofore, it is time it should be so no longer. It is not only opposed to the known facts of modern medical science, but it is a hard and unjust rule to be applied to the unfortunate and providential victims of disease. It seems to be little less than inhumane, and its strict enforcement would probably transfer a large percentage of the inmates of our Insane Hospital from that institution to hard labor in the mines, or the penitentiary. Its fallacy consists in the assumption that no other phase of delusion, proceeding from a diseased brain, can so destroy the volition of an insane person as to render him powerless to do what he knows to be right, or to avoid doing what he may know to be wrong.

This inquiry, as we have said, and here repeat, is a question of fact for the determination of the jury in each particular case. It is not a matter of law to be decided by the courts. We think it sufficient if the insane delusion—by which we mean the delusion proceeding from a diseased mind—sincerely exists at the time of committing the alleged crime, and the defendant believing it to be real, is so influenced by it as either to render him incapable of perceiving the true nature and quality of the act done, by reason of the depravation of the reasoning faculty, or so subverts his will as to destroy his free agency by rendering him powerless to resist by reason of the duress of the disease. In such a case, in other words, there must exist either one of two conditions: (1) Such mental defect as to render the defendant unable to distinguish between right and wrong in relation to the particular act; or (2) the overmastering of defendant's will in consequence of the insane delusion under the influence of which he acts, produced by disease of the mind or brain.

In conclusion of this branch of the subject, that we may not be misunderstood, we think it follows very clearly from what we have said, that the inquiries to be submitted to the jury then, in every criminal trial where the defense of insanity is interposed, are these:

1. Was the defendant at the time of the commission of the alleged crime, as matter of fact, afflicted with a disease of the mind, so as to be either idiotic, or otherwise insane?
2. If such be the case, did he know right from wrong as applied to the particular act in question? If he did not have such knowledge, he is not legally responsible.
3. If he did have such knowledge, he may nevertheless not be legally responsible if the two following conditions concur:

    (1) If, by reason of the duress of such mental disease, he had so far lost the power to choose between the right and wrong, and to avoid doing the act in question, as that his free agency was at the time destroyed.

    (2) And if, at the same time, the alleged crime was so connected with such mental disease, in the relation of cause and effect, as to have been the product of it solely.

The judgment is reversed and the cause remanded. In the meanwhile the prisoners will be held in custody until discharged by due process of law.

Summary

It is not a "new" idea in *Arnold* that "if a man be deprived of his reason, and consequently of his intention, he cannot be guilty; and if that be the case, . . . he is exempted from punishment." Mosaic law, for example, provided for "cities of refuge" for persons who had killed others "without intent." Persons who had killed others accidentally could flee to those cities and be protected from avenging family members. *Arnold* and *Hadfield* concern the evolution of how insanity is construed, but excusing "insane acts" was already a long-established principle in 1800.

A primary consideration within *Pike*, which we alluded to only, was whether "dipsomania" should be construed as insanity. (We redacted *Pike* quite a bit to improve readability; *Pike* is otherwise replete with citations of insanity cases in American courtrooms throughout the 1800s.) *Pike* holds that alcoholism cannot be construed as insanity; the dissenting opinion is one that characterizes the majority opinion in *Parsons*: "When disease is the propelling, uncontrollable power, the man is as innocent as the weapon." *Parsons*, which also reviews quite a bit of much earlier insanity law, concerns not just an impairment of intention, but an impairment of impulse: Why punish defendants who *could not* suppress the intention?

As is obvious from reading these cases, and in the context of the panel interview in *M'Naghten*, insanity law becomes a matter of integrating what is known about human intention, understanding, and impulse control with what the law considers to be fair. Psychology and psychiatry continued to progress through the 1900s and continued to substantially impact insanity law (considered in Section 4). In our next section, we focus more precisely on insanity issues and (American) constitutional protections.

Section 3

Insanity and the U.S. Constitution

Introduction to Section 3

Cases

    Powell v. Texas

    Davis v. United States

    Leland v. Oregon

    Finger v. Nevada

    Clark v. Arizona

Summary

Introduction to Section 3

The first case, *Powell v. Texas* (1968), is a United States Supreme Court decision concerning a defendant who was convicted of being drunk in public. In an earlier decision (*Robinson v. California*, 1962), the Court struck down on Eighth Amendment[1] grounds a California law that allowed conviction for the status of being addicted to narcotics. Based on that holding, Powell appealed his conviction. Although this case is not commonly construed as insanity law, the Court made important points regarding common law concepts of personal responsibility. In *Powell*, the Court made a clear distinction between punishing individuals for their status (being addicted) and punishing individuals for their actions (going into a public place while intoxicated). They considered the "centuries-long evolution" of concepts used to determine moral accountability and concluded that accepting Powell's argument would force the Court into creating a constitutionally mandated "product" test of insanity, which they viewed as "fruitless."

In *Davis v. United States* (1895), the United States Supreme Court dealt with the issues of burden and standard of proof in a federal insanity case. Davis had been convicted following jury instructions that required the defendant to prove he was insane at the time of the offense. In its holding, the Court reversed his conviction and established a process in federal court that remained up to the time of Hinckley's trial. This case discussed the presumption that all persons are sane and the necessity of such a presumption for the efficient operation of justice. It also spelled out that the presumption was rebuttable by "some evidence" after which the prosecution would have the burden of proving (beyond a reasonable doubt) that the defendant belonged to "a class capable of committing crime," that is, the sane.

---

[1] See Appendix B (pp. 291-292).

In *Leland v. Oregon* (1952), the defendant appealed his conviction for first-degree murder to the United States Supreme Court, claiming a Fourteenth Amendment[2] due process violation. Oregon required the defendant to prove his insanity beyond a reasonable doubt. Leland, relying on *Davis*, claimed that such a burden required the defendant to prove his innocence. The Supreme Court distinguished the prosecution's burden of proving every element of the offense including intent from the separate issue of proving insanity, and held that the defendant could be required to prove his insanity. They concluded that placing the burden of proof on the defendant was common and was established in *M'Naghten*. They clarified that the decision in *Davis* only applied to procedures in federal court and did not establish a constitutional requirement for the states to follow.

Next, we consider a decision from the Nevada Supreme Court, *Finger v. Nevada* (2001). Finger was prevented from entering a plea of not guilty by reason of insanity (to the charge of murdering his mother) because the state legislature had abolished the plea in 1995. After he pled guilty but mentally ill, he was sentenced to life in prison and appealed on Eighth and Fourteenth Amendment grounds. The Nevada Supreme Court decision contains an excellent discussion of constitutional issues in the insanity defense, citing the first three cases of this chapter. The court distinguished *mens rea* defenses from insanity and, in striking down the Nevada statute as unconstitutional, makes the intriguing argument that knowledge of wrongfulness constituted an element of some offenses, and legal insanity could not be eliminated by the state legislature.

The last case we consider is *Clark v. Arizona*, decided by the United States Supreme Court (2006). Clark, who killed a police officer and suffered from paranoid schizophrenia, unsuccessfully attempted an insanity defense. Arizona's 1993 revised insanity test contained only the wrongfulness prong of *M'Naghten*. Due to that statutory change, Clark was not allowed to present expert evidence concerning his lack of understanding of the nature and quality of his actions as part of an affirmative insanity defense; nor, as a result of Arizona case law, was he able to present such evidence to rebut the *mens rea* required for first-degree murder. He appealed these prohibitions as violations of due process. In affirming his conviction, the Supreme Court issued an opinion which seems in stark contrast to *Finger*. They gave deference to the state in deciding its insanity test and, as in *Powell*, resisted establishing a constitutional requirement. In addressing the *mens rea* issue, the Court

---

[2] See Appendix B (pp. 291-292).

created a new framework from which to view evidence that might relate to *mens rea*. The Court also expressed concern regarding mental health experts rendering opinions about a defendant's legal capacities, suggesting that such evidence might confuse jurors and allow defendants a means to avoid criminal responsibility without carrying the burden required in an affirmative insanity defense.

Powell v. Texas

392 U.S. 514 (1968)

Facts

After his conviction for drunkenness in a public place, Leroy Powell was fined $50. Expert testimony during trial indicated that he was a "chronic alcoholic" who was subject to a "compulsion" to drink, which, while "not overwhelming," was "an exceedingly strong influence." On appeal, it was argued that because Powell's actions resulted from his alcoholism, punishing the behavior was cruel and unusual.

Issue

This case addresses issues of culpability with respect to medical and psychiatric conditions. More specifically, the case addresses whether it is unconstitutional to convict an alcoholic for drunkenness in a public place.

Holding

No. The Supreme Court ruled that the limited record in this case was "utterly inadequate" to support a new and wide-ranging constitutional principle.

Analysis

Powell argued that because his "compulsion" to drink was associated with a "disease," it was a violation of the principles established in *Robinson v. California* to punish him for that behavior. In *Robinson*, the Supreme Court stated an individual could not be prosecuted for the mere status of addiction. The resulting decision questioned the testimony of a psychiatrist who concluded that Powell was "powerless not to drink," but nevertheless acknowledged that Powell's act of taking his first drink was a voluntary one. The Court juxtaposed the concepts of compulsion and free will, and they noted the debate within the medical community regarding whether alcoholism is a disease.

The Court envisioned chaos should Powell's arguments be upheld, given that similar arguments could be put forth for a virtually unlimited number of psychiatric scenarios. Had Powell prevailed, the Court concluded that the mere presence of a psychiatric disorder might necessarily lead to an acquittal. Thus, they shunned the opportunity to establish an insanity test "in constitutional terms."

Edited Excerpts[1]

Opinion: Mr. Justice Marshall announced the judgment of
the Court and delivered an opinion in which The Chief Justice,
Mr. Justice Black, and Mr. Justice Harlan join.

In late December 1966, appellant was arrested and charged with being found in a state of intoxication in a public place, in violation of Texas Penal Code, which reads as follows: "Whoever shall get drunk or be found in a state of intoxication in any public place, or at any private house except his own, shall be fined not exceeding one hundred dollars." Appellant was tried in the Corporation Court of Austin, Texas, found guilty, and fined $20. He appealed to the County Court at Law No. 1 of Travis County, Texas, where a trial was held. His counsel urged that appellant was "afflicted with the disease of chronic alcoholism," that "his appearance in public while drunk was not of his own volition," and therefore that to punish him criminally for that conduct would be cruel and unusual, in violation of the Eighth and Fourteenth Amendments[2] to the United States Constitution. The trial judge in the county court, sitting without a jury, ruled as a matter of law that chronic alcoholism was not a defense to the charge. He found appellant guilty, and fined him $50. There being no further right to appeal within the Texas judicial system, appellant appealed to this Court; we noted probable jurisdiction.

The principal testimony was that of Dr. David Wade, a Fellow of the American Medical Association, duly certificated in psychiatry. Dr. Wade sketched the outlines of the "disease" concept of alcoholism; noted that there is no generally accepted definition of "alcoholism"; alluded to the ongoing debate within the medical profession over whether alcohol is actually physically "addicting" or merely psychologically "habituating"; and concluded that in either case a "chronic alcoholic" is an "involuntary drinker," who is "powerless not to drink," and who "loses his self-control over his drinking." He testified that he had examined appellant, and that appellant is a "chronic alcoholic," who "by the time he has reached the state of intoxication is not able to control his behavior, and who has reached this point because he has an uncontrollable compulsion to drink."

---

[1] Readers are advised to quote only from the original published cases. See pages vi and vii.
[2] See Appendix B (pp. 291-292).

He added that in his opinion jailing appellant without medical attention would operate neither to rehabilitate him nor to lessen his desire for alcohol.

On cross examination, Dr. Wade admitted that when appellant was sober he knew the difference between right and wrong, and he responded affirmatively to the question whether appellant's act of taking the first drink in any given instance when he was sober was a "voluntary exercise of his will." Qualifying his answer, Dr. Wade stated that "these individuals have a compulsion, and this compulsion, while not completely overpowering, is a very strong influence, an exceedingly strong influence, and this compulsion coupled with the firm belief in their mind that they are going to be able to handle it from now on causes their judgment to be somewhat clouded."

Appellant testified concerning the history of his drinking problem. He reviewed his many arrests for drunkenness; testified that he was unable to stop drinking; stated that when he was intoxicated he had no control over his actions and could not remember them later, but that he did not become violent; and admitted that he did not remember his arrest on the occasion for which he was being tried.

Evidence in the case then closed. The State made no effort to obtain expert psychiatric testimony of its own, or even to explore with appellant's witness the question of appellant's power to control the frequency, timing, and location of his drinking bouts, or the substantial disagreement within the medical profession concerning the nature of the disease, the efficacy of treatment, and the prerequisites for effective treatment. It did nothing to examine or illuminate what Dr. Wade might have meant by his reference to a "compulsion" which was "not completely overpowering," but which was "an exceedingly strong influence," or to inquire into the question of the proper role of such a "compulsion" in constitutional adjudication. Instead, the State contented itself with a brief argument that appellant had no defense to the charge because he "is legally sane and knows the difference between right and wrong." Following this abbreviated exposition of the problem before it, the trial court indicated its intention to disallow appellant's claimed defense of "chronic alcoholism." Thereupon defense counsel submitted, and the trial court entered, the following "findings of fact": "(1) That chronic alcoholism is a disease which destroys the afflicted person's will power to resist the constant, excessive consumption of alcohol. (2) That a chronic alcoholic does not appear in public by his own volition but under a compulsion symptomatic of the disease of chronic alcoholism. (3) That Leroy Powell, defendant herein, is a chronic alcoholic who is afflicted with the disease of chronic alcoholism."

Whatever else may be said of them, those are not "findings of fact" in any recognizable, traditional sense in which that term has been used in a court of law; they are the premises of a syllogism transparently designed to bring this case within the scope of this Court's opinion in *Robinson*. Nonetheless, the dissent would have us adopt these "findings" without critical examination; it would use them as the basis for a constitutional holding that "a person may not be punished if the condition essential to constitute the defined crime is part of the pattern of his disease and is occasioned by a compulsion symptomatic of the disease."

The difficulty with that position, as we shall show, is that it goes much too far on the basis of too little knowledge. In the first place, the record in this case is utterly inadequate to permit the sort of informed and responsible adjudication which alone can support the announcement of an important and wide-ranging new constitutional principle. We know very little about the circumstances surrounding the drinking bout which resulted in this conviction, or about Leroy Powell's drinking problem, or indeed about alcoholism itself. The trial hardly reflects the sharp legal and evidentiary clash between fully prepared adversary litigants which is traditionally expected in major constitutional cases. The State put on only one witness, the arresting officer. The defense put on three—a policeman who testified to appellant's long history of arrests for public drunkenness, the psychiatrist, and appellant himself.

Debate rages within the medical profession as to whether "alcoholism" is a separate "disease" in any meaningful biochemical, physiological, or psychological sense, or whether it represents one peculiar manifestation in some individuals of underlying psychiatric disorders. The trial court's "finding" that Powell "is afflicted with the disease of chronic alcoholism," which "destroys the afflicted person's will power to resist the constant, excessive consumption of alcohol" covers a multitude of sins. Dr. Wade's testimony that appellant suffered from a compulsion which was an "exceedingly strong influence," but which was "not completely overpowering" is at least more carefully stated, if no less mystifying. Presumably a person would have to display both characteristics in order to make out a constitutional defense, should one be recognized. Yet the "findings" of the trial court utterly fail to make this crucial distinction, and there is serious question whether the record can be read to support a finding of either loss of control or inability to abstain.

Dr. Wade testified that when appellant was sober, the act of taking the first drink was a "voluntary exercise of his will," but that this exercise of will was undertaken under the "exceedingly strong influence" of a "compulsion" which was "not completely overpowering." Such concepts, when juxtaposed in this fashion, have little meaning.

It cannot accurately be said that a person is truly unable to abstain from drinking unless he is suffering the physical symptoms of withdrawal. There is no testimony in this record that Leroy Powell underwent withdrawal symptoms either before he began the drinking spree which resulted in the conviction under review here, or at any other time. It is one thing to say that if a man is deprived of alcohol his hands will begin to shake, he will suffer agonizing pains and ultimately he will have hallucinations; it is quite another to say that a man has a "compulsion" to take a drink, but that he also retains a certain amount of "free will" with which to resist. It is simply impossible, in the present state of our knowledge, to ascribe a useful meaning to the latter statement. This definitional confusion reflects, of course, not merely the undeveloped state of the psychiatric art but also the conceptual difficulties inevitably attendant upon the importation of scientific and medical models into a legal system generally predicated upon a different set of assumptions.

One virtue of the criminal process is, at least, that the duration of penal incarceration typically has some outside statutory limit; this is universally true in the case of petty offenses, such as public drunkenness, where jail terms are quite short on the whole. "Therapeutic civil commitment" lacks this feature; one is typically committed until one is "cured." Thus, to do otherwise than affirm might subject indigent alcoholics to the risk that they may be locked up for an indefinite period of time under the same conditions as before, with no more hope than before of receiving effective treatment and no prospect of periodic "freedom."

Faced with this unpleasant reality, we are unable to assert that the use of the criminal process as a means of dealing with the public aspects of problem drinking can never be defended as rational. The picture of the penniless drunk propelled aimlessly and endlessly through the law's "revolving door" of arrest, incarceration, release and re-arrest is not a pretty one. But before we condemn the present practice across-the-board, perhaps we ought to be able to point to some clear promise of a better world for these unfortunate people. Unfortunately, no such promise has yet been forthcoming. If, in addition to the absence of a coherent approach to the problem of treatment, we consider the almost complete absence of facilities and manpower for the implementation of a rehabilitation program, it is difficult to say in the present context that the criminal process is utterly lacking in social value. This Court has never held that anything in the Constitution requires that penal sanctions be designed solely to achieve therapeutic or rehabilitative effects, and it can hardly be said with assurance that incarceration serves such purposes any better for the general run of criminals than it does for public drunks.

Ignorance likewise impedes our assessment of the deterrent effect of criminal sanctions for public drunkenness. The fact that a high percentage of American alcoholics conceal their drinking problems, not merely by avoiding public displays of intoxication but also by shunning all forms of treatment, is indicative that some powerful deterrent operates to inhibit the public revelation of the existence of alcoholism. Quite probably this deterrent effect can be largely attributed to the harsh moral attitude which our society has traditionally taken toward intoxication and the shame which we have associated with alcoholism. Criminal conviction represents the degrading public revelation of what Anglo-American society has long condemned as a moral defect, and the existence of criminal sanctions may serve to reinforce this cultural taboo, just as we presume it serves to reinforce other, stronger feelings against murder, rape, theft, and other forms of antisocial conduct.

Obviously, chronic alcoholics have not been deterred from drinking to excess by the existence of criminal sanctions against public drunkenness. But all those who violate penal laws of any kind are by definition undeterred. The long-standing and still raging debate over the validity of the deterrence justification for penal sanctions has not reached any sufficiently clear conclusions to permit it to be said that such sanctions are ineffective in any particular context or for any particular group of people who are able to appreciate the consequences of their acts.

Appellant claims that his conviction on the facts of this case would violate the Cruel and Unusual Punishment Clause of the Eighth Amendment as applied to the States through the Fourteenth Amendment. The primary purpose of that clause has always been considered, and properly so, to be directed at the method or kind of punishment imposed for the violation of criminal statutes; the nature of the conduct made criminal is ordinarily relevant only to the fitness of the punishment imposed. Appellant, however, seeks to come within the application of the Cruel and Unusual Punishment Clause announced in *Robinson*, which involved a state statute making it a crime to "be addicted to the use of narcotics." This Court held there that "a state law which imprisons a person thus afflicted with narcotic addiction as a criminal, even though he has never touched any narcotic drug within the State or been guilty of any irregular behavior there, inflicts a cruel and unusual punishment."

On its face the present case does not fall within that holding, since appellant was convicted, not for being a chronic alcoholic, but for being in public while drunk on a particular occasion. The State of Texas thus has not sought to punish a mere status, as California did in *Robinson*; nor has it attempted to regulate appellant's behavior in the privacy of his own home. Rather, it has imposed upon appellant a criminal sanction for public behavior which may create substantial health and safety hazards, both for appellant and for members of the general public, and which offends the moral and esthetic sensibilities of a large segment of the community. This seems a far cry from convicting one for being an addict, being a chronic alcoholic, being "mentally ill, or a leper."

Robinson so viewed brings this Court but a very small way into the substantive criminal law. And unless *Robinson* is so viewed it is difficult to see any limiting principle that would serve to prevent this Court from becoming, under the aegis of the Cruel and Unusual Punishment Clause, the ultimate arbiter of the standards of criminal responsibility, in diverse areas of the criminal law, throughout the country.

It is suggested in dissent that *Robinson* stands for the "simple" but "subtle" principle that "criminal penalties may not be inflicted upon a person for being in a condition he is powerless to change." In that view, appellant's "condition" of public intoxication was "occasioned by a compulsion symptomatic of the disease" of chronic alcoholism, and thus, apparently, his behavior lacked the critical element of *mens rea*. Whatever may be the merits of such a doctrine of criminal responsibility, it surely cannot be said to follow from *Robinson*. The entire thrust of *Robinson's* interpretation of the Cruel and Unusual Punishment Clause is that criminal penalties may be inflicted only if the accused has committed some act, has engaged in some behavior, which society has an interest in preventing, or perhaps in historical common law terms, has committed some *actus reus*. It thus does not deal with the question of whether certain conduct cannot constitutionally be punished because it is, in some sense, "involuntary" or "occasioned by a compulsion."

Likewise, as the dissent acknowledges, there is a substantial definitional distinction between a "status," as in *Robinson*, and a "condition," which is said to be involved in this case. Whatever may be the merits of an attempt to distinguish between behavior and a condition, it is perfectly clear that the crucial element in this case, so far as the dissent is concerned, is whether or not appellant can legally be held responsible for his appearance in public in a state of intoxication. The only relevance of *Robinson* to this issue is that because the Court interpreted the statute there involved as making a "status" criminal, it was able to suggest that the statute would cover even a situation in which addiction had been acquired involuntarily.

Ultimately, then, the most troubling aspects of this case, were *Robinson* to be extended to meet it, would be the scope and content of what could only be a constitutional doctrine of criminal responsibility. In dissent it is urged that the decision could be limited to conduct which is "a characteristic and involuntary part of the pattern of the disease as it afflicts" the particular individual, and that "it is not foreseeable" that it would be applied "in the case of offenses such as driving a car while intoxi-

> *If Leroy Powell cannot be convicted of public intoxication, it is difficult to see how a state can convict an individual for murder.*

cated, assault, theft, or robbery." That is limitation by fiat. In the first place, nothing in the logic of the dissent would limit its application to chronic alcoholics. If Leroy Powell cannot be convicted of public intoxication, it is difficult to see how a State can convict an individual for murder, if that individual, while exhibiting normal behavior in all other respects, suffers from a "compulsion" to kill, which is an "exceedingly strong influence," but "not completely overpowering." Even if we limit our consideration to chronic alcoholics, it would seem impossible to confine the principle within the arbitrary bounds which the dissent seems to envision.

It is not difficult to imagine a case involving psychiatric testimony to the effect that an individual suffers from some aggressive neurosis which he is able to control when sober; that very little alcohol suffices to remove the inhibitions which normally contain these aggressions, with the result that the individual engages in assaultive behavior without becoming actually intoxicated; and that the individual suffers from a very strong desire to drink, which is an "exceedingly strong influence" but "not completely overpowering." Without being untrue to the rationale of this case, should the principles advanced in dissent be accepted here, the Court could not avoid holding such an individual constitutionally unaccountable for his assaultive behavior.

Traditional common-law concepts of personal accountability and essential considerations of federalism lead us to disagree with appellant. We are unable to conclude, on the state of this record or on the current state of medical knowledge, that chronic alcoholics in general, and Leroy Powell in particular, suffer from such an irresistible compulsion to drink and to get drunk in public that they are utterly unable to control their performance of either or both of these acts and thus cannot be deterred at all from public intoxication. And in any event this Court has never articulated a general constitutional doctrine of *mens rea*.[3]

We cannot cast aside the centuries-long evolution of the collection of interlocking and overlapping concepts which the common law has utilized to assess the moral accountability of an individual for his antisocial deeds. The doctrines of *actus reus*, *mens rea*, insanity, mistake, justification, and duress have historically provided the tools for a constantly shifting adjustment of the tension between the evolving aims of the criminal law and changing religious, moral, philosophical, and medical views

> *The doctrines of actus reus, mens rea, insanity, mistake, justification, and duress have historically provided the tools for a constantly shifting adjustment of the tension between the evolving aims of the criminal law and changing religious, moral, philosophical, and medical views of the nature of man.*

of the nature of man. This process of adjustment has always been thought to be the province of the States.

Nothing could be less fruitful than for this Court to be impelled into defining some sort of insanity test in constitutional terms. Yet, that task would seem to follow inexorably from an extension of *Robinson* to this case. If a person in the "condition" of being a chronic alcoholic cannot be criminally punished as a constitutional matter for being drunk in public, it would seem to follow that a person who contends that, in terms of one test, "his unlawful act was the product of

> *Nothing could be less fruitful than for this Court to be impelled into defining some sort of insanity test in constitutional terms.*

mental disease or mental defect," (*Durham v. United States*) would state an issue of constitutional dimension with regard to his criminal responsibility had he been tried under some different and perhaps lesser standard, e.g., the right-wrong test of *M'Naghten's* Case. The experimentation of one jurisdiction in that field alone indicates the magnitude of the problem. See, e.g., *Carter v. United States*, *Blocker v. United States*, *McDonald v. United States*, and *Washington v. United States*.

---

[3] It is not suggested that appellant in this case was not fully aware of the prohibited nature of his conduct and of the consequences of taking his first drink.

But formulating a constitutional rule would reduce, if not eliminate, that fruitful experimentation, and freeze the developing productive dialogue between law and psychiatry into a rigid constitutional mold. It is simply not yet the time to write into the Constitution formulas cast in terms whose meaning, let alone relevance, is not yet clear either to doctors or to lawyers.

Affirmed.
Concur: Mr. Justice Black, whom Mr. Justice Harlan joins, concurring.

I agree with MR. JUSTICE MARSHALL that the findings of fact in this case are inadequate to justify the sweeping constitutional rule urged upon us. I could not, however, consider any findings that could be made with respect to "voluntariness" or "compulsion" controlling on the question whether a specific instance of human behavior should be immune from punishment as a constitutional matter. When we say that appellant's appearance in public is caused not by "his own" volition but rather by some other force, we are clearly thinking of a force that is nevertheless "his" except in some special sense. The accused undoubtedly commits the proscribed act and the only question is whether the act can be attributed to a part of "his" personality that should not be regarded as criminally responsible. Almost all of the traditional purposes of the criminal law can be significantly served by punishing the person who in fact committed the proscribed act, without regard to whether his action was "compelled" by some elusive "irresponsible" aspect of his personality. As I have already indicated, punishment of such a defendant can clearly be justified in terms of deterrence, isolation, and treatment. On the other hand, medical decisions concerning the use of a term such as "disease" or "volition," based as they are on the clinical problems of diagnosis and treatment, bear no necessary correspondence to the legal decision whether the overall objectives of the criminal law can be furthered by imposing punishment. For these reasons, much as I think that criminal sanctions should in many situations be applied only to those whose conduct is morally blameworthy, I cannot think the States should be held constitutionally required to make the inquiry as to what part of a defendant's personality is responsible for his actions and to excuse anyone whose action was, in some complex, psychological sense, the result of a "compulsion."

The rule of constitutional law urged by appellant is not required by *Robinson*. In that case we held that a person could not be punished for the mere status of being a narcotics addict. We explicitly limited our holding to the situation where no conduct of any kind is involved. The argument is made that appellant comes within the terms of our holding in

Robinson because being drunk in public is a mere status or "condition." Despite this many-faceted use of the concept of "condition," this argument would require converting *Robinson* into a case protecting actual behavior, a step we explicitly refused to take in that decision.

The reasons for this refusal to permit conviction without proof of an act are difficult to spell out, but they are nonetheless perceived and universally expressed in our criminal law. Evidence of propensity can be considered relatively unreliable and more difficult for a defendant to rebut; the requirement of a specific act thus provides some protection against false charges. Perhaps more fundamental is the difficulty of distinguishing, in the absence of any conduct, between desires of the daydream variety and fixed intentions that may pose a real threat to society; extending the criminal law to cover both types of desire would be unthinkable, since "there can hardly be anyone who has never thought evil. When a desire is inhibited it may find expression in fantasy; but it would be absurd to condemn this natural psychological mechanism as illegal."

In contrast, crimes that require the State to prove that the defendant actually committed some proscribed act involve none of these special problems. In addition, the question whether an act is "involuntary" is, as I have already indicated, an inherently elusive question, and one which the State may, for good reasons, wish to regard as irrelevant. In light of all these considerations, our limitation of our *Robinson* holding to pure status crimes seems to me entirely proper.

> The question whether an act is "involuntary" is an inherently elusive question, and one which the State may wish to regard as irrelevant. (Black, concurring)

If the original boundaries of *Robinson* are to be discarded, any new limits too would soon fall by the wayside and the Court would be forced to hold the States powerless to punish any conduct that could be shown to result from a "compulsion," in the complex, psychological meaning of that term. The result, to choose just one illustration, would be to require recognition of "irresistible impulse" as a complete defense to any crime; this is probably contrary to present law in

> The result would be to require recognition of "irresistible impulse" as a complete defense to any crime. (Black, concurring)

most American jurisdictions. The real reach of any such decision, however, would be broader still, for the basic premise underlying the argument is that it is cruel and unusual to punish a person who is not morally blameworthy. I state the proposition in this sympathetic way because I feel there is much to be said for avoiding the use of criminal sanctions in many such situations. But the question here is one of constitutional law. The legislatures have always been allowed wide freedom to determine the extent to which moral culpability should be a prerequisite to conviction of a crime. The criminal law is a social tool that is employed in seeking a wide variety of goals, and I cannot say the Eighth Amendment's limits on the use of criminal sanctions extend as far as this viewpoint would inevitably carry them.

But even if we were to limit any holding in this field to "compulsions" that are "symptomatic" of a "disease," in the words of the findings of the trial court, the sweep of that holding would still be startling. Such a ruling would make it clear beyond any doubt that a narcotics addict could not be punished for "being" in possession of drugs or, for that matter, for "being" guilty of using them. A wide variety of sex offenders would be immune from punishment if they could show that their conduct was not voluntary but part of the pattern of a disease. More generally speaking, a form of the insanity defense would be made a constitutional requirement throughout the Nation, should the Court now hold it cruel and unusual to punish a person afflicted with any mental disease whenever his conduct was part of the pattern of his disease and occasioned by a compulsion symptomatic of the disease.

> *A form of the insanity defense would be made a constitutional requirement throughout the Nation, should the Court now hold it cruel and unusual to punish a person afflicted with any mental disease whenever his conduct was part of the pattern of his disease and occasioned by a compulsion symptomatic of the disease. (Black, concurring)*

The impact of the holding urged upon us would, of course, be greatest in those States which have until now refused to accept any qualifications to the "right from wrong" test of insanity; apparently at least 30 States fall into this category. But even in States which have recognized insanity defenses similar to the proposed new constitutional rule, or where comparable defenses could be presented in terms of the requirement of a guilty mind (*mens rea*), the proposed new constitutional rule would be devastating, for constitutional questions would be raised by every state effort to regulate the admissibility of evidence relating to "disease" and "compulsion," and by every state attempt to explain these concepts in instructions to the jury. The test urged would make it necessary to determine, not only what constitutes a "disease," but also what is the "pattern" of the disease, what "conditions" are "part" of the pattern, what parts of this pattern result from a "compulsion," and finally which of these compulsions are "symptomatic" of the disease. The resulting confusion and uncertainty could easily surpass that experienced by the District of Columbia Circuit in attempting to give content to its similar, though somewhat less complicated, test of insanity (see *Durham v. United States*). The range of problems created would seem totally beyond our capacity to settle at all, much less to settle wisely, and even the attempt to define these terms and thus to impose constitutional and doctrinal rigidity seems absurd in an area where our understanding is even today so incomplete.

Davis v. United States

160 U.S. 469 (1895)

Facts

Dennis Davis was accused of murder in Indian Territory in Arkansas. The insanity standard contained both cognitive and volitional elements. In an "elaborate charge" to the jury, the trial court carefully explained that the law recognizes a presumption of sanity; no evidence of sanity is necessary. The trial court instructed that the party who raises the defense of insanity has "the responsibility of overturning that presumption."

Issues

Is the presumption of sanity constitutional? Or should sanity be considered an element of the offense which must be proven?

Holding

The Supreme Court found no fault with the general presumption of sanity. They indicated that in the majority of cases, "adducing affirmative evidence" of sanity is unnecessary and would needlessly delay legal proceedings. However, the presumption of sanity is not a "conclusive presumption," but rather a "rebuttable" one. When evidence of insanity is introduced, then it falls upon the government to prove that the accused had the requisite mental state to commit the crime. That the defendant had the requisite mental state becomes an element of the offense which, like all other elements, must be proven beyond a reasonable doubt.

Analysis

It is clear that the Supreme Court had no quarrel with the established presumption of sanity, as it was applied in the vast majority of cases. However, once the issue to sanity was raised, and especially if the evidence was equivocal, the Supreme Court concluded that the prosecution must consider requisite mental state as an element of the offense to be specifically proven beyond a reasonable doubt. The Court could not countenance instructions that the jury must rely on the mere presumption of sanity and reach a conviction. Requiring a defendant to prove that he or she is insane is tantamount to abandoning the presumption of innocence. Such a requirement "is in effect to require him to establish his innocence, by proving that he is not guilty of the crime charged." Such a scheme is unconstitutional.

Edited Excerpts[1]

Opinion: Mr. Justice Harlan delivered the opinion of the court.

Dennis Davis was indicted for the crime of having, on the 18th day of September, 1894, at the Creek Nation, in the Indian Territory, within the Western District of Arkansas, feloniously, wilfully, and of his malice aforethought, killed and murdered one Sol Blackwell. He was found guilty of the charge in the indictment. A motion for a new trial having been overruled, and the court having adjudged that the accused was guilty of the crime of murder, as charged, he was sentenced to suffer the penalty of death by hanging.

At the trial below the government introduced evidence which, if alone considered, made it the duty of the jury to return a verdict of guilty of the crime charged. But there was evidence tending to show that at the time of the killing the accused, by reason of unsoundness or weakness of mind, was not criminally responsible for his acts. In addition to the evidence of a practicing physician of many years standing, and who, for the time, was physician at the jail in which the accused was confined previous to his trial, "other witnesses," the bill of exceptions states, "testified that they had been intimately acquainted with the defendant for a number of years, lived near him, and had been frequently with him, knew his mental condition, and that he was weak-minded, and regarded by his neighbors and people as being what they called half crazy. Other witnesses who had known the defendant for ten to twenty years, witnesses who had worked with him and had been thrown in constant contact with him, said he had always been called half crazy, weak-minded; and in the opinion of the witnesses defendant was not of sound mind." The issue, therefore, was as to the responsibility of the accused for the killing alleged and clearly proved.

We are unable to assent to the doctrine that in a prosecution for murder, the defence being insanity, and the fact of the killing with a deadly weapon being clearly established, it is the duty of the jury to convict where the evidence is equally balanced on the issue as to the sanity of the accused at the time of the killing. On the contrary, he is entitled to an acquittal of

---

[1] Readers are advised to quote only from the original published cases. See pages vi and vii.

the specific crime charged if upon all the evidence there is reasonable doubt whether he was capable in law of committing crime.

No one, we assume, would wish either the courts or juries when trying a case of murder to disregard the humane principle, existing at common law and recognized in all the cases tending to support the charge of the court below, that, "to make a complete crime cognizable by human laws, there must be both a will and an act"; and "as a vicious will without a vicious act is no civil crime, so, on the other hand, an unwarrantable act without a vicious will is no crime at all. So that to constitute a crime against human laws, there must be, first, a vicious will; and, secondly, an unlawful act consequent upon such vicious will." All this is implied in the accepted definition of murder; for it is of the very essence of that heinous crime that it be committed by a person of "sound memory and discretion," and with "malice aforethought," either express or implied. Such was the view of the [trial] court which took care in its charge to say that the crime of murder could only be committed by a sane being, although it instructed the jury that a reasonable doubt as to the sanity of the accused would not alone protect him against a verdict of guilty.

One who takes human life cannot be said to be actuated by malice aforethought, or to have deliberately intended to take life, or to have "a wicked, depraved, and malignant heart," or a heart "regardless of society duty and fatally bent on mischief," unless at the time he had sufficient mind to comprehend the criminality or the right and wrong of such an act. Although the killing of one human being by another human being with a deadly weapon is presumed to be malicious until the contrary appears, yet, "in order to constitute a crime, a person must have intelligence and capacity enough to have a criminal intent and purpose; and if his reason and mental powers are either so deficient that he has no will, no conscience, or controlling mental power, or if, through the overwhelming violence of mental disease, his intellectual power is for the time obliterated, he is not a responsible moral agent, and is not punishable for criminal acts." All admit that the crime of murder necessarily involves the possession by the accused of such mental capacity as will render him criminally responsible for his acts.

Upon whom then must rest the burden of proving that the accused, whose life it is sought to take under the forms of law, belongs to a class capable of committing crime? On principle, it must rest upon those who affirm that he has committed the crime for which he is indicted. That burden is not fully discharged, nor is there any legal right to take the life of the accused, until guilt is made to appear from all the evidence in the case. The plea of not guilty is unlike a special plea in a civil action, which, admitting the case averred, seeks to establish substantive ground of defence by a preponderance of evidence. It is not in confession and avoidance, for it is a plea that controverts the existence of every fact essential to constitute the crime charged. Upon that plea the accused may stand, shielded by the presumption of his innocence, until it appears that he is guilty; and his guilt cannot in the very nature of things be regarded as proved, if the jury entertain a reasonable doubt from all the evidence whether he was legally capable of committing crime.

This view is not at all inconsistent with the presumption which the law, justified by the general experience of mankind as well as by considerations of public safety, indulges in favor of sanity. If that presumption were not indulged the government would always be under the necessity of adducing affirmative evidence of the sanity of an accused. But a requirement of that character would seriously delay and embarrass the enforcement of the laws against crime, and in most cases be unnecessary. Consequently the law presumes that every one charged with crime is sane, and thus supplies in the first instance the required

> **The law presumes that every one charged with crime is sane.**

proof of capacity to commit crime. It authorizes the jury to assume at the outset that the accused is criminally responsible for his acts. But that is not a conclusive presumption, which the law upon grounds of public policy forbids to be overthrown or impaired by opposing proof. It is a disputable or, as it is often designated, a rebuttable presumption resulting from the connection ordinarily existing between certain facts. It is therefore a presumption that is liable to be overcome or to be so far impaired in a particular case that it cannot be safely or properly made the basis of action in that case, especially if the inquiry involves human life. In a certain sense it may be true that where the defence is insanity, and where the case made by the prosecution discloses nothing whatever in excuse or extenuation of the crime charged, the accused is bound to produce some evidence that will impair or weaken the force of the legal presumption in favor of sanity. But to hold that such presumption must absolutely control the jury until it is overthrown or impaired by evidence sufficient to establish the fact of insanity beyond all reasonable doubt or to the reasonable satisfaction of the jury, is in effect to require him to establish his innocence, by proving that he is not guilty of the crime charged.

Strictly speaking, the burden of proof, as those words are understood in criminal law, is never upon the accused to establish his innocence or to disprove the facts necessary to establish the crime for which he is indicted.

It is on the prosecution from the beginning to the end of the trial and applies to every element necessary to constitute the crime. Giving to the prosecution, where the defence is insanity, the benefit in the way of proof of the presumption in favor of sanity, the vital question from the time a plea of not guilty is entered until the return of the verdict, is whether upon all the evidence, by whatever side adduced, guilt is established beyond reasonable doubt. If the whole evidence, including that supplied by the presumption of sanity, does not exclude beyond reasonable doubt the hypothesis of insanity, of which some proof is adduced, the accused is entitled to an acquittal of the specific offence charged. His guilt cannot be said to have been proved beyond a reasonable doubt—his will and his acts cannot be held to have joined in perpetrating the murder charged—if the jury, upon all the evidence, have a reasonable doubt whether he was legally capable of committing crime, or (which is the same thing) whether he wilfully, deliberately, unlawfully, and of malice aforethought took the life of the deceased. As the crime of murder involves sufficient capacity to distinguish between right and wrong, the legal interpretation of every verdict of guilty as charged is that the jury believed from all the evidence beyond a reasonable doubt that the accused was guilty, and was therefore responsible, criminally, for his acts. How then upon principle or consistently with humanity can a verdict of guilty be properly returned, if the jury entertain a reasonable doubt as to the existence of a fact which is essential to guilt, namely, the capacity in law of the accused to commit that crime?

It seems to us that undue stress is placed in some of the cases upon the fact that, in prosecutions for murder the defence of insanity is frequently resorted to and is sustained by the evidence of ingenious experts whose theories are difficult to be met and overcome. Thus it is said, crimes of the most atrocious character often go unpunished, and the public safety is thereby endangered. But the possibility of such results must always attend any system devised to ascertain and punish crime, and ought not to induce the courts to depart from principles fundamental in criminal law, and the recognition and enforcement of which are demanded by every consideration of humanity and justice. No man should be deprived of his life under the forms of law unless the jurors who try him are able, upon their consciences, to say that the evidence before them, by whomsoever adduced, is sufficient to show beyond a reasonable doubt the existence of every fact necessary to constitute the crime charged.

For the reason stated, and without alluding to other matters in respect to which error is assigned, the judgment is reversed and the cause remanded with directions to grant a new trial, and for further proceedings consistent with this opinion.

Reversed.

Leland v. Oregon

343 U.S. 790 (1952)

Facts

Leland was charged with murder of a teenage girl, and he pursued an insanity defense. Based on his confession and other evidence, he was convicted. According to Oregon law at the time, a defendant who pleaded insanity was required to prove that condition beyond a reasonable doubt. Leland argued Oregon's statutory scheme was unconstitutional, because it effectively required a defendant who pleads insanity to bear the burden of proving his or her innocence. He maintained that this scheme required such a defendant to disprove, beyond a reasonable doubt, an element of the offense.

Issue

Did Oregon's requirement that a defendant prove insanity beyond a reasonable doubt violate the Due Process Clause of the Fourteenth Amendment?[1]

Holding

The Supreme Court ruled that under Oregon law, the proof of guilt "was placed squarely upon the state." Only after guilt was established did jurors "consider separately the legal issue of insanity." In the holding, the Court endorsed the well-established presumption of sanity. They observed that 20 states place the burden of proving insanity on the defendant, although they noted that only Oregon required the stringent standard of beyond a reasonable doubt. The Supreme Court found no constitutional flaw with Oregon's law. Although it differed from the procedural rule established in *Davis* for federal courts, it did not violate the protections of the Fourteenth Amendment. The Court concluded that it was acceptable for Oregon to require defendants who plead insanity to prove that insanity beyond a reasonable doubt.

---

[1] See Appendix B (pp. 291-292).

Analysis

The Supreme Court drew a distinction between procedural rules, such as those established in *Davis* or in other states' cases, and the minimal protections mandated by the Constitution. The fact that Oregon was the only state to impose the standard of beyond a reasonable doubt did not make that imposition unconstitutional. The Court was satisfied that the burden of proving the elements of the crime rested with the state, given that insanity was considered separately, after guilt had been established.

In a sharp dissent, Justices Frankfurter and Black conceptualized the mental state necessary for culpability as an element of the offense to be proven by the government. Although they agreed that special procedures were appropriate to address the issue, Oregon's requirement that defendants prove insanity beyond a reasonable doubt placed defendants at too high a risk of erroneous conviction.

Edited Excerpts[2]

Opinion: Mr. Justice Clark delivered the opinion of the Court.

Appellant was charged with murder in the first degree. He pleaded not guilty and gave notice of his intention to prove insanity. Upon trial in the Circuit Court of Multnomah County, Oregon, he was found guilty by a jury. In accordance with the jury's decision not to recommend life imprisonment, appellant received a sentence of death. The Supreme Court of Oregon affirmed. The case is here on appeal.

Oregon statutes required appellant to prove his insanity beyond a reasonable doubt and made a "morbid propensity" no defense. The principal questions in this appeal are raised by appellant's contentions that these statutes deprive him of his life and liberty without due process of law as guaranteed by the Fourteenth Amendment.

The facts of the crime were revealed by appellant's confessions, as corroborated by other evidence. He killed a fifteen-year-old girl by striking her over the head several times with a steel bar and stabbing her twice with a hunting knife. Upon being arrested five days later for the theft of an automobile, he

> **Oregon statutes required appellant to prove his insanity beyond a reasonable doubt.**

asked to talk with a homicide officer, voluntarily confessed the murder, and directed the police to the scene of the crime, where he pointed out the

---

location of the body. On the same day, he signed a full confession and, at his own request, made another in his own handwriting. After his indictment, counsel were appointed to represent him. They have done so with diligence in carrying his case through three courts.

One of the Oregon statutes in question provides: "When the commission of the act charged as a crime is proven, and the defense sought to be established is the insanity of the defendant, the same must be proven beyond a reasonable doubt." Appellant urges that this statute in effect requires a defendant pleading insanity to establish his innocence by disproving beyond a reasonable doubt elements of the crime necessary to a verdict of guilty, and that the statute is therefore violative of that due process of law secured by the Fourteenth Amendment.

In conformity with the applicable state law, the trial judge instructed the jury that, although appellant was charged with murder in the first degree, they might determine that he had committed a lesser crime included in that charged. They were further instructed that his plea of not guilty put in issue every material and necessary element of the lesser degrees of homicide, as well as of the offense charged in the indictment. The jury could have returned any of five verdicts: (1) guilty of murder in the first degree, if they found beyond a reasonable doubt that appellant did the killing purposely and with deliberate and premeditated malice; (2) guilty of murder in the second degree, if they found beyond a reasonable doubt that appellant did the killing purposely and maliciously, but without deliberation and premeditation; (3) guilty of manslaughter, if they found beyond a reasonable doubt that appellant did the killing without malice or deliberation, but upon a sudden heat of passion caused by a provocation apparently sufficient to make the passion irresistible; (4) not guilty, if, after a careful consideration of all the evidence, there remained in their minds a reasonable doubt as to the existence of any of the necessary elements of each degree of homicide; and (5) not guilty by reason of insanity, if they found beyond a reasonable doubt that appellant was insane at the time of the offense charged. A finding of insanity would have freed appellant from responsibility for any of the possible offenses. The verdict which the jury determined—guilty of first degree murder—required the agreement of all twelve jurors; a verdict of not guilty by reason of insanity would have required the concurrence of only ten members of the panel.

It is apparent that the jury might have found appellant to have been mentally incapable of the premeditation and deliberation required to support a first degree murder verdict or of the intent necessary to find him guilty of either first or second degree murder, and yet not have found him to have been legally insane. Although a plea of insanity was made, the prosecution was required to prove beyond a reasonable doubt every element of the crime charged, including, in the case of first degree murder, premeditation, deliberation, malice, and intent. The trial court repeatedly emphasized this requirement in its charge to the jury. Moreover, the judge directed the jury as follows: "I instruct you that the evidence adduced during this trial to prove defendant's insanity shall be considered and weighed by you, with all other evidence, whether or not you find defendant insane, in regard to the ability of the defendant to premeditate, form a purpose, to deliberate, act wilfully, and act maliciously; and if you find the defendant lacking in such ability, the defendant cannot have committed the crime of murder in the first degree."

"I instruct you that should you find the defendant's mental condition to be so affected or diseased to the end that the defendant could formulate no plan, design, or intent to kill in cool blood, the defendant has not committed the crime of murder in the first degree."

These and other instructions, and the charge as a whole, make it clear that the burden of proof of guilt, and of all the necessary elements of guilt, was placed squarely upon the State. As the jury was told, this burden did not shift, but rested upon the State throughout the trial, just as, according to the instructions, appellant was presumed to be innocent until the jury was convinced beyond a reasonable doubt that he was guilty. The jurors were to consider separately the issue of legal sanity *per se*— an issue set apart from the crime charged, to be introduced by a special plea and decided by a special verdict. On this issue appellant had the burden of proof under the statute in question here.

By this statute, originally enacted in 1864, Oregon adopted the prevailing doctrine of the time—that, since most men are sane, a defendant must prove his insanity to avoid responsibility for his acts. That was the rule announced in 1843 in the leading English decision in *M'Naghten's* Case:

"The jurors ought to be told in all cases that every man is to be presumed to be sane, and to possess a sufficient degree of reason to be responsible for his crimes, until the contrary be proved to their satisfaction; and to establish a defence on the ground of insanity, it must be clearly proved that, at the time of the committing of the act, the party accused was laboring under such a defect of reason, from disease of the mind, as not to know the nature and quality of the act he was doing."

This remains the English view today. In most of the nineteenth-century American cases, also, the defendant was required to "clearly" prove insanity, and that was probably the rule followed in most states in 1895, when *Davis v. United States* was decided. In that case this Court, speaking through Mr. Justice Harlan, announced the rule for federal prosecutions to be that an accused is "entitled to an acquittal of the specific crime charged if upon all the evidence there is reasonable doubt whether he was capable in law of committing

> *In most of the nineteenth-century American cases, also, the defendant was required to "clearly" prove insanity, and that was probably the rule followed in most states in 1895, when* Davis v. United States *was decided.*

crime." The decision obviously establishes no constitutional doctrine, but only the rule to be followed in federal courts. As such, the rule is not in question here.

Today, Oregon is the only state that requires the accused, on a plea of insanity, to establish that defense beyond a reasonable doubt. Some twenty states, however, place the burden on the accused to establish his insanity by a preponderance of the evidence or some similar measure of persuasion. While there is an evident distinction between these two rules as to the quantum of proof required, we see no practical difference of such magnitude as to be significant in determining the constitutional question we face here. Oregon merely requires a heavier burden of proof. In each instance, in order to establish insanity as a complete defense to the charges preferred, the accused must prove that insanity. The fact that a practice is followed by a large number of states is not conclusive in a decision as to whether that practice accords with due process, but it is plainly worth considering in determining whether the practice "offends some principle of justice so rooted in the traditions and conscience of our people as to be ranked as fundamental."

Nor is this a case in which it is sought to enforce against the states a right which we have held to be secured to defendants in federal courts by the Bill of Rights. In *Davis* we adopted a rule of procedure for the federal courts which is contrary to that of Oregon. But "its procedure does not run foul of the Fourteenth Amendment because another method may seem to our thinking to be fairer or wiser or to give a surer promise of protection to the prisoner at the bar." We are therefore reluctant to interfere with Oregon's determination of its policy with respect to the burden of proof on the issue of sanity since we cannot say that policy violates generally accepted concepts of basic standards of justice. We have seen that, here, Oregon required the prosecutor to prove beyond a reasonable doubt every element of the offense charged. Only on the issue of insanity as an absolute bar to the charge was the burden placed upon appellant. In all English-speaking courts, the accused is obliged to introduce proof if he would overcome the presumption of sanity.

Much we have said applies also to appellant's contention that due process is violated by the Oregon statute providing that a "morbid propensity to commit prohibited acts, existing in the mind of a person, who is not shown to have been incapable of knowing the wrongfulness of such acts, forms no defense to a prosecution therefor." That statute amounts to no more than a legislative adoption of the "right and wrong" test of legal insanity in preference to the "irresistible impulse" test. Knowledge of right and wrong is the exclusive test of criminal responsibility in a majority of American jurisdictions. The science of psychiatry has made tremendous strides since that test was laid down in *M'Naghten's* Case, but the progress of science has not reached a point where its learning would compel us to

> **Adoption of the irresistible impulse test is not "implicit in the concept of ordered liberty."**

require the states to eliminate the right and wrong test from their criminal law. Moreover, choice of a test of legal sanity involves not only scientific knowledge but questions of basic policy as to the extent to which that knowledge should determine criminal responsibility. This whole problem has evoked wide disagreement among those who have studied it. In these circumstances it is clear that adoption of the irresistible impulse test is not "implicit in the concept of ordered liberty."

Affirmed.

Dissent: Mr. Justice Frankfurter, joined by Mr. Justice Black, dissenting.

For some unrecorded reason, Oregon is the only one of the forty-eight States that has made inroads upon that [requires] the accused to prove beyond a reasonable doubt the absence of one of the essential elements for the commission of murder, namely, culpability for his muscular contraction. Like every other State, Oregon presupposes that an insane person cannot be made to pay with his life for a homicide, though for the public good he may of course be put beyond doing further harm. Unlike every other State, however, Oregon says that the accused person must satisfy a jury beyond a reasonable doubt that, being incapable of committing murder, he has not committed murder.

Whatever tentative and intermediate steps experience makes permissible for aiding the State in establishing the ultimate issues in a prosecution for crime, the State cannot be relieved, on a final show-down, from proving its accusation. To prove the accusation it must prove each of the items which in combination constitute the offense. And it must make such proof beyond a reasonable doubt. This duty of the State of establishing every fact of the equation which adds up to a crime, and of establishing it to the satisfaction of a jury beyond a reasonable doubt is the decisive difference between criminal culpability and civil liability. The only exception is that very limited class of cases variously characterized as *mala prohibita*[3] or public torts or enforcement of regulatory measures. Murder is not a *malum prohibitum* or a public tort or the object of regulatory legislation. To suggest that the legal oddity by which Oregon imposes upon the accused the burden of proving beyond reasonable doubt that he had not the mind capable of committing murder is a mere difference in the measure of proof, is to obliterate the distinction between civil and criminal law.

> *To suggest that the legal oddity by which Oregon imposes upon the accused the burden of proving beyond reasonable doubt that he had not the mind capable of committing murder is a mere difference in the measure of proof, is to obliterate the distinction between civil and criminal law. (Frankfurter, dissenting)*

---

[3] *mala prohibita*, plural of *malum prohibitum*. Statutory crimes, as opposed to obviously wrong actions.

Finger v. Nevada
27 P.3d 66 (2001)

Facts

When Frederick Finger emerged from his house covered in blood, he informed a neighbor that somebody had killed his mother. Police were summoned, and Finger was apprehended after an attempt to flee. Police found the mother dead from a knife wound to the head. Although Finger accused "the Mexican guy who lives in the house" of the crime, Finger was arrested for murder. Records indicated that Finger had a well-documented history of mental illness for over 20 years. He had been diagnosed with schizophrenia, bipolar disorder, and intermittent explosive disorder. He had attacked family members repeatedly, and he had been hospitalized numerous times. Three evaluations regarding his mental state ensued. Finger's request to plead not guilty by reason of insanity was denied on the grounds that the Nevada legislature had abolished the affirmative defense of insanity. Finger thus determined that there were no issues to be resolved at trial. He pleaded guilty but mentally ill and was convicted of second-degree murder. On appeal, he argued that the insanity defense is a fundamental constitutional right.

Issues

Did Nevada's abolishment of the insanity defense violate the Eighth and Fourteenth[1] Amendments of the U.S. Constitution?

Holding

The Nevada Supreme Court held that abolishing the insanity defense is a violation of the Due Process Clause of the Fourteenth Amendment.

Analysis

Following an historical review of the insanity defense, the Nevada Supreme Court concluded the "guilty but mentally ill" process promulgated by the Nevada legislature constituted a *"mens rea* model." Rather than *excusing* an offense, as with the traditional insanity defense,

---

[1] See Appendix B (pp. 291-292).

the *mens rea* model holds that impairment precludes a person from forming the requisite criminal intent necessary for a crime. In other words, defendants could not plead insanity under the legislature's model; they could only argue that the government failed to prove criminal intent beyond a reasonable doubt. Finger contended that the Nevada law was unconstitutional because it permitted the conviction of individuals who could not form necessary intent. He also argued that the concept of intent includes an understanding of wrongfulness. The Nevada Supreme Court explained that insanity is in actuality an extension of the concept of *mens rea*, a "fundamental aspect of criminal law." They noted that the "fundamental principle" of insanity has been recognized for centuries, in various forms. The Nevada Supreme Court concluded that the statutory scheme in question "has the effect of eliminating the concept of wrongfulness from all crimes." Following its analysis of other cases (notably *State v. Herrera*, *State v. Searcy*, *State v. Korell*, and *Powell v. Texas*), the Nevada Supreme Court concluded that the insanity defense is a "well-established and fundamental principle" protected by the Due Process Clause. Although states have considerable latitude regarding procedural issues (i.e., *how* the principle is applied), it was deemed unconstitutional to abolish insanity as a defense.

Edited Excerpts[2]

By the Court, Becker, J.

In April of 1996, appellant Frederick Finger was charged with one count of open murder with the use of a deadly weapon. Finger was accused of murdering his mother, Franziska Brassaw, by stabbing her in the head with a kitchen knife. Finger intended to assert legal insanity as a defense. However, at the time of his arraignment, the district court denied Finger's request to enter a plea of "not guilty by reason of insanity" as that plea had been abolished by the 1995 Nevada Legislature. Subsequently, Finger entered a plea of guilty but mentally ill to a charge of second-degree murder. The district court convicted Finger of second-degree murder and sentenced him to serve life in prison with minimum parole eligibility after ten years.

Finger challenges his conviction on constitutional grounds, alleging that the abolishment of insanity as an affirmative defense violates the Eighth and Fourteenth Amendments to the United States Constitution and [sections] of the Nevada Constitution. Finger asserts that punishing

---

[2] Readers are advised to quote only from the original published cases. See pages vi and vii.

an insane individual constitutes cruel and unusual punishment while prohibiting an accused from asserting a defense of legal insanity violates due process requirements.

While we conclude that neither the United States nor the Nevada Constitutions require that legal insanity be procedurally raised as an affirmative defense or by way of a plea of "not guilty by reason of insanity," both Constitutions prohibit an individual from being convicted of a criminal offense without possessing the requisite criminal intent to commit the crime. For the reasons discussed herein, we conclude that Nevada's current statutory scheme would permit an individual to be convicted of a criminal offense under circumstances where the individual lacked the mental capacity to form the applicable intent to commit the crime, a necessary element of the offense. Such a statutory scheme violates the due process clauses of the United States and Nevada Constitutions. In light of our conclusion that Nevada's scheme does not comport with due process, we need not address Finger's arguments regarding the prohibition against cruel and unusual punishment. Because Finger was prohibited from raising the issue of legal insanity, we remand this matter to the district court with instructions to permit Finger to withdraw his plea of "guilty, but mentally ill," vacate the judgment of conviction, and for further proceedings consistent with this opinion.

On April 10, 1996, at approximately 4:00 a.m., Jeff Jordan, a neighbor of Finger, woke to the sound of a woman screaming. A short time later, Finger pounded on Jordan's door while shouting, "Someone killed my mother! She's hurt real bad! I think she might be dead!" Jordan called 911 then got dressed and opened his door. Finger was not in sight. When the police arrived, Jordan noticed that Finger was now standing some distance down the block. Jordan pointed Finger out to the police. Police officers approached Finger who turned and ran away. The officers pursued and detained Finger. As the officers caught up with Finger, they noticed he was covered in blood. Prior to being detained, Finger announced that "someone beat my mother and killed her" and "the Mexican guy who lives in her house killed her." Because of the large amount of blood found on Finger as well as information received from Jordan, the officers wished to verify the safety of Brassaw or any other occupants inside Finger's residence. Jose Rivera, who shared occupancy of the residence with Finger and Brassaw, granted permission for the officers to enter the house. Upon entering the residence, police discovered Brassaw lying dead on the kitchen floor. Brassaw had been stabbed one time in the head with a kitchen knife, and had bled to death from the wound.

Officers interviewed another neighbor, Lawrence Collins, who related to the officers that he was awakened by talking outside his window. When he looked out the window, he observed Finger mumbling to himself. Collins told the police that he thought Finger said, "I framed my mother," and that Finger was holding an object in his hand. Collins also led police to a bloodied kitchen knife that Collins found in his yard not far from the place where Finger had been standing.

Rivera was also interviewed. He told the police that he was sleeping when he was awakened by the sound of a fight. He opened the door to his room and saw Brassaw staggering as if injured. Rivera then barricaded himself in his room until the noises stopped. Rivera had no blood on his clothes.

Finger gave a voluntary statement to the police. In it he claimed that he heard his mother screaming and that Rivera was stabbing her. He tried to stop Rivera and that's how he ended up with the bloodied kitchen knife and the blood on his clothes. Based upon the witness statements, the lack of blood on Rivera's clothes, the amount of blood on Finger's clothes, and his statement to detectives, Finger was arrested for the murder.

Finger has an extensive history of mental illness. He was first determined to be mentally ill in 1972 at the age of seventeen. Finger has been diagnosed as suffering from schizophrenia, manic depressive disorder with homicidal and suicidal tendencies, intermittent explosive disorder, and paranoia. Finger periodically suffers from visual and auditory hallucinations. In addition, Finger had a long history of violence and co-dependency with his mother and had been institutionalized in mental heath facilities several times due to delusions and attacks on his mother or other members of his family.

Upon interviewing Finger, it was immediately apparent to defense counsel that Finger was of questionable mental capacity. Counsel sought psychiatric evaluations. Two of the three evaluations concluded that Finger was unable to aid in his own defense. Based upon the evaluations, the district court committed Finger to the Lakes Crossing Center for the Criminally Insane until such time as he was found competent to participate in judicial proceedings.

In the course of these evaluations, Finger gave two different versions of what happened to his mother. The first version was consistent with his statements to the police. Finger claimed that Rivera had killed his mother, but could not give a coherent explanation for the blood on his clothes or his possession of the knife. The second version was an admission that he had stabbed his mother because she had been plotting to kill him and he decided to kill her before she had the opportunity to carry out her plot.

On December 18, 1996, Finger was deemed competent and Finger's case was remanded for a preliminary hearing. The hearing was conducted and Finger was bound over for trial. In the district court, Finger filed a motion seeking leave to enter a plea of not guilty by reason of insanity. Finger's counsel filed the motion because the 1995 Nevada Legislature had amended the laws concerning the treatment of insanity as a defense to criminal culpability. Counsel believed, based upon the legislative history of the amendments, that he would be prohibited from arguing that Finger should be acquitted of the murder charges on the grounds of legal insanity.

The motion was never argued and no order disposing of the motion was ever entered by the district court. Instead, the record reflects that at the time of his arraignment, Finger requested permission from the district court to enter a plea of not guilty by reason of insanity. The State objected and the district court denied the request without explanation. There is no indication in the record that the district court considered the legal issues raised in the written motion.

After the district court denied his request, Finger declined to enter a plea. The district court then entered a plea of not guilty and set a trial date. Based upon the district court's denial of his request to plead not guilty by reason of insanity and, by inference, his ability to raise insanity as a complete defense to the murder charge, Finger determined that there were no issues to be resolved by a trial. Therefore, Finger entered his plea of guilty but mentally ill, deciding to raise the constitutional issues relating to legal insanity. Based upon his plea, Finger was convicted of second-degree murder. This appeal followed.

Finger contends that the ability of an accused to pursue a defense of legal insanity is a fundamental right under the due process clauses of the United States and Nevada Constitutions. He asserts that various amendments to the provisions of the criminal procedure statutes enacted by the 1995 Legislature changed the substantive and pro-

> *Finger contends that the ability of an accused to pursue a defense of legal insanity is a fundamental right.*

cedural law regarding how the issue of legal insanity is treated in a criminal case and that these changes have resulted in an unconstitutional statutory scheme.

Finger asserts two additional grounds for relief. Finger contends that Nevada's statutory treatment scheme improperly discriminates between individuals who enter a plea of guilty but mentally ill and individuals with mental illnesses who are convicted after a jury trial in violation of the equal protection clause of the Federal and State Constitutions. Further, Finger alleges that the statutory scheme creates an improper chilling effect upon a defendant's right to a jury trial, because a mentally ill defendant will be forced to plead guilty if he or she wishes to avail themselves of appropriate treatment options in prison.

In 1995 the Legislature abolished the plea of "not guilty by reason of insanity" and created a new plea of "guilty but mentally ill." In addition, the Legislature amended the statutes that define what types of individuals can be punished for the violation of a criminal law. Finally, the Legislature enacted language declaring that an act committed by a person while in a state of insanity is no less criminal by reason of insanity and repealing the statute authorizing commitment of the criminally insane. At the same time, however, the Legislature permitted insanity to be taken into consideration whenever purpose, motive, or intent is a necessary element of a criminal offense.

Under the post-1995 statutory scheme, an individual pleading "guilty but mentally ill" is still subject to the same punishment as an individual who enters an unconditional plea of guilty or is found guilty upon trial. In the case of guilty but mentally ill defendants, however, the district court may suggest that the prison system provide certain types of treatment to the convicted individual. The status of an "insane" individual, however, is unclear. The Legislature deleted the term "insanity" from a number of statutes that define criminal culpability and criminal defenses. Insanity as it relates to liability for a criminal offense is now found only in NRS 193.220, which provides that: "No act committed by a person while in a state of insanity or voluntary intoxication shall be deemed less criminal by reason of his condition, but whenever the actual existence of any particular purpose, motive or intent is a necessary element to constitute a particular species or degree of crime, the fact of his insanity or intoxication may be taken into consideration in determining the purpose, motive or intent."

Finger argues that language of NRS 193.220, together with the elimination of insanity as an affirmative defense, permits persons to be convicted of crimes even though they did not possess the mental ability to form the criminal intent designated as an element of an offense. Finger contends that such a conviction violates the due process clauses of the Federal and State Constitutions.

On its face, NRS 193.220 is a contradiction in terms. It states that a person who is insane cannot be relieved of criminal culpability, i.e., acquitted, as a result of that insanity. Yet it also recognizes that insanity can be considered when determining whether or not an element of the crime has been proven beyond a reasonable doubt. Normally, when faced with such a statute, a court will construe the statute in favor of the accused. Thus we could construe NRS 193.220 to simply be a change in the procedure by which the issue of legal insanity is presented to the jury, rather than a change in the substantive law of insanity. In part, this is the dissent's position.

For hundreds of years, societies recognized that insane individuals are incapable of understanding when their conduct violates a legal or moral standard, and they were therefore relieved of criminal liability for their actions. Such individuals did not escape responsibility for their actions; they were still locked away, but in asylums, not prisons.

This concept of treating individuals differently based upon their mental capacity is called legal insanity. It recognizes that a "crime" involves something more than just the commission of a particular act, it also involves a certain mental component. This mental component is usually referred to as the *mens rea* of a crime, or criminal intent. The term "*mens rea*" refers to the mental state of a person at the time of the commission of the criminal act. Most serious crimes, either at common law or by statute, require a particular degree of *mens rea*, or criminal intent, to be proven as a material element of the offense. This is usually demonstrated by the use of such words as "knowingly," "willfully," or "deliberately." Where a person is unable to form the required criminal intent, the *mens rea*, that person is considered to be legally insane.

As early as the sixth century B.C., commentary on the Hebrew scriptures distinguished between harmful acts traceable to fault and those that occur without fault. To those ancient scholars, the paradigm of the latter type of act was one committed by a child, who was seen as incapable of weighing the moral implications of personal behavior, even when willful; retarded and insane persons were likened to children.

Although the general concept of legal insanity in relation to criminal culpability is centuries old, the definition of what constitutes legal insanity and how it should be presented to a jury under the American legal system is not so ancient. *M'Naghten* created a very strict guideline for determining insanity. The fact that a person had mental health problems did not necessarily mean that he or she could meet the *M'Naghten* test for insanity. In order to be considered legally insane under *M'Naghten*, a defendant must labor under a delusion so great that he is incapable of appreciating his surroundings. This delusion must do one of two things: (1) rob the defendant of the ability to understand what he is doing; or (2) deprive the defendant of the ability to appreciate that his action is wrong, that is, not authorized by law. For example, persons who think that they are shooting at a target shaped like a human being would meet the first factor of the standard. They would not understand the nature and quality of their act (i.e., shooting at a person, not a target). Similarly, persons who thought they were soldiers in the middle of a battlefield and that the individuals they were killing were enemy forces would meet the second factor of *M'Naghten*. Such persons would know they were shooting and killing human beings, but would not understand that it was wrong because of their delusional belief they were in the middle of a war.

While such severe delusional states do exist, they are not the kind of mental illness most commonly encountered in the criminal justice system. Beginning in the early 1900s, some legal scholars and mental health professionals began to advocate for an expanded definition of legal insanity. They felt the *M'Naghten* rule was too limited and that people with severe mental illnesses were being improperly convicted of crimes. The *M'Naghten* rule looks only to the cognitive condition of the defendant's state of mind. That is, the ability of the defendant to perceive reality and make rational choices based upon that perception. If you can form the criminal intent to do an act, then the reasons why you think you must do the act are irrelevant. Advocates for change believed that individuals who suffered from partial delusions, such as a conspiracy complex, should not be subject to criminal incarceration, but should be committed to a treatment facility for the mentally ill. Although such individuals had the mental capacity to form the required *mens rea* or criminal intent, advocates argued that these individuals could not control their acts and that to handle such individuals through the criminal justice system was inhumane. This is referred to as the "volitional" component of legal insanity.

This advocacy resulted in some courts adopting a new standard for legal insanity, the Irresistible Impulse Test. Under this theory, a defendant is legally insane if he or she suffers from a mental condition that creates overwhelming compulsions urging him or her to commit the illegal acts. For example, if a person was under a delusion that God wanted certain people killed and, based upon hearing the voice of God, that individual immediately began killing people around them, then that person would be legally insane under the Irresistible Impulse Test, but not under the *M'Naghten* standard. The individual knew that he was killing human beings and that he was not authorized by law to take a human life, but he could not resist what he perceived to be the will of God and acted under the impulse of his delusion.

Discussions and debates over the definition of legal insanity continued into the 1950s. Additional tests were proposed or adopted. In *Durham v.*

United States, the Circuit Court of Appeals for the District of Columbia held that a person is not responsible for actions that are the product of a mental disease or defect. Under the *Durham* standard, individuals were legally insane if they would not have committed the criminal act but for the existence of a mental disease or defect. In other words, if I did not have a delusion, I would not have committed the criminal act.

However, *Durham* was criticized as being too expansive. Another proposal, developed by the American Law Institute (ALI), combined elements of the *M'Naghten* rule, the Irresistible Impulse test, and *Durham*. Under this theory, a person is not responsible for criminal conduct committed during a time when, as a result of a severe mental disease or defect, that person lacks substantial capacity either to appreciate the criminality of his or her conduct or to conform his or her conduct to the requirements of law. The ALI Model Penal Code, however, excluded conditions that manifested only through repeated criminal or anti-social conduct, in other words, you are not legally insane simply because you commit violent acts. To be considered legally insane under the ALI Model Penal Code, a person does not have to be totally incapacitated, as with the *M'Naghten* rule, but they must have a substantial impairment of their mental capacity as opposed to simply having some impairment as under *Durham*.

In addition to discussing what test to use in determining legal insanity, courts and scholars have also debated over the procedural method for asserting the issue. Under *M'Naghten*, insanity is considered an affirmative defense which must be proven by the defendant. The burden of proof can be either: (1) by a preponderance of the evidence, (2) by clear and convincing evidence, or (3) beyond a reasonable doubt. (See *Leland v. Oregon*.) In contrast, other jurisdictions have determined that insanity is not an affirmative defense, but an issue of presumptions. A person is presumed to be sane. This presumption can be rebutted by the introduction of evidence tending to show that the defendant is legally insane. Once such evidence is presented, the prosecution has the burden of proving the defendant's sanity beyond a reasonable doubt. (See *Davis v. United States*.)

Combining definitions of legal insanity with the procedural mechanism for asserting the subject leads to a range of methods for dealing with the issue. The most restrictive method is the *M'Naghten* definition of legal insanity combined with a defendant having to prove legal insanity beyond a reasonable doubt as an affirmative defense. The least restrictive would be the use of the *Durham* test of legal insanity combined with the requirement that the prosecution must prove sanity beyond a reasonable doubt once a defendant introduces evidence rebutting the presumption of sanity.

The trend to expand the definition of legal insanity continued into the early 1980s. It ceased, however, as a result of John Hinckley's acquittal in the attempted assassination and shooting of President Ronald Reagan. Hinckley asserted the insanity defense, alleging he was under an irresistible compulsion brought on by a mental disease or defect. Hinckley would not have been able to assert his defense under the *M'Naghten* rule, but was successful in convincing a jury that he was legally insane under the lesser standards embodied by [*Brawner*] that governed his trial. In response to the Hinckley case, many jurisdictions made changes to their laws regarding the concept of legal insanity. Some adopted a compromise approach between *M'Naghten* and the Irresistible Impulse or *Durham* tests. Others changed the burden and standards of proof relating to the insanity defense. Some did both. In addition to the above changes, two new approaches to dealing with mentally ill defendants were considered. The first of these new theories incorporates the idea that a person can be found guilty, but mentally ill, of a criminal offense. It was originally intended as an additional verdict or plea, not as a replacement for the insanity defense. It gives the criminal justice system an alternative to either finding mentally ill persons guilty of a criminal offense or totally acquitting them of any criminal liability.

This allows states to maintain a stricter definition of insanity, but still provide for a verdict with different penalty implications for persons with mental health conditions that did not rise to the level of legal insanity. It has sometimes been described as a codification of the rule of diminished capacity. In such a case, the state mandates different treatment for such individuals than would be accorded to them under a more traditional finding of guilt. Thus a jury would be less inclined, out of sympathy for the defendant's mental condition, to improperly acquit a defendant because they would have another option.

The second theory to be developed after Hinckley involved abolishing legal insanity as a defense. Insanity is only admissible as it relates to a material element of a criminal offense, such as intent. Only where the level of mental illness completely negates a necessary element would a defendant be entitled to an acquittal. In addition, the definition of legal insanity under this theory is narrowed to include only the first part of the *M'Naghten* rule. Under this new theory, *mens rea*, or criminal intent, is viewed more in the context of strict liability, that is, so long as you had the intent to commit a particular act, you would be held liable for that act even though the definition of the crime might require a more specific mental state, such as an element of malice. Professor Joshua Dressler best described the difference by using the following example: "If D is prosecuted for intentionally killing V, D may introduce evidence that, due to mental illness, she believed she was squeezing a lemon rather than strangling V and, therefore, that she lacked the intent to kill. Evidence of D's mental condition would be inadmissible, however, to show that she did not realize that taking a life is morally or legally wrong, that she acted on the basis of an irresistible impulse to kill, or even that she killed V because she hallucinated that V was trying to kill her."

This approach has been designated by legal scholars as the *mens rea* model because it defines *mens rea*, or criminal intent, only in terms of the decision to do a certain act and eliminates the concept of the appreciation of the wrongfulness of the act. As long as a defendant can appreciate the nature and quality of his act, he is not legally insane and is capable of forming the necessary *mens rea*. Therefore, the person who thought he was shooting at a target would still be legally insane, but the individual who believes he is killing an enemy soldier would not qualify as insane under the law. Under this approach, because the latter individual is capable of recognizing he was killing a human being, he possesses the requisite intent to kill.

The *mens rea* model alters the focus of criminal intent, without actually changing the elements of the crimes themselves. It assumes that all crimes require the simple intent to do an act and it ignores the fact that most crimes have a required element of knowledge, willfulness, or something beyond the mere performance of an act. It treats all criminal intent more like an aspect of strict liability. Idaho, Montana, and Utah have adopted some form of the *Mens Rea* Approach.

As can be seen from the above discussion, federal and state laws regarding the insanity defense cover a broad spectrum of theories with respect to the treatment accorded to a mentally ill defendant. They are the product of society's continuing struggle over the need to protect the public from the actions of such individuals versus our recognition that a severely mentally ill individual may not possess the same level of culpability as a person who has no mental health problems.

Prior to the 1995 amendments, Nevada took a very strict approach to the issue of legal insanity. Nevada was not one of the states that reacted to the Hinckley decision and instituted new procedures or laws regarding legal insanity. Such actions were not necessary since Nevada already adhered to a very narrow view of legal insanity. In 1995, at the urging of the Nevada District Attorney's Association, the Nevada Legislature considered several amendments to the laws involving the insanity defense. The prosecutors believed that too many courts were allowing defendants to present evidence of mental health problems and argue for an insanity

acquittal even when that evidence did not relate to, or support, a
M'Naghten defense. Instead such evidence appeared to be more aligned
with concepts of the Irresistible Impulse, *Durham*, or ALI Model Penal
Code tests, theories of legal insanity which were not recognized under
Nevada law. This was particularly true when lay and expert witnesses
were allowed to give opinions regarding the defendant's sanity without
understanding the legal standard for determining insanity under
M'Naghten. While the Association acknowledged that no one had been
acquitted improperly, the admission of such evidence, and the need for
the prosecution to hire its own experts to rebut such evidence, was a
costly and time-consuming process. To correct this situation, the
Association proposed the adoption of a legislative scheme based on the
Idaho, Montana, and Utah statutes that embraced the *mens rea* model.
Insanity would no longer be treated as an affirmative defense, legal insanity
would be abolished, and a new plea, "guilty but mentally ill," would be
created.

Under the new system, a defendant who entered a plea of guilty but
mentally ill would still be convicted of a criminal offense. Prior to
sentencing, the judge would then determine whether or not the defendant
was suffering from a mental illness and, if so, what type of treatment
regime should be suggested to the division of parole and probation or the
prison for supervising the defendant's sentence. Given the confusion in
our case law and the testimony presented at the hearings, the Legislature
determined to abolish the concept of legal insanity as a defense to
culpability and enacted laws following the *mens rea* model.

Finger contends that NRS 193.220, if interpreted in accordance with
the *mens rea* model as intended by the Legislature, is unconstitutional
because it would permit an individual to be convicted of a criminal offense
without being able to form the necessary criminal intent. Finger argues
that due process requires that the concept of *mens rea*, at least with the
most serious crimes, incorporates an element of wrongfulness; that is, a
person not only intends to do the specific act, but also understands the act
is wrong because it is not permitted by law. Finger also contends that due
process requires that a defendant be able to present the issue of legal
insanity by asserting legal insanity as an affirmative defense.

The State argues that while insanity is no longer a defense, the
provisions of NRS 193.220 permit a defendant to introduce evidence
regarding insanity as it relates to the ability of the defendant to form
intent. If the Legislature requires the *mens rea* of a crime to include an
element of wrongfulness, then both tests under *M'Naghten* apply. If the
criminal statute does not specify such a requirement, then individuals

would only be legally insane if they failed to know and understand the nature and quality of their acts or the first test of *M'Naghten*. An individual who lacks the required intent could not be convicted of a criminal offense. Thus NRS 193.220 is constitutional because there is no requirement that legal insanity be asserted by way of an affirmative defense, only that a person who is legally insane cannot be convicted of an offense.

The State, however, has referenced the statutory schemes and cases from Idaho, Montana, and Utah in its arguments. In doing so, the State appears to be adopting the concept inherent in the *mens rea* model that knowledge that one's actions are "wrong" is not generally an element of a crime, even a specific intent crime, and it is not a requirement of murder. Moreover, the *mens rea* model, adopted by the Nevada Legislature, assumes that "wrongfulness" is never an element of intent, regardless of the crime. If this is so, then the State's argument that the 1995 legislative amendments only affect the method by which the issue of insanity is addressed must fail.

> *The* mens rea *model assumes that "wrongfulness" is never an element of intent, regardless of the crime.*

The Due Process Clause mandates protection of those principles deemed "fundamental to the American scheme of justice." The history of American jurisprudence reflects that it is a fundamental principle of our law that a defendant who is incapable of forming the requisite intent, or *mens rea*, to commit a crime cannot be convicted of a crime. One who does not possess the necessary criminal intent is not subject to criminal punishment.

> *One who does not possess the necessary criminal intent is not subject to criminal punishment.*

The contention that an injury can amount to a crime only when inflicted by intention (i.e., culpable mental state) is no provincial or transient notion. It is as universal and persistent in mature systems of law as belief in freedom of the human will and a consequent ability and duty of the normal individual to choose between good and evil. A relation between some mental element and punishment for a harmful act is almost as instinctive as the child's familiar exculpatory "But I didn't mean to," and has afforded the rational basis for a tardy and unfinished substitution of deterrence and reformation in place of retaliation and vengeance as the motivation for public prosecution (*Morissette v. United States*).

Mens rea is a fundamental aspect of criminal law. Thus it follows that the concept of legal insanity, that a person is not culpable for a criminal act because he or she cannot form the necessary *mens rea*, is also a fundamental principle. Indeed the term "legal insanity" simply means that a person has a complete defense to a criminal act based upon the person's inability to form the requisite criminal intent. Congress, even in the face of the public outrage following the *Hinckley* trial, refused to

> **Congress, even in the face of the public outrage following the Hinckley *trial, refused to completely abolish the concept of legal insanity, recognizing that culpability is a prerequisite to a criminal prosecution.***

completely abolish the concept of legal insanity, recognizing that culpability is a prerequisite to a criminal prosecution. While courts and scholars may debate what standard or definition should apply in determining what constitutes legal insanity, or by what method it should be raised, all have agreed that due process requires that a defendant be able to present evidence and argue that he or she lacked the *mens rea* to commit the criminal act.

It is because legal insanity is a corollary of *mens rea*, the mental state that imposes criminal responsibility upon an individual, that legal insanity is a fundamental principle under the Due Process Clause. What constitutes a "fundamental principle" is largely a matter of historical development. Historical practice overwhelmingly supports the conclusion that legal insanity is a fundamental principle. As Justice Stewart notes in his dis-

> **It is because legal insanity is a corollary of mens rea *that legal insanity is a fundamental principle under the Due Process Clause.***

senting opinion in *State v. Herrera*: "Recognition of insanity as a defense is a core principle that has been recognized for centuries by every civilized system of law in one form or another. Historically, the defense has been formulated differently, but given the extent of knowledge concerning principles of human nature at any given point in time, the essence of the defense, however formulated, has been that a defendant must have the mental capacity to know the nature of his act and that it was wrong."

Legal insanity has been an established concept in English common law for centuries. Since the reign of Edward II (1307-1321), English law acknowledged that an individual who does not know what he is doing or that what he is doing is wrong cannot be held criminally liable.

The same conclusion was reached by the American Bar Association's Standing Committee on Association Standards for Criminal Justice. Commenting on the *mens rea* model, the Committee stated that: "This approach, which would permit evidence of mental condition on the requisite mental element of the crime but eliminate mental nonresponsiblity as an independent, exculpatory doctrine, has been proposed in several bills in Congress and adopted in Montana, Idaho and Utah. The ABA has rejected it out of hand. Such a jarring reversal of hundreds of years of moral and legal history would constitute an unfortunate and unwarranted overreaction to the *Hinckley* verdict."

The State does not contest that the need to establish criminal intent beyond a reasonable doubt is a fundamental principle. Instead the State argues that NRS 193.220 does not interfere with or negate this principle. We disagree. The *mens rea* model has the effect of eliminating the concept of wrongfulness from all crimes, in effect changing the criminal intent to be established regardless of the statutory definition of the offense. This would permit an individual to be convicted of a crime where the State failed to prove an element of the offense beyond a reasonable doubt.

The United States Supreme Court has never held that a defense of insanity is a fundamental principle under the Due Process Clause. In *Powell*, the Supreme Court was considering the constitutionality of a statute that made it a crime to be drunk in a public place. The court concluded this was not an unconstitutional status crime. In the opinion, the court stated that: "We cannot cast aside the centuries-long evolution of the collection of inter-locking and overlapping concepts which the common law has utilized to assess the moral accountability of an individual for his antisocial deeds. The doctrines of *actus reus, mens rea,* insanity, mistake, justification, and duress have historically provided the tools for a constantly shifting adjustment of the tension between the evolving aims of the criminal law and changing religious, moral, philosophical, and medical views of the nature of man. This process of adjustment has always been thought to be the province of the States." In addition to this comment from *Powell*, Justice Rehnquist's dissenting opinion in *Ake v. Oklahoma* [includes]: "It is highly doubtful that due process requires a State to make available an insanity defense to a criminal defendant, but in any event if such a defense is afforded the burden of proving insanity can be placed on the defendant." Justice O'Connor's commentary in *Powell*, [however,] when read in context, [supports] the Supreme Court's longstanding policy to generally permit the states to determine the details of how to implement well-established doctrines. In other words, how a state chooses to present the issue of legal insanity is left up to state law. *Powell* cannot be read to stand for the proposition that the concept of legal insanity, i.e., an inability to form the requisite *mens rea*, is not a fundamental principle of our jurisprudence entitled to protection under the Due Process Clause.

The ideas embodied in *Powell* regarding giving the state's discretion on the procedural method for determining legal insanity are also expressed in *Leland v. Oregon*. In *Leland*, the High Court upheld Oregon's legal insanity statute. The statute required that a defendant prove legal insanity beyond a reasonable doubt. Oregon also followed the *M'Naghten* rule. The defendant was challenging Oregon's requirement that he prove, as an affirmative defense, that he was legally insane beyond a reasonable doubt. This, he argued, was an impermissible shift to the defendant of the burden of proof. The Supreme Court found that this scheme did not violate "generally accepted concepts of basic standards of justice" because the state still had the burden to prove every element of the crime beyond a reasonable doubt.

In reaching this conclusion, the High Court's discussion of legal insanity implies that it viewed the issues of legal insanity and *mens rea* to be intertwined. Due Process requires that the prosecution prove the *mens rea*, or intent, of a crime beyond a reasonable doubt. Legal insanity negates criminal intent, but how the issue of legal insanity is raised is a procedural issue left to the judgment of the individual state and requiring a defendant to establish legal insanity as an affirmative defense was a permissible method for accomplishing this task. While the court did not adopt any one procedure or test for establishing legal insanity, it implied that legal insanity is a fundamental principle of our system of justice.

It is also interesting to note that the Supreme Court in *Leland* did not withdraw from any of the language in *Davis* that discusses the importance of legal insanity. The Court only found that the procedure for litigating the issue of legal insanity set forth in *Davis* was not constitutionally mandated. In *Davis*, Justice Harlan stated that: "We are unable to assent to the doctrine that in a prosecution for murder, the defence being insanity, and the fact of the killing with a deadly weapon being clearly established, it is the duty of the jury to convict where the evidence is equally balanced on the issue as to the sanity of the accused at the time of the killing. On the contrary, he is entitled to an acquittal of the specific crime charged if, upon all the evidence, there is reasonable doubt whether he was capable in law of committing crime."

The significance of the isolated comments in *Powell* and *Ake* becomes more tenuous in the face of other statements of the High Court affirming the importance of legal insanity as a defense to criminal culpability. Justice O'Connor relied upon the protections afforded by the defense of insanity when determining that the imposition of the death penalty upon a mentally retarded defendant did not constitute cruel and unusual punishment. The Court acknowledged that there is a constitutional prohibition against executing a legally insane person, but that mental retardation did not equate to legal insanity. Further, Justice O'Connor noted that there were sufficient safeguards to ensure that a mentally incompetent individual who was incapable of forming the requisite *mens rea* would not be convicted, among them the insanity defense.

The common law prohibition against punishing "idiots" for their crimes suggests that it may indeed be "cruel and unusual" punishment to execute persons who are profoundly or severely retarded and wholly lacking the capacity to appreciate the wrongfulness of their actions. Because of the protections afforded by the insanity defense today, such a person is not likely to be convicted or face the prospect of punishment (*Penry v. Lynaugh*). Given the Supreme Court's discussion of insanity in *Leland, Morissette*, and *Penry*, we cannot agree with the analysis of federal law contained in the majority opinions of *Herrera, Searcy*, and *Korell*.

Proponents of abolishing the insanity defense appear to assume that wrongfulness, that is the knowledge that you are acting in an unauthorized manner, is not a necessary component of the crime of murder. But murder is generally not defined as just the killing of another human being. In Nevada, as in most states, murder requires something more than the intent to kill. Nevada defines murder as the "unlawful killing of a human being, with *malice aforethought*, either express or implied." Express malice involves the deliberate intention to unlawfully take away the life of a fellow creature, while malice is implied when, for example, the circumstances of the killing show an abandoned and malignant heart.

An individual who labors under the total delusion that they are a soldier in a war and are shooting at enemy soldiers is not capable of forming the intent to kill with malice aforethought. His delusional state prohibits him from forming the requisite *mens reas*, because he believes that his killing is authorized by law. He is legally insane under *M'Naghten*. Anytime a statute requires something more than the intent to commit a particular act, then legal insanity must be a viable defense to the crime and involves both tests under the *M'Naghten* rule.

We conclude that legal insanity is a well-established and fundamental principle of the law of the United States. It is therefore protected by the

Due Process Clauses of both the United States and Nevada Constitutions. The Legislature may not abolish insanity as a complete defense to a criminal offense. Thus the provisions of [Nevada statutes] abolishing the insanity defense are unconstitutional and unenforceable.

We take this opportunity to clarify our previous case law. To qualify as being legally insane, a defendant must be in a delusional state such that he cannot know or understand the nature and capacity of his act, or his delusion must be such that he cannot appreciate the wrongfulness of his act, that is, that the act is not authorized by law. So, if a jury believes he was suffering from a delusional state, and if the facts as he believed them to be in his delusional state would justify his actions, he is insane and entitled to acquittal. If, however, the delusional facts would not amount to a legal defense, then he is not insane. Persons suffering from a delusion that someone is shooting at them, so they shot back in self-defense are insane under *M'Naghten*. Persons who are paranoid and believe that the victim is going to get them some time in the future, so they hunt down the victim first, are not.

We also take this opportunity to clarify the proper use of lay opinion in cases involving legal insanity. Legal insanity has a precise and extremely narrow definition in Nevada law. To allow a lay witness to testify that someone is "insane" assumes that the witness fully understands the complexity of the insanity defense as outlined in *M'Naghten* and *State v. Lewis*. A lay witness can certainly testify as to their observations of a defendant's behavior and can use other words, such as "crazy" or "abnormal." But a lay witness should not be permitted to use the word "insane" since that is a term of art. We expressly disapprove of any language in our case law that holds to the contrary.

In addition we stress the need for experts and juries to be correctly advised on the *M'Naghten* standard. The ability to understand right from wrong under *M'Naghten* is directly linked to the nature of the defendant's delusional state. Delusional beliefs can only be the grounds for legal insanity when the facts of the delusion, if true, would justify the commission of the criminal act. This is a very narrow standard. Unless a defendant presents evidence that complies with this standard, he or she is not entitled to have the jury instructed on the issue of insanity. Evidence that does not rise to the level of legal insanity may, of course, be considered in evaluating whether or not the prosecution has proven each element of an offense beyond a reasonable doubt, for example, in determining whether a killing is first- or second-degree murder or manslaughter or some other argument regarding diminished capacity.

Clark v. Arizona

548 U.S. _____ (2006)

Facts

In June 2000, Eric Clark (age 17) shot and killed a Flagstaff police officer who had stopped Clark's truck for loud music in a residential neighborhood. Clark was initially found incompetent to stand trial. Two years later, after treatment, he was found competent and had a bench trial. Clark did not contest the shooting, but his defense relied on "undisputed paranoid schizophrenia." He attempted to present mental illness evidence both to raise an affirmative defense of insanity and to rebut the prosecution's evidence of requisite intent. (Arizona's law made it first-degree murder to *intentionally or knowingly* kill a law enforcement officer.) Clark argued he did not know he was killing a police officer, because he had a delusion that Flagstaff was populated by aliens who could only be stopped by bullets. The prosecution argued Clark had earlier told others he wanted to kill a police officer, intentionally lured the officer to the scene, and evaded police and hid evidence afterward. Both sides presented experts who agreed Clark suffered from paranoid schizophrenia but disagreed on whether his illness prevented him from appreciating the wrongfulness of his actions. Arizona's insanity test, revised in 1993, included only the "wrongfulness" prong of the *M'Naghten* standard and not the "nature and quality" prong. Furthermore, based on *State v. Mott*, a 1997 decision, Arizona did not allow mental health testimony to negate specific intent (*mens rea*). Clark was found guilty and sentenced to life. He appealed, arguing that the two prongs of *M'Naghten* were "so rooted in the traditions and conscience of our people as to be ranked as fundamental." He also argued that the *Mott* rule, disallowing expert evidence on *mens rea*, violated due process. The Arizona Court of Appeals affirmed his conviction, and the Arizona Supreme Court denied further review. The U.S. Supreme Court granted certiorari.

Issue

(a) Does due process prohibit Arizona from using an insanity test stated solely in terms of the capacity to tell whether the act was right or wrong? (b) Does restricting defense mental health evidence to the issue of insanity and eliminating its use directly on the issue of the mental element of the crime violate due process?

Holding

Due process was not violated. The lower court judgment was affirmed.

Analysis

In reference to the first issue, the Court reasoned that there were four "traditional strains" of insanity tests that combined to create several diverse American standards. These strains were cognitive incapacity (nature and quality), moral incapacity (wrongfulness), volitional incapacity (irresistible impulse), and product-of-mental-illness (*Durham*, see Section 4). Since state and federal standards included several combinations, including four states with no insanity defense, the first prong of *M'Naghten* (cognitive incapacity) could not be considered "fundamental." Furthermore, "cognitive incapacity is itself enough to demonstrate moral incapacity," making those with the former a subset of those with the latter. Therefore, Arizona's abridged *M'Naghten* standard did not violate due process.

In addressing the second issue, the Court explained there were three types of evidence that might bear on *mens rea*: observational evidence, mental disease evidence, and capacity evidence. The latter two types were usually provided by mental health experts, but the *Mott* rule allowed only the first type. All criminal cases have presumptions of both innocence and sanity. The "force of the presumption" is determined by the showing needed to overcome it. The prosecution must overcome the innocence presumption by evidence beyond a reasonable doubt of all elements of the crime, but the force of the sanity presumption varies across jurisdictions. The Court reasoned that allowing the defendant to present expert evidence on *mens rea* would, in actuality, make the sanity presumption only as strong as the evidence necessary to convince a fact finder of reasonable doubt concerning *mens rea*. In other words, the defendant could avoid criminal responsibility without proving insanity by clear and convincing or even a preponderance of the evidence, by merely creating reasonable doubt about intent.

The Court concluded that expert mental disease and capacity evidence regarding intent has the potential to confuse jurors, pointing to disagreement among mental health professionals about diagnoses and the effects of mental disease on capacities. Unlike "observational evidence," the Court reasoned that such "capacity evidence" includes judgments which are "fraught with multiple perils." In formulating this opinion, the majority argued that an expert's "judgment addressing the basic categories of capacity requires a leap from the concepts of psychology, which are devised for thinking about treatment, to the concepts of legal sanity, which are devised for thinking about criminal responsibility."

Edited Excerpts[1]

Justice Souter delivered the opinion of the Court

The case presents two questions: whether due process prohibits Arizona's use of an insanity test stated solely in terms of the capacity to tell whether an act charged as a crime was right or wrong; and whether Arizona violates due process in restricting consideration of defense evidence of mental illness and incapacity to its bearing on a claim of insanity, thus eliminating its significance directly on the issue of the mental element of the crime charged (known in legal shorthand as the *mens rea*, or guilty mind). We hold that there is no violation of due process in either instance.

In the early hours of June 21, 2000, Officer Jeffrey Moritz of the Flagstaff Police responded in uniform to complaints that a pickup truck with loud music blaring was circling a residential block. When he located the truck, the officer turned on the emergency lights and siren of his marked patrol car, which prompted petitioner Eric Clark, the truck's driver (then 17), to pull over. Officer Moritz got out of the patrol car and told Clark to stay where he was. Less than a minute later, Clark shot the officer, who died soon after but not before calling the police dispatcher for help. Clark ran away on foot but was arrested later that day with gunpowder residue on his hands; the gun that killed the officer was found nearby, stuffed into a knit cap.

Clark was charged with first-degree murder for intentionally or knowingly killing a law enforcement officer in the line of duty. In March 2001, Clark was found incompetent to stand trial and was committed to a state hospital for treatment, but two years later the same trial court found his competence restored and ordered him to be tried. Clark waived his right to a jury, and the case was heard by the court.

At trial, Clark did not contest the shooting and death, but relied on his undisputed paranoid schizophrenia at the time of the incident in denying that he had the specific intent to shoot a law enforcement officer or knowledge that he was doing so. Accordingly, the prosecutor offered

---

[1] Readers are advised to quote only from the original published cases. See pages vi and vii.

circumstantial evidence that Clark knew Officer Moritz was a law enforcement officer. The evidence showed that the officer was in uniform at the time, that he caught up with Clark in a marked police car with emergency lights and siren going, and that Clark acknowledged the symbols of police authority and stopped. The testimony for the prosecution indicated that Clark had intentionally lured an officer to the scene to kill him, having told some people a few weeks before the incident that he wanted to shoot police officers. At the close of the State's evidence, the trial court denied Clark's motion for judgment of acquittal for failure to prove intent to kill a law enforcement officer or knowledge that Officer Moritz was a law enforcement officer.

> **The testimony for the prosecution indicated that Clark had intentionally lured an officer to the scene to kill him, having told some people a few weeks before the incident that he wanted to shoot police officers.**

In presenting the defense case, Clark claimed mental illness, which he sought to introduce for two purposes. First, he raised the affirmative defense of insanity, putting the burden on himself to prove by clear and convincing evidence, that "at the time of the commission of the criminal act [he] was afflicted with a mental disease or defect of such severity that [he] did not know the criminal act was wrong." Second, he aimed to rebut the prosecution's evidence of the requisite *mens rea*, that he had acted intentionally or knowingly to kill a law enforcement officer.

The trial court ruled that Clark could not rely on evidence bearing on insanity to dispute the *mens rea*. The court cited *State v. Mott* (1997), which "refused to allow psychiatric testimony to negate specific intent," and held that "Arizona does not allow evidence of a defendant's mental disorder short of insanity to negate the *mens rea* element of a crime."

> **There was lay and expert testimony that Clark thought Flagstaff was populated with "aliens" (some impersonating government agents), the "aliens" were trying to kill him, and bullets were the only way to stop them.**

As to his insanity, then, Clark presented testimony from classmates, school officials, and his family describing his increasingly bizarre behavior over the year before the shooting. Witnesses testified, for example, that paranoid delusions led Clark to rig a fishing line with beads and wind chimes at home to alert him to intrusion by invaders, and to keep a bird in his automobile to warn of airborne poison. There was lay and expert testimony that Clark thought Flagstaff was populated with "aliens" (some impersonating government agents), the "aliens" were trying to kill him, and bullets were the only way to stop them. A psychiatrist testified that Clark was suffering from paranoid schizophrenia with delusions about "aliens" when he killed Officer Moritz, and he concluded that Clark was incapable of luring the officer or understanding right from wrong and that he was thus insane at the time of the killing. In rebuttal, a psychiatrist for the State gave his opinion that Clark's paranoid schizophrenia did not keep him from appreciating the wrongfulness of his conduct, as shown by his actions before and after the shooting (such as circling the residential block with music blaring as if to lure the police to intervene, evading the police after the shooting, and hiding the gun).

At the close of the defense case consisting of this evidence bearing on mental illness, the trial court denied Clark's renewed motion for a directed verdict grounded on failure of the prosecution to show that Clark knew the victim was a police officer. The judge then issued a special verdict of first-degree murder, expressly finding that Clark shot and caused the death of Officer Moritz beyond a reasonable doubt and that Clark had not shown that he was insane at the time. The judge noted that though Clark was indisputably afflicted with paranoid schizophrenia at the time of the shooting, the mental illness "did not distort his perception of reality so severely that he did not know his actions were wrong." For this conclusion, the judge expressly relied on "the facts of the crime, the evaluations of the experts, [Clark's] actions and behavior both before and after the shooting, and the observations of those that knew [Clark]." The sentence was life imprisonment without the possibility of release for 25 years.

Clark moved to vacate the judgment and sentence, arguing, among other things, that Arizona's insanity test and its *Mott* rule each violate due process. As to the insanity standard, Clark claimed (as he had argued earlier) that the Arizona Legislature had impermissibly narrowed its standard in 1993 when it eliminated the first part of the two-part insanity test announced in *M'Naghten's* Case. The court denied the motion.

The Court of Appeals of Arizona affirmed Clark's conviction, treating the conclusion on sanity as supported by enough evidence to withstand review for abuse of discretion, and holding the State's insanity scheme consistent with due process. As to the latter, the Court of Appeals reasoned that there is no constitutional requirement to recognize an insanity defense at all, the bounds of which are left to the State's discretion. Beyond that, the appellate court followed *Mott*, reading it as barring the trial court's consideration of evidence of Clark's mental illness and capacity directly on the element of *mens rea*. The Supreme Court of Arizona denied further review.

We granted certiorari to decide whether due process prohibits Arizona from thus narrowing its insanity test or from excluding evidence of mental illness and incapacity due to mental illness to rebut evidence of the requisite criminal intent. We now affirm.

Clark first says that Arizona's definition of insanity, being only a fragment of the Victorian standard from which it derives, violates due process. The landmark English rule in *M'Naghten's* Case states that "the jurors ought to be told that to establish a defence on the ground of insanity, it must be clearly proved that, at the time of the committing of the act, the party accused was laboring under such a defect of reason, from disease of the mind, as not to know the nature and quality of the act he was doing; or, if he did know it, that he did not know he was doing what was wrong."

The first part asks about cognitive capacity: whether a mental defect leaves a defendant unable to understand what he is doing. The second part presents an ostensibly alternative basis for recognizing a defense of insanity understood as a lack of moral capacity: whether a mental disease or defect leaves a defendant unable to understand that his action is wrong.

When the Arizona Legislature first codified an insanity rule, it adopted the full *M'Naghten* statement (subject to modifications in details that do not matter here). In 1993, the legislature dropped the cognitive incapacity part, leaving only moral incapacity as the nub of the stated definition. Under current Arizona law, a defendant will not be adjudged insane unless he demonstrates that "at the time of the commission of the criminal act [he] was afflicted with a mental disease or defect of such severity that [he] did not know the criminal act was wrong."

Clark challenges the 1993 amendment excising the express reference to the cognitive incapacity element. He insists that the side-by-side *M'Naghten* test represents the minimum that a government must provide in recognizing an alternative to criminal responsibility on grounds of mental illness or defect, and he argues that elimination of the *M'Naghten* reference to nature and quality "offends [a] principle of justice so rooted in the traditions and conscience of our people as to be ranked as fundamental" (*Patterson v. New York*).

The claim entails no light burden, and Clark does not carry it. History shows no deference to *M'Naghten* that could elevate its formula to the level of fundamental principle, so as to limit the traditional recognition of a State's capacity to define crimes and defenses.

Even a cursory examination of the traditional Anglo-American approaches to insanity reveals significant differences among them, with four traditional strains variously combined to yield a diversity of American standards. The main variants are the cognitive incapacity, the moral incapacity, the volitional incapacity, and the product-of-mental-illness tests. The first two emanate from the alternatives stated in the *M'Naghten* rule. The volitional incapacity or irresistible impulse test, which surfaced over two centuries ago, asks whether a person was so lacking in volition due to a mental defect or illness that he could not have controlled his actions. And the product-of-mental-illness test was used as early as 1870, and simply asks whether a person's action was a product of a mental disease or defect. Seventeen States and the Federal Government have adopted a recognizable version of the *M'Naghten* test with both its cognitive incapacity and moral incapacity components. One State has adopted only *M'Naghten's* cognitive incapacity test, and 10 (including Arizona) have adopted the moral incapacity test alone. Fourteen jurisdictions, inspired by the Model Penal Code, have in place an amalgam of the volitional incapacity test and some variant of the moral incapacity test, satisfaction of either (generally by showing a defendant's substantial lack of capacity) being enough to excuse. Three States combine a full *M'Naghten* test with a volitional incapacity formula. And New Hampshire alone stands by the product-of-mental-illness test. The alternatives are multiplied further by variations in the prescribed insanity verdict: a significant number of these jurisdictions supplement the traditional "not guilty by reason of insanity" verdict with an alternative of "guilty but mentally ill." Finally, four States have no affirmative insanity defense, though one provides for a "guilty and mentally ill" verdict. These four, like a number of others that recognize an affirmative insanity defense, allow consideration of evidence of mental illness directly on the element of *mens rea* defining the offense.

    With this varied background, it is clear that no particular formulation has evolved into a baseline for due process, and that the insanity rule, like the conceptualization of criminal offenses, is substantially open to state choice. Indeed, the legitimacy of such choice is the more obvious when one considers the interplay of legal concepts of mental illness or deficiency required for an insanity defense, with the medical concepts of mental abnormality that influence the expert opinion testimony by psychologists and psychiatrists commonly introduced to support or contest insanity claims. For medical definitions devised to justify treatment, like legal ones devised to excuse from conventional criminal responsibility, are subject to flux and disagreement. There being such fodder for reasonable debate about what the cognate legal and medical tests should be, due process imposes no single canonical formulation of legal insanity.

Nor does Arizona's abbreviation of the *M'Naghten* statement raise a proper claim that some constitutional minimum has been shortchanged. Clark's argument of course assumes that Arizona's former statement of the *M'Naghten* rule, with its express alternative of cognitive incapacity, was constitutionally adequate (as we agree). That being so, the abbreviated rule is no less so, for cognitive incapacity is relevant under that statement, just as it was under the more extended formulation, and evidence going to cognitive incapacity has the same significance under the short form as it had under the long.

Though Clark is correct that the application of the moral incapacity test (telling right from wrong) does not necessarily require evaluation of a defendant's cognitive capacity to appreciate the nature and quality of the acts charged against him, his argument fails to recognize that cognitive incapacity is itself enough to demonstrate moral incapacity. Cognitive incapacity, in other words, is a sufficient condition for establishing a defense of insanity, albeit not a necessary one. As a defendant can therefore make out moral incapacity by demonstrating cognitive incapacity, evidence bearing on whether the defendant knew the nature and quality of his actions is both relevant and admissible. In practical terms, if a defendant did not know what he was doing when he acted, he could not have known that he was performing the wrongful act charged as a crime. Indeed, when the two-part rule was still in effect, the Supreme Court of Arizona held that a jury instruction on insanity containing the moral incapacity part but not a full recitation of the cognitive incapacity part was fine, as the cognitive incapacity part might be "treated as adding nothing to the requirement that the accused know his act was wrong."

The Court of Appeals of Arizona acknowledged as much in this case, too, and thus aligned itself with the long-accepted understanding that the cognitively incapacitated are a subset of the morally incapacitated within the meaning of the standard *M'Naghten* rule.

Clark, indeed, adopted this very analysis himself in the trial court. The trial court apparently agreed, for the judge admitted Clark's evidence of cognitive incapacity for consideration under the State's moral incapacity formulation. And Clark can point to no evidence bearing on insanity that was excluded. His psychiatric expert and a number of lay witnesses testified to his delusions, and this evidence tended to support a description of Clark as lacking the capacity to understand that the police officer was a human being. There is no doubt that the trial judge considered the evidence as going to an issue of cognitive capacity, for in finding insanity not proven he said that Clark's mental illness "did not distort his perception of reality so severely that he did not know his actions were wrong."

We are satisfied that neither in theory nor in practice did Arizona's 1993 abridgment of the insanity formulation deprive Clark of due process.

Clark's second claim of a due process violation challenges the rule adopted by the Supreme Court of Arizona in *Mott*. This case ruled on the admissibility of testimony from a psychologist offered to show that the defendant suffered from battered women's syndrome and therefore lacked the capacity to form the *mens rea* of the crime charged against her. The opinion variously referred to the testimony in issue as "psychological testimony," and "expert testimony," and implicitly equated it with "expert psychiatric evidence," and "psychiatric testimony." The state court held that testimony of a professional psychologist or psychiatrist about a defendant's mental incapacity owing to mental disease or defect was admissible, and could be considered, only for its bearing on an insanity defense; such evidence could not be considered on the element of *mens rea*, that is, what the State must show about a defendant's mental state (such as intent or understanding) when he performed the act charged against him.

Understanding Clark's claim requires attention to the categories of evidence with a potential bearing on *mens rea*. First, there is "observation evidence" in the everyday sense, testimony from those who observed what Clark did and heard what he said; this category would also include testimony that an expert witness might give about Clark's tendency to think in a certain way and his behavioral characteristics. This evidence may support a professional diagnosis of mental disease and in any event is the kind of evidence that can be relevant to show what in fact was on Clark's mind when he fired the gun. Observation evidence in the record covers Clark's behavior at home and with friends, his expressions of belief around the time of the killing that "aliens" were inhabiting the bodies of local people (including government agents), his driving around the neighborhood before the police arrived, and so on. Contrary to the dissent's characterization, observation evidence can be presented by either lay or expert witnesses.

Second, there is "mental-disease evidence" in the form of opinion testimony that Clark suffered from a mental disease with features described by the witness. As was true here, this evidence characteristically but not always comes from professional psychologists or psychiatrists who testify as expert witnesses and base their opinions in part on examination of a defendant, usually conducted after the events in question. The thrust of this evidence was that, based on factual reports, professional observations, and tests, Clark was psychotic at the time in question, with a condition that fell within the category of schizophrenia.

Third, there is evidence we will refer to as "capacity evidence" about a defendant's capacity for cognition and moral judgment (and ultimately also his capacity to form *mens rea*). This, too, is opinion evidence. Here, as it usually does, this testimony came from the same experts and concentrated on those specific details of the mental condition that make the difference between sanity and insanity under the Arizona definition. In their respective testimony on these details the experts disagreed: the defense expert gave his opinion that the symptoms or effects of the disease in Clark's case included inability to appreciate the nature of his action and to tell that it was wrong, whereas the State's psychiatrist was of the view that Clark was a schizophrenic who was still sufficiently able to appreciate the reality of shooting the officer and to know that it was wrong to do that.

A caveat about these categories is in order. They attempt to identify different kinds of testimony offered in this case in terms of explicit and implicit distinctions made in *Mott*. What we can say about these categories goes to their cores, however, not their margins. Exact limits have thus not been worked out in any Arizona law that has come to our attention, and in this case, neither the courts in their rulings nor counsel in objections invoked or required precision in applying the *Mott* rule's evidentiary treatment, as we explain below. Necessarily, then, our own decision can address only core issues, leaving for other cases any due process claims that may be raised about the treatment of evidence whose categorization is subject to dispute.

It is clear that *Mott* itself imposed no restriction on considering evidence of the first sort, the observation evidence. We read the *Mott* restriction to apply, rather, to evidence addressing the two issues in testimony that characteristically comes only from psychologists or psychiatrists qualified to give opinions as expert witnesses: mental-disease evidence (whether at the time of the crime a defendant suffered from a mental disease or defect, such as schizophrenia) and capacity evidence (whether the disease or defect left him incapable of performing or experiencing a mental process defined as necessary for sanity such as appreciating the nature and quality of his act and knowing that it was wrong).

Mott was careful to distinguish this kind of opinion evidence from observation evidence generally and even from observation evidence that an expert witness might offer, such as descriptions of a defendant's tendency to think in a certain way or his behavioral characteristics; the

Arizona court made it clear that this sort of testimony was perfectly admissible to rebut the prosecution's evidence of *mens rea*. Thus, only opinion testimony going to mental defect or disease, and its effect on the cognitive or moral capacities on which sanity depends under the Arizona rule, is restricted.

In this case, the trial court seems to have applied the *Mott* restriction to all evidence offered by Clark for the purpose of showing what he called his inability to form the required *mens rea*. Thus, the trial court's restriction may have covered not only mental-disease and capacity evidence as just defined, but also observation evidence offered by lay (and expert) witnesses who described Clark's unusual behavior. Clark's objection to the application of the *Mott* rule does not, however, turn on the distinction between lay and expert witnesses or the kinds of testimony they were competent to present.

There is some, albeit limited, disagreement between the dissent and ourselves about the scope of the claim of error properly before us. To start with matters of agreement, all Members of the Court agree that Clark's general attack on the *Mott* rule covers its application in confining consideration of capacity evidence to the insanity defense.

The point on which we disagree with the dissent, however, is this: Did Clark apprise the Arizona courts that he believed the trial judge had erroneously limited the consideration of observation evidence, whether from lay witnesses like Clark's mother or (possibly) the expert witnesses who observed him? This sort of evidence was not covered by the *Mott* restriction, and confining it to the insanity issue would have been an erroneous application of *Mott* as a matter of Arizona law. We think no such objection was made in a way the Arizona courts could have understood it, and that no such issue is before us now. We think the only issue properly before us is the challenge to *Mott* on due process grounds, comprising objections to limits on the use of mental-disease and capacity evidence.

At no point did the trial judge specify any particular evidence that he refused to consider on the *mens rea* issue. Nor did defense counsel specify any observation or other particular evidence that he claimed was admissible but wrongly excluded on the issue of *mens rea*, so as to produce a clearer ruling on what evidence was being restricted on the authority of *Mott* and what was not. He made no "offer of proof" in the trial court, although his brief in the Arizona Court of Appeals stated at one point that it was not inconsistent with *Mott* to consider nonexpert evidence indicating mental illness on the issue of *mens rea*, and argued that the trial judge had failed to do so. Similarly, we read the Arizona Court of Appeals to have done nothing more than rely on *Mott* to reject the claim that due process forbids restricting evidence bearing on "ability to form *mens rea*" (i.e., mental-disease and capacity evidence) to the insanity determination.

In sum, the trial court's ruling, with its uncertain edges, may have restricted observation evidence admissible on *mens rea* to the insanity defense alone, but we cannot be sure. But because a due process challenge to such a restriction of observation evidence was, by our measure, neither pressed nor passed upon in the Arizona Court of Appeals, we do not consider it. What we do know, and now consider, is Clark's claim that *Mott* denied due process because it "precluded Eric from contending that factual inferences" of the "mental states which were necessary elements of the crime charged" "should not be drawn because the behavior was explainable, instead, as a manifestation of his chronic paranoid schizophrenia." We consider the claim, as Clark otherwise puts it, that "Arizona's prohibition of 'diminished capacity' evidence by criminal defendants violates" due process.

Clark's argument that the *Mott* rule violates the Fourteenth Amendment[2] guarantee of due process turns on the application of the presumption of innocence in criminal cases, the presumption of sanity, and the principle that a criminal defendant is entitled to present relevant and favorable evidence on an element of the offense charged against him.

The first presumption is that a defendant is innocent unless and until the government proves beyond a reasonable doubt each element of the offense charged including the mental element or *mens rea*. Before the last century, the *mens rea* required to be proven for particular offenses was often described in general terms like "malice" ("an unwarrantable act without a vicious will is no crime at all"), but the modern tendency has been toward more specific descriptions, as shown in the Arizona statute defining the murder charged against Clark: The State had to prove that in acting to kill the victim, Clark intended to kill a law enforcement officer on duty or knew that the victim was such an officer on duty. As applied to *mens rea* (and every other element), the force of the presumption of innocence is measured by the force of the showing needed to overcome it, which is proof beyond a reasonable doubt that a defendant's state of mind was in fact what the charge states.

The presumption of sanity is equally universal in some variety or other, being (at least) a presumption that a defendant has the capacity to form the *mens rea* necessary for a verdict of guilt and the consequent criminal responsibility. This presumption dispenses with a requirement on the government's part to include as an element of every criminal charge an allegation that the defendant had such a capacity. The force of this

---

[2] See Appendix B (pp. 291-292).

presumption, like the presumption of innocence, is measured by the quantum of evidence necessary to overcome it; unlike the presumption of innocence, however, the force of the presumption of sanity varies across the many state and federal jurisdictions, and prior law has recognized considerable leeway on the part of the legislative branch in defining the presumption's strength through the kind of evidence and degree of persuasiveness necessary to overcome it.

There are two points where the sanity or capacity presumption may be placed in issue. First, a State may allow a defendant to introduce (and a fact finder to consider) evidence of mental disease or incapacity for the bearing it can have on the government's burden to show *mens rea*. In such States the evidence showing incapacity to form the guilty state of mind, for example, qualifies the probative force of other evidence, which considered alone indicates that the defendant actually formed the guilty state of mind. If it is shown that a defendant with mental disease thinks all blond people are robots, he could not have intended to kill a person when he shot a man with blond hair, even though he seemed to act like a man shooting another man. In jurisdictions that allow mental-disease and capacity evidence to be considered on par with any other relevant evidence when deciding whether the prosecution has proven *mens rea* beyond a reasonable doubt, the evidence of mental disease or incapacity need only support what the fact finder regards as a reasonable doubt about the capacity to form (or the actual formation of) the *mens rea*, in order to require acquittal of the charge. Thus, in these States the strength of the presumption of sanity is no greater than the strength of the evidence of abnormal mental state that the fact finder thinks is enough to raise a reasonable doubt.

The second point where the force of the presumption of sanity may be tested is in the consideration of a defense of insanity raised by a defendant. Insanity rules like *M'Naghten* and variants are attempts to define, or at least to indicate, the kinds of mental differences that overcome the presumption of sanity or capacity and therefore excuse a defendant from customary criminal responsibility even if the prosecution has otherwise overcome the presumption of innocence by convincing the fact finder of all the elements charged beyond a reasonable doubt. The burden that must be carried by a defendant who raises the insanity issue, again, defines the strength of the sanity presumption. A State may provide, for example, that whenever the defendant raises a claim of insanity by some quantum of credible evidence, the presumption disappears and the government must prove sanity to a specified degree of certainty (whether beyond reasonable doubt or something less). Or a jurisdiction may place the burden of persuasion on a defendant to prove insanity as the applicable law defines it, whether by a preponderance of the evidence or to some more convincing degree. In any case, the defendant's burden defines the presumption of sanity, whether that burden be to burst a bubble or to show something more.

The third principle implicated by Clark's argument is a defendant's right as a matter of simple due process to present evidence favorable to himself on an element that must be proven to convict him. As already noted, evidence tending to show that a defendant suffers from mental disease and lacks capacity to form *mens rea* is relevant to rebut evidence that he did in fact form the required *mens rea* at the time in question; this is the reason that Clark claims a right to require the fact finder in this case to consider testimony about his mental illness and his incapacity directly, when weighing the persuasiveness of other evidence tending to show *mens rea*, which the prosecution has the burden to prove.

As Clark recognizes, however, the right to introduce relevant evidence can be curtailed if there is a good reason for doing that. And if evidence may be kept out entirely, its consideration may be subject to limitation, which Arizona claims the power to impose here. State law says that evidence of mental disease and incapacity may be introduced and considered, and if sufficiently forceful to satisfy the defendant's burden of proof under the insanity rule it will displace the presumption of sanity and excuse from criminal responsibility. But mental-disease and capacity evidence may be considered only for its bearing on the insanity defense, and it will avail a defendant only if it is persuasive enough to satisfy the defendant's burden as defined by the terms of that defense. The mental-disease and capacity evidence is thus being channeled or restricted to one issue and given effect only if the defendant carries the burden to convince the fact finder of insanity; the evidence is not being excluded entirely, and the question is whether reasons for requiring it to be channeled and restricted are good enough to satisfy the standard of fundamental fairness that due process requires. We think they are.

The first reason supporting the *Mott* rule is Arizona's authority to define its presumption of sanity (or capacity or responsibility) by choosing an insanity definition and by placing the burden of persuasion on defendants who claim incapacity as an excuse from customary criminal responsibility. No one, certainly not Clark here, denies that a State may place a burden of persuasion on a defendant claiming insanity. And Clark presses no objection to Arizona's decision to require persuasion to a clear and convincing degree before the presumption of sanity and normal responsibility is overcome.

But if a State is to have this authority in practice as well as in theory, it must be able to deny a defendant the opportunity to displace the presumption of sanity more easily when addressing a different issue in the course of the criminal trial. Yet, as we have explained, just such an opportunity would be available if expert testimony of mental disease and incapacity could be considered for whatever a fact finder might think it was worth on the issue of *mens rea*. As we mentioned, the presumption of sanity would then be only as strong as the evidence a fact finder would accept as enough to raise a reasonable doubt about *mens rea* for the crime charged; once reasonable doubt was found, acquittal would be required, and the standards established for the defense of insanity would go by the boards.

Now, a State is of course free to accept such a possibility in its law. After all, it is free to define the insanity defense by treating the presumption of sanity as a bursting bubble, whose disappearance shifts the burden to the prosecution to prove sanity whenever a defendant presents any credible evidence of mental disease or incapacity. In States with this kind of insanity rule, the legislature may well be willing to allow such evidence to be considered on the *mens rea* element for whatever the fact finder thinks it is worth. What counts for due process, however, is simply that a State that wishes to avoid a second avenue for exploring capacity, less stringent for a defendant, has a good reason for confining the consideration of evidence of mental disease and incapacity to the insanity defense.

It is obvious that Arizona's *Mott* rule reflects such a choice. The State Supreme Court pointed out that the State had declined to adopt a defense of diminished capacity (allowing a jury to decide when to excuse a defendant because of greater than normal difficulty in conforming to the law). The court reasoned that the State's choice would be undercut if evidence of incapacity could be considered for whatever a jury might think sufficient to raise a reasonable doubt about *mens rea*, even if it did not show insanity. In other words, if a jury were free to decide how much evidence of mental disease and incapacity was enough to counter evidence of *mens rea* to the point of creating a reasonable doubt, that would in functional terms be analogous to allowing jurors to decide upon some degree of diminished capacity to obey the law, a degree set by them, that would prevail as a stand-alone defense.

A State's insistence on preserving its chosen standard of legal insanity cannot be the sole reason for a rule like *Mott*, however, for it fails to answer an objection the dissent makes in this case. An insanity rule gives a defendant already found guilty the opportunity to excuse his conduct by showing he was insane when he acted, that is, that he did not have the mental capacity for conventional guilt and criminal responsibility. But, as the dissent argues, if the same evidence that affirmatively shows he was not guilty by reason of insanity (or "guilty except insane" under Arizona law) also shows it was at least doubtful that he could form *mens rea*, then he should not be found guilty in the first place; it thus violates due process when the State impedes him from using mental-disease and capacity evidence directly to rebut the prosecution's evidence that he did form *mens rea*.

Are there, then, characteristics of mental-disease and capacity evidence giving rise to risks that may reasonably be hedged by channeling the consideration of such evidence to the insanity issue on which, in States like Arizona, a defendant has the burden of persuasion? We think there are: in the controversial character of some categories of mental disease, in the potential of mental-disease evidence to mislead, and in the danger of according greater certainty to capacity evidence than experts claim for it.

To begin with, the diagnosis may mask vigorous debate within the profession about the very contours of the mental disease itself. And Members of this Court have previously recognized that the end of such debate is not imminent. Though we certainly do not [condemn mental-disease evidence wholesale], the consequence of this professional ferment is a general caution in treating psychological classifications as predicates for excusing otherwise criminal conduct.

Next, there is the potential of mental-disease evidence to mislead jurors (when they are the fact finders) through the power of this kind of evidence to suggest that a defendant suffering from a recognized mental disease lacks cognitive, moral, volitional, or other capacity, when that may not be a sound conclusion at all. Even when a category of mental disease is broadly accepted and the assignment of a defendant's behavior to that category is uncontroversial, the classification may suggest something very significant about a defendant's capacity, when in fact the classification tells us little or nothing about the ability of the defendant to form *mens rea* or to exercise the cognitive, moral, or volitional capacities that define legal sanity. The limits of the utility of a professional disease diagnosis are evident in the dispute between the two testifying experts in this case; they agree that Clark was schizophrenic, but they come to opposite conclusions on whether the mental disease in his particular case left him bereft of cognitive or moral capacity. Evidence of mental disease, then, can easily mislead; it is very easy to slide from evidence that an individual with a professionally recognized mental disease is very different, into doubting that he has the capacity to form *mens rea*, whereas that doubt may not be justified. And of course, in the cases mentioned before, in which the categorization is doubtful or the category of mental disease is itself subject to controversy, the risks are even greater that opinions about mental disease may confuse a jury into thinking the opinions show more than they do. Because allowing mental-disease evidence on *mens rea* can thus easily mislead, it is not unreasonable to address that tendency by confining consideration of this kind of evidence to insanity, on which a defendant may be assigned the burden of persuasion.

There are, finally, particular risks inherent in the opinions of the experts who supplement the mental-disease classifications with opinions on incapacity: on whether the mental disease rendered a particular defendant incapable of the cognition necessary for moral judgment or *mens rea* or otherwise incapable of understanding the wrongfulness of the conduct charged. Unlike observational evidence bearing on *mens rea*, capacity evidence consists of judgment, and judgment fraught with multiple perils: A defendant's state of mind at the crucial moment can be elusive no matter how conscientious the inquiry, and the

> **Unlike observational evidence bearing on mens rea, capacity evidence consists of judgment, fraught with multiple perils.**

law's categories that set the terms of the capacity judgment are not the categories of psychology that govern the expert's professional thinking. Although such capacity judgments may be given in the utmost good faith, their potentially tenuous character is indicated by the candor of the defense expert in this very case. Contrary to the State's expert, he testified that Clark lacked the capacity to appreciate the circumstances realistically and to understand the wrongfulness of what he was doing, but he said that "no one knows exactly what was on [his] mind" at the time of the shooting. And even when an expert is confident that his understanding of the mind is reliable, judgment addres-

> **And even when an expert is confident that his understanding of the mind is reliable, judgment addressing the basic categories of capacity requires a leap from the concepts of psychology, which are devised for thinking about treatment, to the concepts of legal sanity, which are devised for thinking about criminal responsibility.**

sing the basic categories of capacity requires a leap from the concepts of psychology, which are devised for thinking about treatment, to the concepts of legal sanity, which are devised for thinking about criminal responsibility. In sum, these empirical and conceptual problems add up to a real risk that an expert's judgment in giving capacity evidence will come with an apparent authority that psychologists and psychiatrists do not claim to have. We think that this risk, like the difficulty in assessing the significance of mental-disease evidence, supports the State's decision to channel such expert testimony to consideration on the insanity defense, on which the party seeking the benefit of this evidence has the burden of persuasion.

It bears repeating that not every State will find it worthwhile to make the judgment Arizona has made, and the choices the States do make about dealing with the risks posed by mental-disease and capacity evidence will reflect their varying assessments about the presumption of sanity as expressed in choices of insanity rules. The point here simply is that Arizona has sensible reasons to assign the risks as it has done by channeling the evidence.

Arizona's rule serves to preserve the State's chosen standard for recognizing insanity as a defense and to avoid confusion and misunderstanding on the part of jurors. For these reasons, there is no violation of due process under *Chambers* and its progeny, and no cause to claim that channeling evidence on mental disease and capacity offends any "principle of justice so rooted in the traditions and conscience of our people as to be ranked as fundamental."

The judgment of the Court of Appeals of Arizona is, accordingly, affirmed.

It is so ordered.

Justice Kennedy, with whom Justice Stevens and Justice Ginsburg join, dissenting.

In my submission the Court is incorrect in holding that Arizona may convict petitioner Eric Clark of first-degree murder for the intentional or knowing killing of a police officer when Clark was not permitted to introduce critical and reliable evidence showing he did not have that intent or knowledge. The Court is wrong, too, when it concludes the issue cannot be reached because of an error by Clark's counsel. Its reasons and conclusions lead me to file this respectful dissent.

Clark claims that the trial court erred in refusing to consider evidence of his chronic paranoid schizophrenia in deciding whether he possessed the knowledge or intent required for first-degree murder. Seizing upon a theory invented here by the Court itself, the Court narrows Clark's claim so he cannot raise the point everyone else thought was involved in the case. The Court says the only issue before us is whether there is a right to introduce mental-disease evidence or capacity evidence, not a right to introduce observation evidence. This restructured evidentiary universe, with no convincing authority to support it, is unworkable on its own terms. Even were that not so, however, the Court's tripartite structure is something not addressed by the state trial court, the state appellate court, counsel on either side in those proceedings, or the briefs the parties filed with us. The Court refuses to consider the key part of Clark's claim because his counsel did not predict the Court's own invention. It is unrealistic, and most unfair, to hold that Clark's counsel erred in failing to anticipate so novel an approach. If the Court is to insist on its approach, at a minimum the case should be remanded to determine [if] Clark is bound by his counsel's purported waiver.

The Court's error, of course, has significance beyond this case. It adopts an evidentiary framework that, in my view, will be unworkable in many cases. The Court classifies Clark's behavior and expressed beliefs as observation evidence but insists that its description by experts must be mental-disease evidence or capacity evidence. These categories break down quickly when it is understood how the testimony would apply to the question of intent and knowledge at issue here. The most common type of schizophrenia, and the one Clark suffered from, is paranoid schizophrenia. The existence of this functional psychosis is beyond dispute, but that does not mean the lay witness understands it or that a disputed issue of fact concerning its effect in a particular instance is not something for the expert to address. Common symptoms of the condition are delusions accompanied by hallucinations, often of the auditory type, which can cause disturbances of perception. Clark's expert testified that people with schizophrenia often play radios loudly to drown out the voices in their heads. Clark's attorney argued to the trial court that this, rather than a desire to lure a policeman to the scene, explained Clark's behavior just before the killing. The observation that schizophrenics play radios loudly is a fact regarding behavior, but it is only a relevant fact if Clark has schizophrenia.

Even if this evidence were, to use the Court's term, mental-disease evidence, because it relies on an expert opinion, what would happen if the expert simply were to testify, without mentioning schizophrenia, that people with Clark's symptoms often play the radio loudly? This seems to be factual evidence, as the term is defined by the Court, yet it differs from mental-disease evidence only in forcing the witness to pretend that no one has yet come up with a way to classify the set of symptoms being described. More generally, the opinion that Clark had paranoid schizophrenia—an opinion shared by experts for both the prosecution and defense—bears on efforts to determine, as a factual matter, whether he knew he was killing a police officer. The psychiatrist's explanation of Clark's condition was essential to understanding how he processes sensory data and therefore to deciding what information was in his mind at the time of the shooting. Simply put, knowledge relies on cognition, and cognition can be affected by schizophrenia. The mental-disease evidence at trial was also intertwined with the observation evidence because it lent needed credibility. Clark's parents and friends testified Clark thought the people in his town were aliens trying to kill him. These claims might not be believable without a psychiatrist confirming the story based on his experience with people who have exhibited similar behaviors. It makes little sense to divorce the observation evidence from the explanation that makes it comprehensible.

The central theory of Clark's defense was that his schizophrenia made him delusional. He lived in a universe where the delusions were so dominant, the theory was, that he had no intent to shoot a police officer or knowledge he was doing so. It is one thing to say he acted with intent or knowledge to pull the trigger. It is quite another to say he pulled the trigger to kill someone he knew to be a human being and a police officer. If the trier of fact were to find Clark's evidence sufficient to discount the case made by the State, which has the burden to prove knowledge or intent as an element of the offense, Clark would not be guilty of first-degree murder under Arizona law.

The Court attempts to diminish Clark's interest by treating mental-illness evidence as concerning only "judgment," rather than fact. This view appears to derive from the Court's characterization of Clark's claim as raising only general incapacity. This is wrong for the reasons already discussed. It fails to recognize, moreover, the meaning of the offense element in question here. The *mens rea* element of intent or knowledge may, at some level, comprise certain moral choices, but it rests in the first instance on a factual determination. That is the fact Clark sought to put in issue. Either Clark knew he was killing a police officer or he did not.

The issue is not, as the Court insists, whether Clark's mental illness acts as an "excuse from customary criminal responsibility," but whether his mental illness, as a factual matter, made him unaware that he was shooting a police officer. If it did, Clark needs no excuse, as then he did not commit the crime as Arizona defines it. For the elements of first-degree murder, where the question is knowledge of particular facts—that one is killing a police officer—the determination depends not on moral responsibility but on empirical fact. Clark's evidence of mental illness had a direct and substantial bearing upon what he knew, or thought he knew, to be the facts when he pulled the trigger; this lay at the heart of the matter.

The Court says mental-illness evidence "can easily mislead," and may "tell us little or nothing about the ability of the defendant to form *mens rea*." These generalities do not, however, show how relevant or misleading the evidence in this case would be (or explain why Arizona Rules of Evidence [are] insufficient for weighing these factors). As explained above, the evidence of Clark's mental illness bears directly on *mens rea*, for it suggests Clark may not have known he was killing a human being. It is striking that while the Court discusses at length the likelihood of misjudgment from placing too much emphasis on evidence of mental illness, it ignores the risk of misjudging an innocent man guilty from refusing to consider this highly relevant evidence at all. Clark's expert, it is true, said no one could know exactly what was on Clark's mind at the time of the shooting. The expert testified extensively, however, about the effect of Clark's delusions on his perceptions of the world around him, and about whether Clark's behavior around the time of the shooting was consistent with delusional thinking. This testimony was relevant to determining whether Clark knew he was killing a human being. It also bolstered the testimony of lay witnesses, none of which was deemed unreliable or misleading by the state courts.

Putting aside the lack of any legitimate state interest for application of the rule in this case, its irrationality is apparent when considering the evidence that is allowed. Arizona permits the defendant to introduce, for example, evidence of "behavioral tendencies" to show he did not have the required mental state. While defining mental illness is a difficult matter, the State seems to exclude the evidence one would think most reliable by allowing unexplained and uncategorized tendencies to be introduced while excluding relatively well-understood psychiatric testimony regarding well-documented mental illnesses. It is unclear, moreover, what would have happened in this case had the defendant wanted to testify that he thought Officer Moritz was an alien. If disallowed, it would be tantamount to barring Clark from testifying on his behalf to explain his own actions. If allowed, then Arizona's rule would simply prohibit the corroboration necessary to make sense of Clark's explanation. In sum, the rule forces the jury to decide guilt in a fictional world with undefined and unexplained behaviors but without mental illness. This rule has no rational justification and imposes a significant burden upon a straightforward defense: He did not commit the crime with which he was charged.

These are the reasons for my respectful dissent.

Summary

In February 2002, the U.S. Supreme Court declined to hear an appeal of *Finger* from the state of Nevada. Consequently, in the state of Nevada it remains a recognized constitutional right for a defendant to assert an insanity defense. Given the Supreme Court's opinion in *Clark*, it is unlikely that they would hold any specific insanity defense as a constitutional right. *Powell* and *Robinson* (which is well worth reading) can be read to show that the Court recognizes that individuals cannot be punished for being mentally ill, even though behavior that results from a mental disorder might be punishable. In *Powell*, as in *Clark*, the Court resists recognizing a constitutional right for certain sorts of insanity defenses. It may be that the Court's denial to hear Nevada's appeal of *Finger* also reflects their determination to resist defining a constitutional basis for an insanity defense, while affirming the rights of individual states to resolve the matters for themselves (in the case of Nevada, via the judiciary).

The Court's holdings in *Davis* and *Leland* have been trumped by elements of the Insanity Defense Reform Act (IDRA). Insanity is now an affirmative defense in federal courts as well as in many states. In *Clark*, the Court reiterates that there is always a presumption of sanity. Insanity defenses are potentially emotionally charged and, as is seen in *M'Naghten*, the IDRA, and the abolition of insanity defenses in some states, subject to shifting political winds. The judiciary remains ambivalent about the proper role for mental health experts in such defenses as demonstrated in *Clark*, as well as in the cases reviewed in the next Section.

Section 4

The D.C. Experiment

Introduction to Section 4
Cases
  Durham v. United States
  McDonald v. United States
  United States v. Brawner
Summary

Introduction to Section 4

During the last half of the 19th and the first half of the 20th centuries, most jurisdictions in the United States used some form of the *M'Naghten* "right-wrong" insanity test. Some jurisdictions added the *Parsons* "irresistible impulse" prong to *M'Naghten* to allow for the consideration of volition. Mental health professionals continued to criticize these tests as too simplistic and too rigid. In response to the perceived inadequacy of these standards, the United States Court of Appeals for the District of Columbia Circuit undertook a radical departure from the other Federal Circuits in 1954.

In *Durham v. United States* (1954), the Court of Appeals reviewed the currently used tests of insanity, "right-wrong" and "irresistible impulse," and found them wanting. The "right-wrong" test was thought to ignore the realities of mental disorders by focusing on a single, atypical symptom. The "irresistible impulse" test was thought to disallow losses of control that followed long periods of "brooding" rather than rapid impulsive actions. In their place, the Court adopted a much broader "product" test similar to that developed by New Hampshire in response to *Pike*. To be excused, the criminal behavior had to be the "product" of a "mental disease" or "mental defect." The Court also attempted to define those terms and distinguish one from the other in a manner not dissimilar to the distinctions made in England centuries earlier between "lunacy" and "idiocy."

The substantial change adopted by the D.C. Circuit in *Durham* was intended to open the courtroom for broader testimony by psychiatrists in their own terms. And it did. Psychiatrists, led by attorneys, somewhat arbitrarily and rather freely, began to broaden their views of what constituted a mental disease or defect and state openly whether an act was the product of such a condition. In *McDonald v. United States* (1962), the Court of Appeals attempted to rein in the expanding concepts of mental disease and defect by defining them as "abnormal" conditions that cause "substantial" impairment. Additionally, the Court clarified that these were legal facts to be determined by the deliberations of a jury, not medical facts to be determined by the diagnosis of a psychiatrist.

In spite of the Court of Appeals' efforts in *McDonald* and subsequent cases, the problem of experts testifying in conclusory terms and encroaching on the function of the jury continued. The "product" test appeared to be particularly vulnerable to this problem. In the meantime, most other federal circuits had adopted some variant of the new insanity standard proposed by the American Law Institute (ALI) in its Model Penal Code (1955). In *United States v. Brawner* (1972), the D.C. Circuit concluded that their experiment with the "product" test had resulted in an unproductive "trial by label." They also chose to adopt the ALI standard as the test of insanity for their Circuit. This standard, with both a cognitive and volitional prong, the definition of mental disease and defect (from *Durham* and *McDonald*), and the burden and standard of proof (from *Davis* and *Durham*), remained intact for the following decade until John Hinckley's trial for the attempted assassination of President Reagan led to the sweeping changes described in the first section of this book.

Durham v. United States
214 F.2d 862 (1954)

Facts

Monte Durham was convicted in a bench trial of a 1951 housebreaking. He had a long history of arrests, imprisonment, and psychiatric hospitalizations, and he had been released from St. Elizabeths Hospital only two months prior to the housebreaking. He was initially found incompetent to stand trial and was readmitted to St. Elizabeths for treatment. After being determined competent in a somewhat unusual proceeding, he was tried without a jury. Durham presented a defense of insanity. At that time the District of Columbia employed the "right-wrong test" of insanity, supplemented by the "irresistible impulse test." A psychiatrist testified that Durham was of "unsound mind" at the time of the crime, but the District Judge ruled there was no testimony on Durham's mental state on the date of the offense and, therefore, the defense had not overcome the presumption of sanity (which would have shifted the burden of proving sanity beyond a reasonable doubt to the prosecution).

Issues

(a) Did the trial court err in applying the rules governing the burden of proof in a defense of insanity? (b) Should the existing tests of criminal responsibility be replaced?

Holding

(a) The trial court incorrectly applied the rules governing the burden of proof, and the judgment was reversed and the case remanded for a new trial. (b) The existing tests of insanity were obsolete and inadequate and were replaced with a "product test."

Analysis

The Appeals Court pointed out that a defendant must present only "some evidence" of insanity to shift the burden and require the Court to consider "the whole evidence." This error led to the decision being reversed. The Appeals Court then addressed the insanity standard to be used in the retrial as well as all subsequent insanity cases in the District of Columbia. The Court reviewed the history of insanity standards and concluded the current test was inadequate because the "right-wrong test" failed to take "sufficient account of psychic realities" by focusing exclusively on one atypical symptom of mental disorder. The "irresistible impulse test" was also considered inadequate for failing to give recognition to "mental illness characterized by brooding and reflection." Concluding a broader test was necessary, the Court adopted a test similar to that used in New Hampshire "that an accused is not criminally responsible if his unlawful act was the product of a mental disease or mental defect." The Court also defined a mental "disease" as a condition that was "capable of either improving or deteriorating" and a mental "defect" as not capable of such change and as "either congenital, or the result of injury, or the residual effect of physical or mental disease." The Court emphasized the jury would still have the responsibility of making moral judgments concerning whether a defendant could be blamed and punished, but their task would be "guided by wider horizons of knowledge concerning mental life."

Edited Excerpts[1]

Opinion by Bazelon

Monte Durham was convicted of housebreaking by the District Court sitting without a jury. The only defense asserted at the trial was that Durham was of unsound mind at the time of the offense. We are now urged to reverse the conviction (1) because the trial court did not correctly apply existing rules governing the burden of proof on the defense of insanity, and (2) because existing tests of criminal responsibility are obsolete and should be superseded.

Durham has a long history of imprisonment and hospitalization. In 1945, at the age of 17, he was discharged from the Navy after a psychiatric examination had shown that he suffered "from a profound personality disorder which renders him unfit for Naval service." In 1947 he pleaded guilty to violating the National Motor Theft Act and was placed on probation for one to three years. He attempted suicide, was taken to Gallinger Hospital for observation, and was transferred to St. Elizabeths Hospital, from which he was discharged after two months. In January of 1948, as a result of a conviction in the District of Columbia Municipal Court for passing bad checks, the District Court revoked his probation and he commenced service of his Motor Theft sentence. His conduct

---

[1] Readers are advised to quote only from the original published cases. See pages vi and vii.

within the first few days in jail led to a lunacy inquiry in the Municipal Court where a jury found him to be of unsound mind. Upon commitment to St. Elizabeths, he was diagnosed as suffering from "psychosis with psychopathic personality." After 15 months of treatment, he was discharged in July 1949 as "recovered" and was returned to jail to serve the balance of his sentence. In June 1950 he was conditionally released. He violated the conditions by leaving the District. When he learned of a warrant for his arrest as a parole violator, he fled to the "South and Midwest obtaining money by passing a number of bad checks." After he was found and returned to the District, the Parole Board referred him to the District Court for a lunacy inquisition, wherein a jury again found him to be of unsound mind. He was readmitted to St. Elizabeths in February 1951. This time the diagnosis was "without mental disorder, psychopathic personality." He was discharged for the third time in May 1951. The housebreaking which is the subject of the present appeal took place two months later, on July 13, 1951.

According to his mother and the psychiatrist who examined him in September 1951, he suffered from hallucinations immediately after his May 1951 discharge from St. Elizabeths. Following the present indictment, in October 1951, he was adjudged of unsound mind upon the affidavits of two psychiatrists that he suffered from "psychosis with psychopathic personality." He was committed to St. Elizabeths for the fourth time and given subshock insulin therapy. This commitment lasted 6 months—until February 1953—he was released to the custody of the District Jail on the certificate of Dr. Silk, Acting Superintendent of St. Elizabeths, that he was "mentally competent to stand trial and able to consult with counsel to properly assist in his own defense."

He was thereupon brought before the court on the charge involved here. The prosecutor told the court: "So I take this attitude, in view of the fact that he has been over there (St. Elizabeths) a couple of times and these cases that were charged against him were dropped, I don't think I should take the responsibility of dropping these cases against him; then Saint Elizabeths would let him out on the street, and if that man committed a murder next week then it is my responsibility. So we decided to go to trial on one case, that is the case where we found him right in the house, and let him bring in the defense, if he wants to, of unsound mind at the time the crime was committed, and then Your Honor will find him on that, and in your decision send him back to Saint Elizabeths Hospital, and then if they let him out on the street it is their responsibility."

Shortly thereafter, when the question arose whether Durham could be considered competent to stand trial merely on the basis of Dr. Silk's statement, the court said to defense counsel: "I am going to ask you this, Mr. Ahern: I have taken the position that if once a person has been found of unsound mind after a lunacy hearing, an *ex parte* certificate of the superintendent of Saint Elizabeths is not sufficient to set aside that finding and I have held another lunacy hearing. That has been my custom. However, if you want to waive that you may do it, if you admit that he is now of sound mind."

The court accepted counsel's waiver on behalf of Durham, although it had been informed by the prosecutor that a letter from Durham claimed need of further hospitalization, and by defense counsel that "the defendant does say that even today he thinks he does need hospitalization; he told me this morning." Upon being so informed, the court said, "Of course, if I hold he is not mentally competent to stand trial I send him back to Saint Elizabeths Hospital and they will send him back again in two or three months." In this atmosphere Durham's trial commenced.

His conviction followed the trial court's rejection of the defense of insanity in these words: "I don't think it has been established that the defendant was of unsound mind as of July 13, 1951, in the sense that he didn't know the difference between right and wrong or that even if he did, he was subject to an irresistible impulse by reason of the derangement of mind. While, of course, the burden of proof on the issue of mental capacity to commit a crime is upon the Government, just as it is on every other issue, nevertheless, the Court finds that there is not sufficient basis to contradict the usual presumption of the usual inference of sanity. There is no testimony concerning the mental state of the defendant as of July 13, 1951, and therefore the usual presumption of sanity governs. While if there was some testimony as to his mental state as of that date, the burden of proof would be on the Government to overcome it. There has been no such testimony, and the usual presumption of sanity prevails. Mr. Ahern, I think you have done very well by your client and defended him very ably, but I think under the circumstances there is nothing that anybody could have done."

We think this reflects error requiring reversal.

In *Tatum v. United States* we said, "when lack of mental capacity is raised as a defense to a charge of crime, the law accepts the general experience of mankind and presumes that all people, including those accused of crime, are sane." So long as this presumption prevails, the prosecution is not required to prove the defendant's sanity, like any other fact, must be proved as part of the prosecution's case beyond a reasonable doubt. Here it appears that the trial judge recognized this rule but failed to find "some evidence." We hold that the court erred and that the requirement of "some evidence" was satisfied. The psychiatric testimony was unequivocal that Durham was of unsound mind at the time of the crime. Dr. Gilbert, the only expert witness heard, so stated at least four times. Intensive questioning by the court failed to produce any retraction of Dr. Gilbert's testimony that the "period of insanity would have embraced the date July 13, 1951." And though the prosecution sought unsuccessfully in its cross- and recross-examination of Dr. Gilbert to establish that Durham was a malingerer who feigned insanity whenever he was trapped for his misdeeds, it failed to present any expert testimony to support this theory. In addition to Dr. Gilbert's testimony, there was testimony by Durham's mother to the effect that in the interval between his discharge from St. Elizabeths in May 1951, and the crime "he seemed afraid of people" and had urged her to put steel bars on his bedroom windows.

Apparently the trial judge regarded this psychiatric testimony as "no testimony" on two grounds: (1) it did not adequately cover Durham's condition on July 13, 1951, the date of the offense; and (2) it was not directed to Durham's capacity to distinguish between right and wrong. We are unable to agree that for either of these reasons the psychiatric testimony could properly be considered "no testimony."

Moreover, any conclusion that there was "no testimony" regarding Durham's mental condition at the time of the crime disregards the testimony of his mother. Her account of his behavior after his discharge from St. Elizabeths in May 1951 was directly pertinent to the issue of his sanity at the time of the crime.

On re-direct examination, Dr. Gilbert was asked whether he would say that Durham "knew the difference between right and wrong on July 13, 1951; that is, his ability to distinguish between what was right and what was wrong." He replied: "As I have stated before, if the question of the right and wrong were propounded to him he could give you the right answer." Then the court interrupted to ask:

"The Court. No, I don't think that is the question, Doctor—not whether he could give a right answer to a question, but whether he, himself, knew the difference between right and wrong in connection with governing his own actions. If you are unable to answer, why, you can say so; I mean, if you are unable to form an opinion."

"The Witness. I can only answer this way: That I can't tell how much the abnormal thinking and the abnormal experiences in the form of hallucinations and delusions—delusions of persecution—had to do with his antisocial behavior. I don't know how anyone can answer that question categorically, except as one's experience leads him to know that most mental cases can give you a categorical answer of right and wrong, but what influence these symptoms have on abnormal behavior or antisocial behavior —".

"The Court. Well, your answer is that you are unable to form an opinion, is that it?"

"The Witness. I would say that that is essentially true, for the reasons that I have given."

The inability of the expert to give categorical assurance that Durham was unable to distinguish between right and wrong did not destroy the effect of his previous testimony that the period of Durham's "insanity" embraced July 13, 1951. It is plain from our decision in *Tatum* that this previous testimony was adequate to prevent the presumption of sanity from becoming conclusive and to place the burden of proving sanity upon the Government. None of the testimony before the court in *Tatum* was couched in terms of "right and wrong."

Finally, even assuming *arguendo*[2] that the court, contrary to the plain meaning of its words, recognized that the prosecution had the burden of proving Durham's sanity, there would still be a fatal error. For once the issue of insanity is raised by the introduction of "some evidence," the presumption of sanity is no longer absolute. It is incumbent upon the trier of fact to weigh and consider "the whole evidence, including that supplied by the presumption of sanity" on the issue of "the capacity in law of the accused to commit" the crime.

It has been ably argued by counsel for Durham that the existing tests in the District of Columbia for determining criminal responsibility, i.e., the so-called right-wrong test supplemented by the irresistible impulse test, are not satisfactory criteria for determining criminal responsibility.

Here, manifestly, the court as the trier of fact did not and could not weigh "the whole evidence," for it found there was "no testimony concerning the mental state" of Durham.

For the foregoing reasons, the judgment is reversed and the case is remanded for a new trial.

It has been ably argued by counsel for Durham that the existing tests in the District of Columbia for determining criminal responsibility, i.e., the so-called right-wrong test supplemented by the irresistible impulse test, are not satisfactory criteria for determining criminal responsibility.

---

[2] *arguendo.* For the sake of argument.

We are argued to adopt a different test to be applied on the retrial of this case. This contention has behind it nearly a century of agitation for reform.

The right-wrong test, approved in this jurisdiction in 1882, was the exclusive test of criminal responsibility in the District of Columbia until 1929 when we approved the irresistible impulse test as a supplementary test in *Smith v. United States*. The right-wrong test has its roots in England. There, by the first quarter of the eighteenth century, an accused escaped punishment if he could not distinguish "good and evil," that is, if he "doth not know what he is doing, no more than a wild beast." Later in the same century, the "wild beast" test was abandoned and "right and wrong" was substituted for "good and evil." And toward the middle of the nineteenth century, the House of Lords in the famous *M'Naghten* case restated what had become the accepted "right-wrong" test in a form which has since been followed, not only in England but in most American jurisdictions.

> **As early as 1838, Isaac Ray, one of the founders of the American Psychiatric Association, in his now classic** Medical Jurisprudence of Insanity, *called knowledge of right and wrong a* "fallacious" *test of criminal responsibility.*

As early as 1838, Isaac Ray, one of the founders of the American Psychiatric Association, in his now classic *Medical Jurisprudence of Insanity*, called knowledge of right and wrong a "fallacious" test of criminal responsibility.[3] This view has long since been substantiated by enormous developments in knowledge of mental life. In 1928, Mr. Justice Cardozo said to the New York Academy of Medicine: "Everyone concedes that the present legal definition of insanity has little relation to the truths of mental life."

Medicolegal writers in large number, *The Report of the Royal Commission on Capital Punishment 1949-1953*, and *The Preliminary Report by the Committee on Forensic Psychiatry of the Group for the Advancement of Psychiatry* present convincing evidence that the right-and-wrong test is "based on an entirely obsolete and misleading conception of the nature of insanity." The science of psychiatry now recognizes that a man is an integrated personality and that reason, which is only one element in that personality, is not the sole determinant of his conduct.

---

[3] "That the insane mind is not entirely deprived of this power of moral discernment, but in many subjects is perfectly rational, and displays the exercise of a sound and well balanced mind is one of those facts now so well established, that to question it would only betray the height of ignorance and presumption."

The right-wrong test, which considers knowledge or reason alone, is therefore an inadequate guide to mental responsibility for criminal behavior. As Professor Sheldon Glueck of the Harvard Law School points out in discussing the right-wrong tests, which he calls the knowledge tests: "It is evident that the knowledge tests unscientifically abstract out of the mental make-up but one phase or element of

> *The science of psychiatry now recognizes that a man is an integrated personality and that reason, which is only one element in that personality, is not the sole determinant of his conduct.*

mental life, the cognitive, which, in this era of dynamic psychology, is beginning to be regarded as not the most important factor in conduct and its disorders. In brief, these tests proceed upon the following questionable assumptions of an outworn era in psychiatry: (1) that lack of knowledge of the 'nature or quality' of an act (assuming the meaning of such terms to be clear), or incapacity to know right from wrong, is the sole or even the most important symptom of mental disorder; (2) that such knowledge is the sole instigator and guide of conduct, or at least the most important element therein, and consequently should be the sole criterion of responsibility when insanity is involved; and (3) that the capacity of knowing right from wrong can be completely intact and functioning perfectly even though a defendant is otherwise demonstrably of disordered mind."

Nine years ago we said: "The modern science of psychology does not conceive that there is a separate little man in the top of one's head called reason whose function it is to guide another unruly little man called instinct, emotion, or impulse in the way he should go" (*Holloway v. United States*[4]).

---

[4] More recently, the Royal Commission, after an exhaustive survey of legal, medical, and lay opinion in many Western countries, including England and the United States made a similar finding. It reported: "The gravamen of the charge against the *M'Naghten* Rules is that they are not in harmony with modern medical science, which, as we have seen, is reluctant to divide the mind into separate compartments—the intellect, the emotions and the will—but looks at it as a whole and considers that insanity distorts and impairs the action of the mind as a whole." The Commission lends vivid support to this conclusion by pointing out that "It would be impossible to apply modern methods of care and treatment in mental hospitals, and at the same time to maintain order and discipline, if the great majority of the patients, even among the grossly insane, did not know what is forbidden by the rules and that, if they break them, they are liable to forfeit some privilege. Examination of a number of individual cases in which a verdict of guilty but insane (the nearest English equivalent of our acquittal by reason of insanity) was returned, and rightly returned, has convinced us that there are few indeed where the accused can truly be said not to have known that his act was wrong."

By its misleading emphasis on the cognitive, the right-wrong test requires court and jury to rely upon what is, scientifically speaking, inadequate, and most often, invalid and irrelevant testimony in determining criminal responsibility.

The fundamental objection to the right-wrong test, however, is not that criminal irresponsibility is made to rest upon an inadequate, invalid, or indeterminable symptom or manifestation, but that it is made to rest upon any particular symptom. In attempting to define insanity in terms of a symptom, the courts have assumed an impossible role,[5] not merely one for which they have no special competence. As the Royal Commission emphasizes, it is dangerous "to abstract particular mental faculties, and to lay it down that unless these particular faculties are destroyed or gravely impaired, an accused person, whatever the nature of his mental disease, must be held to be criminally responsible." In this field of law as in others, the fact finder should be free to consider all information advanced by relevant scientific disciplines.

Despite demands in the name of scientific advances, this court refused to alter the right-wrong test at the turn of the century.[6] But in 1929, we reconsidered in response to "the cry of scientific experts" and added the irresistible impulse test as a supplementary test for mining criminal responsibility. Without "hesitation" we declared, in *Smith v. United States*, "it to be the law of this District that, in cases where insanity is interposed as a defense, and the facts are sufficient to call for the application of the rule of irresistible impulse, the jury should be so charged." We said: "The modern doctrine is that the degree of insanity which will relieve the accused of the consequences of a criminal act must be such as to create in his mind an uncontrollable impulse to commit the offense charged. This

---

[5] Professor John Whitehorn of the Johns Hopkins Medical School, who recently prepared an informal memorandum on this subject for a Commission on Legal Psychiatry appointed by the Governor of Maryland, has said: "Psychiatrists are challenged to set forth a crystal-clear statement of what constitutes insanity. It is impossible to express this adequately in words, alone, since such diagnostic judgments involve clinical skill and experience which cannot wholly be verbalized. The medical profession would be baffled if asked to write into the legal code universally valid criteria for the diagnosis of the many types of psychotic illness which may seriously disturb a person's responsibility, and even if this were attempted, the diagnostic criteria would have to be rewritten from time to time, with the progress of psychiatric knowledge."

[6] See, e.g., *Taylor v. United States*, where we rejected "emotional insanity" as a defense, citing with approval the following from the trial court's instruction to the jury: "Whatever may be the cry of scientific experts, the law does not recognize, but condemns the doctrine of emotional insanity—that a man may be sane up until a moment before he commits a crime, insane while he does it, and sane again soon afterwards. Such a doctrine would be dangerous in the extreme. The law does not recognize it; and a jury cannot without violating their oaths."

impulse must be such as to override the reason and judgment and obliterate the sense of right and wrong to the extent that the accused is deprived of the power to choose between right and wrong. The mere ability to distinguish right from wrong is no longer the correct test either in civil or criminal cases, where the defense of insanity is interposed. The accepted rule in this day and age, with the great advancement in medical science as an enlightening influence on this subject, is that the accused must be capable, not only of distinguishing between right and wrong, but that he was not impelled to do the act by an irresistible impulse, which means before it will justify a verdict of acquittal that his reasoning powers were so far dethroned by his diseased mental condition as to deprive him of the will power to resist the insane impulse to perpetrate the deed, though knowing it to be wrong." As we have already indicated, this has since been the test in the District.

Although the *Smith* case did not abandon the right-wrong test, it did liberate the fact finder from exclusive reliance upon that discredited criterion by allowing the jury to inquire also whether the accused suffered from an undefined "diseased mental condition which deprived him of the will power to resist the insane impulse." The term "irresistible impulse," however, carries the misleading implication that "diseased mental conditions" produce only sudden, momentary, or spontaneous inclinations to commit unlawful acts.

As the Royal Commission found: "In many cases this is not true at all. The sufferer from (melancholia, for example) experiences a change of mood which alters the whole of his existence. He may believe, for instance, that a future of such degradation and misery awaits both him and his family that death for all is a less dreadful alternative. Even the thought that the acts he contemplates are murder and suicide pales into insignificance in contrast with what he otherwise expects. The criminal act, in such circumstances, may be the reverse of impulsive. It may be coolly and carefully prepared; yet it is still the act of a madman. This is merely an illustration; similar states of mind are likely to lie behind the criminal act when murders are committed by persons suffering from schizophrenia or paranoid psychoses due to disease of the brain."[7]

We find that as an exclusive criterion the right-wrong test is inadequate in that (a) it does not take sufficient account of psychic realities and scientific knowledge, and (b) it is based upon one symptom and so cannot

---

[7] The New Mexico Supreme Court in recently adopting a broader criminal insanity rule, observed: "insanity takes the form of the personality of the individual and, if his tendency is toward depression, his wrongful act may come at the conclusion of a period of complete lethargy, thoroughly devoid of excitement."

validly be applied in all circumstances. We find that the "irresistible impulse" test is also inadequate in that it gives no recognition to mental illness characterized by brooding and reflection and so relegates acts caused by such illness to the application of the inadequate right-wrong test. We conclude that a broader test should be adopted.

In the District of Columbia, the formulation of tests of criminal responsibility is entrusted to the courts and, in adopting a new test, we invoke our inherent power to make the change prospectively. The rule we now hold must be applied on the retrial of this case and in future cases is not unlike that followed by the New Hampshire court since 1870 (*State v. Pike*).

> *The rule we now hold is simply that an accused is not criminally responsible if his unlawful act was the product of mental disease or mental defect.*

It is simply that an accused is not criminally responsible if his unlawful act was the product of mental disease or mental defect.

We use "disease" in the sense of a condition which is considered capable of either improving or deteriorating. We use "defect" in the sense of a condition which is not considered capable of either improving or deteriorating and which may be either congenital, or the result of injury, or the residual effect of a physical or mental disease.

Whenever there is "some evidence" that the accused suffered from a diseased or defective mental condition at the time the unlawful act was committed, the trial court must provide the jury with guides for determining whether the accused can be held criminally responsible. We do not, and indeed could not, formulate an instruction which would be either appropriate or binding in all cases. But under the rule now announced, any instruction should in some way convey to the jury the sense and substance of the following: If you the jury believe beyond a reasonable doubt that the accused was not suffering from a diseased or defective mental condition at the time he committed the criminal act charged, you may find him guilty. If you believe he was suffering from a diseased or defective mental condition when he committed the act, but believe beyond a reasonable doubt that the act was not the product of such mental abnormality, you may find him guilty. Unless you believe beyond a reasonable doubt either that he was not suffering from a diseased or defective mental condition, or that the act was not the product of such abnormality, you must find the accused not guilty by reason of insanity. Thus your task would not be completed upon finding, if you did find, that the accused suffered from a mental disease or defect. He would still be responsible for his unlawful act if there was no causal connection between such mental abnormality and the act.[8] These questions must be determined by you from the facts which you find to be fairly deducible from the testimony and the evidence in this case.

The questions of fact under the test we now lay down are as capable of determination by the jury as, for example, the questions juries must determine upon a claim of total disability under a policy of insurance where the state of medical knowledge concerning the disease involved, and its effects, is obscure or in conflict. In such cases, the jury is not required to depend on arbitrarily selected "symptoms, phases or manifestations" of the disease as criteria for determining the ultimate questions of fact upon which the claim depends. Similarly, upon a claim of criminal irresponsibility, the jury will not be required to rely on such symptoms as criteria for determining the ultimate question of fact upon which such claim depends. Testimony as to such "symptoms, phases or manifestations," along with other relevant evidence, will go to the jury upon the ultimate questions of fact which it alone can finally determine. Whatever the state of psychiatry, the psychiatrist will be permitted to carry out his principal court function which, as we noted in *Holloway v. United States*, "is to inform the jury of the character of the accused's mental disease or defect." The jury's range of inquiry will not be limited to, but may include, for example, whether an accused, who suffered from a mental disease or defect did not know the difference between right and wrong, acted under the compulsion of an irresistible impulse, or had "been deprived of or lost the power of his will."

Finally, in leaving the determination of the ultimate question of fact to the jury, we permit it to perform its traditional function which, as we said in *Holloway*, is to apply "our inherited ideas of moral responsibility to individuals prosecuted for crime." Juries will continue to make moral judgments, still operating under the fundamental precept that "our collective conscience does not allow punishment where it cannot impose blame." But in making such judgments, they will be guided by wider

---

[8] There is no *a priori* reason why every person suffering from any form of mental abnormality or disease, or from any particular kind of mental disease, should be treated by the law as not answerable for any criminal offence which he may commit, and be exempted from conviction and punishment. Mental abnormalities vary infinitely in their nature and intensity and in their effects on the character and conduct of those who suffer from them. Where a person suffering from a mental abnormality commits a crime, there must always be some likelihood that the abnormality has played some part in the causation of the crime; and, generally speaking, the graver the abnormality the more probable it must be that there is a causal connection between them. But the closeness of this connection will be shown by the facts brought in evidence in individual cases and cannot be decided on the basis of any general medical principle.

horizons of knowledge concerning mental life. The question will be simply whether the accused acted because of a mental disorder, and not whether he displayed particular symptoms which medical science has long recognized do not necessarily, or even typically, accompany even the most serious mental disorder.

> *The question will be simply whether the accused acted because of a mental disorder, and not whether he displayed particular symptoms which medical science has long recognized do not necessarily, or even typically, accompany even the most serious mental disorder.*

The legal and moral traditions of the western world require that those who, of their own free will and with evil intent (sometimes called *mens rea*), commit acts which violate the law, shall be criminally responsible for those acts. Our traditions also require that where such acts stem from and are the product of a mental disease or defect as those terms are used herein, moral blame shall not attach, and hence there will not be criminal responsibility. The rule we state in this opinion is designed to meet these requirements.

Reversed and remanded for a new trial.

McDonald v. United States

312 F.2d 874 (1962)

Facts

Ernest McDonald was charged with second-degree murder for aiding and abetting his employer, Davis, in shooting the victim, Jenkins. During the course of the jury trial, a psychiatrist and psychologist testified that the defendant had a mental defect, "a state of mental development which does not reach the level of average intelligence," based on a measured I.Q. of 68. Based on their conclusion that McDonald had a mental defect, the experts stated McDonald would have less than normal ability to distinguish right from wrong in complex situations, would act impulsively, and would be strongly influenced by someone who befriended him (such as Davis). The psychiatrist testified that McDonald's relationship with Davis was, to some extent, a "product" of his mental deficiency. McDonald was convicted of manslaughter and sentenced to 5 to 15 years. He appealed on two grounds related to the jury charge: (a) that the court failed to state that if acquitted by reason of insanity he would be confined to a mental hospital (see *Lyles v. United States*), and (b) the court failed twice in enumerating the alternative verdicts to include "not guilty because of insanity." The Government argued the expert evidence regarding insanity was insufficient to require the instructions.

Issues

(a) Did the court err in not giving the *Lyles* instruction? (b) Did the court err in not instructing the jury that one of the alternative verdicts was not guilty by reason of insanity?

Holding

Yes for both issues. The court should have given the *Lyles* instruction and should have instructed the jury that a not guilty by reason of insanity verdict was an option. The conviction was reversed and the case remanded.

Analysis

The Appeals Court concluded the evidence reached the "some evidence" standard (see *Davis v. United States*), establishing the possibility of a not guilty by reason of insanity verdict; and a *Lyles* instruction was required in the absence of an "affirmative" appearance on the record that the defendant did not want it. Therefore the conviction was reversed.

More importantly, in considering the testimony of the experts, the Court clarified that the jury is not bound by psychiatric conclusions about what is a disease or defect. They clarified that it is for the jury alone, considering all lay and expert testimony, to determine if the defendant was sufficiently disabled to have a mental disease or defect. To guide their considerations, the Court ruled that the jury should be told "a mental disease or defect includes any abnormal condition of the mind which substantially affects mental or emotional processes and substantially impairs behavior controls."

> **Mental disease or defect includes any abnormal condition of the mind which substantially affects mental or emotional processes and substantially impairs behavior controls.**

Edited Excerpts[1]

Opinion by Per curiam[2]

Appellant was convicted of manslaughter and sentenced to from five to fifteen years' imprisonment. He had been charged with second degree murder for aiding and abetting his employer, Davis, in the shooting of one Jenkins during an altercation. In this case a psychiatrist and a psychologist testified that the defendant had a "mental defect," principally because his I.Q. rating shown by various tests was below the "average" intelligence range of 90 to 110. His overall I.Q. was 68. Neither witness was able to say whether appellant's mental defect stemmed from organic injury or from some other cause. But the psychiatrist testified that some organic pathology can only be established by autopsy and that McDonald's defect probably prevented him from progressing beyond the sixth grade.

The witnesses also explained generally how mental defect affects behavior. The psychologist testified that a person suffering from a mental defect would have less ability than normal persons to distinguish between right and wrong in complex situations; would tend to act impulsively under stress; and would readily become dependent upon and be strongly

---

[1] Readers are advised to quote only from the original published cases. See pages vi and vii.
[2] *Per curiam*. A decision of an appeals court in which no individual judge is the author.

influenced by someone who befriended him. The witness testified further that McDonald had a mental defect, which she defined as "a state of mental development which does not reach the level of average intelligence," and that "if McDonald had a person on whom he was dependent and if that person should produce a gun and threaten another McDonald would not be as able as the average adult to assess and evaluate the situation and the consequences of whatever action he might take." McDonald's testimony suggests that he was financially and socially dependent upon Davis. The psychiatrist stated that McDonald would lack the ability of normal persons to foresee the consequences of his acts and offered an opinion that appellant's relationship to Davis was to some extent a product of his mental deficiency.

Evidence of a 68 I.Q. rating, standing alone and without more, is not evidence of a "mental defect," thus invoking the *Durham* charge. Our eight-year experience under *Durham* suggests a judicial definition, however broad and general, of what is included in the terms "disease" and "defect." In *Durham*, rather than define either term, we simply sought to distinguish disease from defect. Our purpose now is to make it very clear that neither the court nor the jury is bound by *ad hoc* definitions or conclusions as

> **What psychiatrists may consider a "mental disease or defect" for clinical purposes, where their concern is treatment, may or may not be the same as mental disease or defect for the jury's purpose in determining criminal responsibility.**

to what experts state is a disease or defect. What psychiatrists may consider a "mental disease or defect" for clinical purposes, where their concern is treatment, may or may not be the same as mental disease or defect for the jury's purpose in determining criminal responsibility. Consequently, for that purpose the jury should be told that a mental disease or defect includes any abnormal condition of the mind which substantially affects mental or emotional processes and substantially impairs behavior controls. Thus the jury would consider testimony concerning the development, adaptation, and functioning of these processes and controls.

We emphasize that, since the question of whether the defendant has a disease or defect is ultimately for the triers of fact, obviously its resolution cannot be controlled by expert opinion. The jury must determine for itself, from all the testimony, lay and expert, whether the nature and degree of the disability are sufficient to establish a mental disease or defect as we have now defined those terms. What we have said, however, should in no way be construed to limit the latitude of expert testimony.

Reversed and remanded.

United States v. Brawner

471 F.2d 969 (1972)

Facts

After a day of drinking, Archie Brawner attended a party at which several fights occurred. After his jaw was injured, Brawner left the party. According to one witness, Brawner stated he would return and added, "Someone is going to die tonight." He returned with a gun and fired several shots through the apartment door, killing Billy Ford. At trial, experts said Brawner had a neurological disorder; diagnoses included "epileptic personality disorder" and "explosive personality." Defense and government experts disagreed on a causal connection between the mental disorder and the offense. Brawner was convicted of second-degree murder and carrying a dangerous weapon. He appealed the conviction, and the Court of Appeals reconsidered the insanity standard to be applied in the District of Columbia.

Issue

Should the District of Columbia adopt a new rule (in place of the *Durham* "product test") to govern the insanity defense?

Holding

Yes, the District of Columbia adopted the American Law Institute (ALI) formulation from its Model Penal Code. The ALI standard reads: "A person is not responsible for criminal conduct if at the time of such conduct as a result of a mental disease or defect he lacks substantial capacity either to appreciate the criminality [wrongfulness] of his conduct or to conform his conduct to the requirements of the law."

Analysis

The Court reviewed its reasoning in the development of the *Durham* rule and subsequent modifications in *McDonald*, *Washington v. United States*, and *Carter v. United States*. The former was intended to allow experts to "testify in their own terms concerning matters within their domain," but instead opened the door to "trial by label" and "undue dominance by experts giving testimony." The latter cases attempted to minimize this effect and maintain the proper domain of the jury. The ALI standard would still require a "meaningful relationship" between the mental illness and the offense, but it attenuated "testimonial mystique," in which experts dominate the jury or encroach on its function. In adopting the ALI standard, the D.C. Circuit maintained the rules established in *McDonald* to define mental disease and defect as they apply to the insanity standard.

Edited Excerpts[1]

Opinion by Leventhal, Circuit Judge

The principal issues raised on this appeal from a conviction for second degree murder and carrying a dangerous weapon relate to appellant's defense of insanity. In the course of our reconsideration of the rule governing the insanity defense, we have studied the opinions of other courts, particularly but not exclusively the opinions of the other Federal circuits, and the views of the many scholars who have thoughtfully pondered the underlying issues.

We have stretched our canvas wide; and the focal point of the landscape before us is the formulation of the American Law Institute. The ALI's primary provision is stated thus in its Model Penal Code.

Section 4.01 Mental Disease or Defect Excluding Responsibility. (1) A person is not responsible for criminal conduct if at the time of such conduct as a result of mental disease or defect he lacks substantial capacity either to appreciate the criminality (wrongfulness) of his conduct or to conform his conduct to the requirements of the law.

We have decided to adopt the ALI rule as the doctrine excluding responsibility for mental disease or defect, for application prospectively to trials begun after this date.

We highlight, as most notable of these, our decision to retain the definition of "mental illness or defect" that we evolved in our 1962 *McDonald* opinion. Others are prompted by the submissions which raised, as points of objection to the ALI rule, matters that we think can be fairly taken into account by clarifying comments.

Passing by various minor disagreements among the witnesses, the record permits us to reconstruct the events of September 8, 1967, as follows: After a morning and afternoon of wine-drinking, appellant Archie W. Brawner, Jr. and his uncle Aaron Ross, went to a party at the home of three acquaintances. During the evening, several fights broke

---

[1] Readers are advised to quote only from the original published cases. See pages vi and vii.

out. In one of them, Brawner's jaw was injured when he was struck or pushed to the ground. The time of the fight was approximately 10:30 p.m. After the fight, Brawner left the party. He told Mr. Ross that some boys had jumped him. Mr. Ross testified that Brawner "looked like he was out of his mind." Other witnesses who saw him after the fight testified that Brawner's mouth was bleeding and that his speech was unclear (but the same witness added, "I heard every word he said"); that he was staggering and angry; and that he pounded on a mailbox with his fist. One witness testified that Brawner said, "I'm going to get my boys" and come back, and that "Someone is going to die tonight."

Half an hour later, at about eleven p.m., Brawner was on his way back to the party with a gun. One witness testified that Brawner said he was going up there to kill his attackers or be killed. Upon his arrival at the address, Brawner fired a shot into the ground and entered the building. He proceeded to the apartment where the party was in progress and fired five shots through the closed metal hallway door. Two of the shots struck Billy Ford, killing him. Brawner was arrested a few minutes later, several blocks away. The arresting officer testified that Brawner appeared normal, and did not appear to be drunk, that he spoke clearly, and had no odor of alcohol about him.

After the Government had presented the evidence of its non-expert witnesses, the trial judge ruled that there was insufficient evidence on "deliberation" to go to the jury: accordingly, a verdict of acquittal was directed on first degree murder.

The expert witnesses, called by both defense and prosecution, all agreed that Brawner was suffering from an abnormality of a psychiatric or neurological nature. The medical labels were variously given as "epileptic personality disorder," "psychologic brain syndrome associated with a convulsive disorder," "personality disorder associated with epilepsy," or, more simply, "an explosive personality." There was no disagreement that the epileptic condition would be exacerbated by alcohol, leading to more frequent episodes and episodes of greater intensity, and would also be exacerbated by a physical blow to the head. The experts agreed that epilepsy *per se* is not a mental disease or defect, but a neurological disease which is often associated with a mental disease or defect. They further agreed that Brawner had a mental, as well as a neurological, disease.

Where the experts disagreed was on the part which that mental disease or defect played in the murder of Billy Ford. The position of the witnesses called by the Government is that Brawner's behavior on the night of September 8 was not consistent with an epileptic seizure, and was not suggestive of an explosive reaction in the context of a psychiatric disorder. In the words of Dr. Platkin of St. Elizabeths Hospital, "He was just mad."

The experts called by the defense maintained the contrary conclusion. Thus, Dr. Eugene Stanmeyer, a psychologist at St. Elizabeths, was asked on direct by counsel for defense, whether, assuming accused did commit the act which occurred, there was a causal relationship between the assumed act and his mental abnormality. Dr. Stanmeyer replied in the affirmative, that there was a cause and effect relationship.

Later, the prosecutor asked the Government's first expert witness Dr. Weickhardt: "Did you come to any opinion concerning whether or not the crimes in this case were causally related to the mental illness which you diagnosed?" An objection to the form of the question was overruled. The witness then set forth that in his opinion there was no causal relationship between the mental disorder and the alleged offenses. Brawner claims that the trial court erred when it permitted a prosecution expert to testify in this manner.

History looms large in obtaining a sound perspective for a subject like this one. But the cases are numerous. And since our current mission is to illuminate the present, rather than to linger over the past, it suffices for our purposes to review a handful of our opinions on the insanity defense.

The landmark opinion was written by Judge Bazelon in *Durham*. Prior to *Durham* the law of the District of Columbia was established by *United States v. Lee* and *Smith v. United States*, which, taken together, stated a traditional test of insanity, in terms of right and wrong and irresistible impulse. *Durham* adopted the "product rule," pioneered in *Pike*, and exculpated from criminal responsibility those whose forbidden acts were the product of a mental disease or defect.

Few cases have evoked as much comment as *Durham*. It has sparked widespread interest in the legal-judicial community and focused attention on the profound problems involved in defining legal responsibility in case of mental illness. It has been hailed as a guide to the difficult and problem-laden intersection of law and psychiatry, ethics, and science. It has been scored as an unwarranted loophole through which the cunning criminal might escape from the penalty of the law. We view it more modestly, as the court's effort, designed in the immemorial manner of the case method that has built the common law, to alleviate two serious problems with the previous rule.

The first of these was a problem of language which raised an important symbolic issue in the law. We felt that the language of the old right-wrong/irresistible impulse rule for insanity was antiquated, no longer reflecting the community's judgment as to who ought to be held criminally liable for socially destructive acts. We considered the rule as restated to have more fruitful, accurate, and considered reflection of the sensibilities of the community as revised and expanded in the light of continued study of abnormal human behavior.

The second vexing problem that *Durham* was designed to reach related to the concern of the psychiatrists called as expert witnesses for their special knowledge of the problem of insanity, who often and typically felt that they were obliged to reach outside of their professional expertise when they were asked, under the traditional insanity rule established in 1843 by *M'Naghten*, whether the defendant knew right from wrong. They further felt that the narrowness of the traditional test, which framed the issue of responsibility solely in terms of cognitive impairment, made it impossible to convey to the judge and jury the full range of information material to an assessment of defendant's responsibility.

Discerning scholarship now available asserts that the experts' fears and concerns reflected a misapprehension as to the impact of the traditional standard in terms of excluding relevant evidence. Wigmore[2] states the rule to be that when insanity is in issue, "any and all conduct of the person is admissible in evidence." And the cases support Wigmore's view. The almost unvarying policy of the courts has been to admit any evidence of aberrational behavior so long as it is probative of the defendant's mental condition, without regard to the supposed restrictions of the test used to define insanity for the jury. Moreover if the term "know" in the traditional test of "know right from wrong" is taken as denoting affective knowledge, rather than merely cognitive knowledge, it yields a rule of greater flexibility than was widely supposed to exist.

We need not occupy ourselves here and now with the question whether, and to what extent, the *M'Naghten* Rule, ameliorated by the irresistible impulse doctrine, is susceptible of application to include medical insights and information as justice requires. In any event, the experts felt hemmed in by the traditional test; they felt that they could not give the jury and judge the necessary information in response to the questions which the traditional test posed.

The Rule as reformulated in *Durham* permitted medical experts to testify on medical matters properly put before the jury for its consideration, and to do so without the confusion that many, perhaps most, experts experienced from testimony structured under the *M'Naghten* Rule. That was a positive contribution to jurisprudence—and one that was retained

---

[2] John Henry Wigmore, 1863-1943, legal scholar.

when the American Law Institute undertook to analyze the problem and proposed a different formulation.

A difficulty arose under the *Durham* rule in application. The rule was devised to facilitate the giving of testimony by medical experts in the context of a legal rule, with the jury called upon to reach a composite conclusion that had medical, legal, and moral components. However the pristine statement of the *Durham* rule opened the door to "trial by label." *Durham* did distinguish between "disease," as used "in the sense of a condition which is considered capable of either improving or deteriorating," and "defect," as referring to a condition not capable of such change "and which may be either congenital or the result of injury, or the residual effect of a physical or mental disease." But the court failed to explicate what abnormality of mind was an essential ingredient of these concepts. In the absence of a definition of "mental disease or defect," medical experts attached to them the meanings which would naturally occur to them—medical meanings—and gave testimony accordingly. The problem was dramatically highlighted by the weekend flip flop case, *In re Rosenfield*. The petitioner was described as a sociopath. A St. Elizabeths psychiatrist testified that a person with a sociopathic personality was not suffering from a mental disease. That was Friday afternoon. On Monday morning, through a policy change at St. Elizabeths Hospital, it was determined as an administrative matter that the state of a psychopathic or sociopathic personality did constitute a mental disease.

The concern that medical terminology not control legal outcomes culminated in *McDonald*, where this court recognized that the term, mental disease or defect, has various meanings, depending upon how and why it is used, and by whom. Mental disease means one thing to a physician bent on treatment, but something different, if somewhat overlapping, to a court of law. We provided a legal definition of mental disease or defect, and held that it included "any abnormal condition of the mind which substantially affects mental or emotional processes and substantially impairs behavior controls."

While the *McDonald* standard of mental disease was not without an attribute of circularity, it was useful in the administration of justice because it made plain that clinical and legal definitions of mental disease were distinct, and it helped the jury to sort out its complex task and to focus on the matters given it to decide.

The *Durham* rule also required explication along other lines, notably the resolution of the ambiguity inherent in the formulation concerning actions that were the "product" of mental illness. It was supplemented in *Carter v. United States* (1957): "The simple fact that a person has a mental disease or defect is not enough to relieve him of responsibility for a crime. There must be a relationship between the disease and the criminal act; and the relationship must be such as to justify a reasonable inference that the act would not have been committed if the person had not been suffering from the disease." Thus *Carter* clarified that the mental illness must not merely have entered into the production of the act, but must have played a necessary role. *Carter* identified the "product" element of the rule with the "but for" variety of causation.

The pivotal "product" term continued to present problems, principally that it put expert testimony on a faulty footing. Assuming that a mental disease, in the legal sense, had been established, the fate of the defendant came to be determined by what came to be referred to by the legal jargon of "productivity." On the other hand, it was obviously sensible, if not imperative, that the experts having pertinent knowledge should speak to the crucial question whether the mental abnormality involved is one associated with aberrant behavior. But since "productivity" was so decisive a factor in the decisional equation, a ruling permitting experts to testify expressly in language of "product" raised in a different context the concern lest the ultimate issue be in fact turned over to the experts rather than retained for the jurors representing the community.

The problem was identified by then Circuit Judge Burger in his concurring opinion in *Blocker*: "The hazards in allowing experts to testify in precisely or even substantially the terms of the ultimate issue are apparent. This is a course which, once allowed, risks the danger that lay jurors, baffled by the intricacies of expert discourse and unintelligible technical jargon may be tempted to abdicate independent analysis of the facts on which the opinion rests."

As early as *Carter*, we had warned that the function of an expert was to explain the origin, development, and manifestations of mental disorders, in terms that would be coherent and meaningful to the jury. "Unexplained medical labels are not enough." Even after *McDonald*, however, we continued to see cases where the testimony of the experts was limited to the use of conclusory labels, without the explication of the underlying analysis. We do not say this was deliberated by the experts. It seems in large measure to have reflected tactical decisions of counsel, and perhaps problems of communications between the disciplines.

It was in this context that the court came to the decision in *Washington v. United States*, which forbade experts from testifying as to productivity altogether. Chief Judge Bazelon's opinion illuminates the basis of the ruling, as one intended "to help the psychiatrists understand their role in court, and thus eliminate a fundamental cause of unsatisfactory expert testimony," namely, the tendency of the expert to use "concepts which can become slogans, hiding facts and representing nothing more than the witness's own conclusion about the defendant's criminal responsibility."

The American Law Institute's Model Penal Code expressed a rule which has become the dominant force in the law pertaining to the defense of insanity. The ALI rule is eclectic in spirit, partaking of the moral focus of *M'Naghten*, the practical accommodation of the "control rules" (a term more exact and less susceptible of misunderstanding than "irresistible impulse" terminology), and responsive, at the same time, to a relatively modern, forward-looking view of what is encompassed in "knowledge."

For convenience, we quote again the basic rule propounded by the ALI's Model Penal Code: "A person is not responsible for criminal conduct if at the time of such conduct as a result of mental disease or defect he lacks substantial capacity either to appreciate the criminality [wrongfulness] of his conduct or to conform his conduct to the requirements of the law."

A subsidiary rule in paragraph (2), stating what has come to be known as the "caveat" paragraph, has had a mixed reception in the courts and discussion of that problem will be deferred.

The core rule of the ALI has been adopted, with variations, by all save one of the Federal circuit courts of appeals, and by all that have come to reconsider the doctrine providing exculpation for mental illness. Their opinions have been exceptionally thoughtful and thorough in their expositions of the interests and values protected. These opinions show that the ALI rule has proved peculiarly subject to successful adaptation, permitting variations but within a framework of uniformity.

The first was *Currens*, where Chief Judge Biggs of the Third Circuit defined the test: "The jury must be satisfied that at the time of committing the prohibited act the defendant, as a result of mental disease or defect, lacked substantial capacity to conform his conduct to the requirements of the law which he is alleged to have violated."

This formula is explicitly derived from the ALI rule. It takes an additional step, however, in that it treats cognitive impairments as "surplusage" to a test of criminal responsibility. The premise is that an abnormality in the cognitive function is neither sufficient nor necessary. If it does not result in a substantial incapacity of the volitional function, it is not sufficient in law; and a substantial incapacity of the volitional function results in exculpation even though it does not involve the cognitive faculties.

Thus *Currens* capped the history of the insanity defense—which began with impairment of knowledge and proceeded to impairment of control—

by dropping the knowledge feature as merely one aspect of the ultimate control element. Though not without considerable force and logic *Currens* has not been followed by the other Federal courts, which adhere more closely to the ALI model.

A principal reason for our decision to depart from the *Durham* rule is the undesirable characteristic, surviving even the *McDonald* modification, of undue dominance by the experts giving testimony. The difficulty is rooted in the circumstance that there is no generally accepted understanding, either in the jury or the community it represents, of the concept requiring that the crime be the "product" of the mental disease.

> *A principal reason for our decision to depart from the* Durham *rule is the undesirable characteristic, surviving even the* McDonald *modification, of undue dominance by the experts giving testimony.*

When the court used the term "product" in *Durham* it likely assumed that this was a serviceable, and indeed a natural, term for a rule defining criminal responsibility—a legal reciprocal, as it were, for the familiar term "proximate cause," used to define civil responsibility. But if concepts like "product" are, upon refinement, reasonably understood, or at least appreciated, by judges and lawyers, and perhaps philosophers, difficulties developed when it emerged that the "product" concept did not

> *The difficulty is rooted in the circumstance that there is no generally accepted understanding, either in the jury or the community it represents, of the concept requiring that the crime be the "product" of the mental disease.*

signify a reasonably identifiable common ground that was also shared by the nonlegal experts, and the laymen serving on the jury as the representatives of the community.

The doctrine of criminal responsibility is such that there can be no doubt "of the complicated nature of the decision to be made—intertwining moral, legal, and medical judgments." Hence, jury decisions have been accorded unusual deference even when they have found responsibility in the face of a powerful record, with medical evidence uncontradicted, pointing toward exculpation. The "moral" elements of the decision are not defined exclusively by religious considerations but by the totality of underlying conceptions of ethics and justice shared by the community, as expressed by its jury surrogate. The essential feature of a jury "lies in the interposition between the accused and his accuser of the common sense judgment of a group of laymen, and in the community participation and shared responsibility that results from that group's determination of guilt or innocence."

The expert witnesses—psychiatrists and psychologists—are called to adduce relevant information concerning what may for convenience be referred to as the "medical" component of the responsibility issue. But the difficulty—as emphasized in *Washington v. United States*—is that the medical expert comes, by testimony given in terms of a non-medical construct ("product"), to express conclusions that in essence embody ethical and legal conclusions. There is, indeed, irony in a situation under which the *Durham* rule, which was adopted in large part to permit experts to testify in their own terms concerning matters within their domain which the jury should know, resulted in testimony by the experts in terms not their own to reflect unexpressed judgments in a domain that is properly not theirs but the jury's. The irony is heightened when the jurymen, instructed under the esoteric "product" standard, are influenced significantly by "product" testimony of expert witnesses really reflecting ethical and legal judgments rather than a conclusion within the witnesses' particular expertise.

It is easier to identify and spotlight the irony than to eradicate the mischief. The objective of *Durham* is still sound—to put before the jury the information that is within the expert's domain, to aid the jury in making a broad and comprehensive judgment. But when the instructions and appellate decisions define the "product" inquiry as the ultimate issue, it is like stopping the tides to try to halt the emergence of this term in the language of those with a central role in the trial—the lawyers who naturally seek to present testimony that will influence the jury who will be charged under the ultimate "product" standard, and the expert witnesses who have an awareness, gained from forensic psychiatry and related disciplines, of the ultimate "product" standard that dominates the proceeding.

The experts have meaningful information to impart, not only on the existence of mental illness or not, but also on its relationship to the incident charged as an offense. In the interest of justice this valued information should be available, and should not be lost or blocked by requirements that unnaturally restrict communication between the experts and the jury. The more we have pondered the problem the more convinced we have become that the sound solution lies not in further shaping of the *Durham* "product" approach in more refined molds, but in adopting the ALI's formulation as the linchpin of our jurisprudence.

The ALI's formulation retains the core requirement of a meaningful relationship between the mental illness and the incident charged. The language in the ALI rule is sufficiently in the common ken that its use in the courtroom, or in preparation for trial, permits a reasonable three-way communication—between (a) the law-trained, judges and lawyers; (b) the experts; and (c) the jurymen—without insisting on a vocabulary that is either stilted or stultified, or conducive to a testimonial mystique permitting expert dominance and encroachment on the jury's function. There is no indication in the available literature that any such untoward development has attended the reasonably widespread adoption of the ALI rule in the Federal courts and a substantial number of state courts.

In our further discussion of ALI and *McDonald*, we shall sometimes refer to "mental disease" as the core concept, without specifically referring to the possibility of exculpation by reason of a non-altering "mental defect." The *McDonald* rule has helped accomplish the objective of securing expert testimony needed on the subject of mental illness, while guarding against the undue dominance of expert testimony or specialized labels. It has thus permitted the kind of communication without encroachment, as between experts and juries, that has prompted us to adopt the ALI rule, and hence will help us realize our objective. This advantage overrides the surface disadvantage of any clumsiness in the blending of the *McDonald* component, defining mental disease, with the rest of the ALI rule, a matter we discuss further below.

Adoption of the ALI rule furthers uniformity of judicial approach—a feature eminently desirable, not as a mere glow of "togetherness," but as an appreciation of the need and value of judicial communication. In all likelihood, this court's approach under *Durham*, at least since *McDonald*, has differed from that of other courts in vocabulary more than substance. Uniformity of vocabulary has an important value, however, as is evidenced from the familiar experience of meanings that "get lost in translation." No one court can amass all the experience pertinent to the judicial administration of the insanity defense. It is helpful for courts to be able to learn from each other without any blockage due to jargon. It is an impressive virtue of the common law, that its distinctive reliance on judicial decisions to establish the corpus of the law furthers a multiparty conversation between men who have studied a problem in various places at various times.

Though it provides a general uniformity, the ALI rule leaves room for variations. Thus, we have added an adjustment in the *McDonald* definition of mental disease, which we think fully compatible with both the spirit and text of the ALI rule. In the interest of good administration, we now undertake to set forth, with such precision as the subject will permit, other elements of the ALI rule as adopted by this court.

The two main components of the rule define (1) mental disease, (2) the consequences thereof that exculpate from responsibility.

The first component of our rule, derived from *McDonald*, defines mental disease or defect as an abnormal condition of the mind, and a condition which substantially (a) affects mental or emotional processes and (b) impairs behavioral controls. The second component, derived from the Model Penal Code, tells which defendant with a mental disease lacks criminal responsibility for particular conduct: it is the defendant who, as a result of this mental condition, at the time of such conduct, either (i) lacks substantial capacity to appreciate that his conduct is wrongful, or (ii) lacks substantial capacity to conform his conduct to the law.

The first component establishes eligibility for an instruction concerning the defense for a defendant who presents evidence that his abnormal condition of the mind has substantially impaired behavioral controls. The second component completes the instruction and defines the ultimate issue, of exculpation, in terms of whether his behavioral controls were not only substantially impaired but impaired to such an extent that he lacked substantial capacity to conform his conduct to the law.

The rule contains a requirement of causality, as is clear from the term "result." Exculpation is established not by mental disease alone but only if "as a result" defendant lacks the substantial capacity required for responsibility. Presumably the mental disease of a kleptomaniac does not entail as a "result" a lack of capacity to conform to the law prohibiting rape.

Under the ALI rule the issue is not whether defendant is so disoriented or void of controls that he is never able to conform to external demands, but whether he had that capacity at the time of the conduct. The question is not properly put in terms of whether he would have capacity to conform in some untypical restraining situation—as with an attendant or policeman at his elbow. The issue is whether he was able to conform in the unstructured condition of life in an open society, and whether the result of his abnormal mental condition was a lack of substantial internal controls.

The schizophrenic is disoriented from reality; the disorientation is extreme; but it is rarely total. Most psychotics will respond to a command of someone in authority within the mental hospital; they thus have some capacity to conform to a norm. But this is very different from the question whether they have the capacity to conform to requirements that are not thus immediately symbolized by an attendant or policeman at the elbow. Nothing makes the inquiry into responsibility more unreal for the psychiatrist than limitation of the issue to some ultimate extreme of total incapacity, when clinical experience reveals only a graded scale with marks along the way.

As to the option of terminology noted in the ALI code, we adopt the formulation that exculpates a defendant whose mental condition is such that he lacks substantial capacity to appreciate the wrongfulness of his conduct. We prefer this

> *Nothing makes the inquiry into responsibility more unreal for the psychiatrist than limitation of the issue to some ultimate extreme of total incapacity, when clinical experience reveals only a graded scale with marks along the way.*

on pragmatic grounds to "appreciate the criminality of his conduct" since the resulting jury instruction is more like that conventionally given to and applied by the jury. While such an instruction is of course subject to the objection that it lacks complete precision, it serves the objective of calling on the jury to provide a community judgment on a combination of factors. And since the possibility of analytical differences between the two formulations is insubstantial in fact in view of the control capacity test, we are usefully guided by the pragmatic considerations pertinent to jury instructions.

When the question arose as to whether "wrong" means moral or legal wrong, the American courts split. One group, following *M'Naghten*, held the offender sane if he knew the act was prohibited by law. A second group, following the lead of Judge Cardozo in *People v. Schmidt*, ruled that the defense was available to a defendant who knew the killing was legally wrong but thought it morally right because he was so ordered by God. In *Sauer v. United States* (1957), Judge Barnes summed up the practicalities: "The practice has been to state merely the word 'wrong' and leave the decision for the jury. While not entirely condonable, such practice is explained in large measure by an awareness that the jury will eventually exercise a moral judgment as to the sanity of the accused."

This issue rarely arose under *M'Naghten*, and its substantiality was reduced if not removed by the control capacity test, since anyone under a delusion as to God's mandate would presumably lack substantial capacity to conform his conduct to the requirements of the law. We are not informed of any case where a mental illness left a person with capacity to appreciate wrongfulness but not a capacity to appreciate criminality. If such a case ever arises, supported by credible evidence, the court can then consider its correct disposition more meaningfully, in the light of a concrete record.

Section 4.01 of the Model Penal Code as promulgated by ALI contains what has come to be known as the "caveat paragraph": "The terms "mental disease or defect" do not include an abnormality manifested only by repeated criminal or otherwise anti-social conduct." The purpose of this provision was to exclude a defense for the so-called "psychopathic personality." Our own approach is influenced by the fact that our rule already includes a definition of mental disease (from *McDonald*). Under that definition, as we have pointed out, the mere existence of "a long criminal record does not excuse crime" (*Williams v. United States*). We do not require the caveat paragraph as an insurance against exculpation of the deliberate and persistent offender. Our *McDonald* rule guards against the danger of misunderstanding and injustice that might arise, say, from an expert's classification that reflects only a conception defining all criminality as reflective of mental illness. There must be testimony to show both that the defendant was suffering from an abnormal condition of the mind and that it substantially affected mental or emotional processes and substantially impaired behavioral controls. In this context, our pragmatic approach is to adopt the caveat paragraph as a rule for application by the judge, to avoid miscarriage of justice, but not for inclusion in instructions to the jury.

Our adoption of the ALI rule does not depart from the doctrines this court has built up over the past twenty years to assure a broad presentation to the jury concerning the condition of defendant's mind and its consequences. Thus we adhere to our rulings admitting expert testimony of psychologists, as well as psychiatrists, and to our many decisions contemplating that expert testimony on this subject will be accompanied by presentation of the facts and premises underlying the opinions and conclusions of the experts, and that the Government and defense may present, in Judge Blackmun's words, "all possibly relevant evidence" bearing on cognition, volition, and capacity.

Finally, we have not accepted suggestions to adopt a rule that disentangles the insanity defense from a medical model, and announces a standard exculpating anyone whose capacity for control is insubstantial, for whatever cause or reason. There may be logic in these submissions, but we are not sufficiently certain of the nature, range, and implications of the conduct involved to attempt an all-embracing unified field theory. The applicable rule can be discerned as the cases arise in regard to other conditions—somnambulism or other automatisms; blackouts due, e.g., to overdose of insulin; drug addiction. Whether these somatic conditions should be governed by a rule comparable to that herein set forth for mental disease would require, at a minimum, a judicial determination, which takes medical opinion into account, finding convincing evidence of an ascertainable condition characterized by "a broad consensus that free will does not exist."

At the risk of repetition, but out of abundance of caution, and in order to obviate needless misunderstanding, we reiterate that this opinion retains the "abnormal mental condition" concept that marks the threshold of *McDonald*. Assuming the introduction of evidence showing "abnormal mental condition," the judge will consider an appropriate instruction making it clear to the jury that even though defendant did not have an abnormal mental condition that absolves him of criminal responsibility, e.g., if he had substantial capacity to appreciate the wrongfulness of his act or to control his behavior he may have had a condition that negates the specific mental state required for a higher degree of crime, e.g., if the abnormal mental condition existing at the time of the homicide deprived him of the capacity for the premeditation required for first degree murder.

To avoid needless confusion, we contemplate strict adherence to the term "abnormal mental condition," and do not contemplate use of terms such as "mental unsoundness," which might confuse a juror who considered that any defendant committing a wanton act is "unsound," and, presumably, suffering from "mental unsoundness."

The case is remanded for further consideration by the District Court in accordance with this opinion. So ordered.

Summary

Some readers may wish to pursue a study of the D.C. Circuit Court of Appeals and the efforts of Judge Bazelon and his colleagues to develop proper relationships between mental health professionals and the courts. The trouble was not necessarily a recalcitrant group of doctors who could not resist insinuating themselves into legal decision making; the significant problem was of prosecutors and defense attorneys posing questions designed to get doctors to make legal statements. There are a number of cases in the D.C. Circuit from *Durham* to *Brawner* that address various facets of the insanity defense, expert testimony, and disposition of acquittees. (We present a case in Section 7 [*Marble*] that is the last in a series of D.C. cases that explores whether defendants should have choice in foregoing an insanity defense.) We encourage interested readers to read these cases and others in their unexpurgated forms. It is fair to say that the Court gave up its efforts creative in *Brawner*, perhaps finding the ALI standard as the best it could hope for. Ultimately, of course, the Insanity Defense Reform Act effectively overturned *Brawner* and forced the Court to return to the *M'Naghten* standard it had rejected in *Durham*.

Section 5

What Is "Wrongfulness"?

Introduction to Section 5

Cases

  United States v. Sullivan

  United States v. Segna

  United States v. Dubray

Summary

189

Introduction to Section 5

At least as early as 1812, the time of *Bellingham's* trial (cited in *Parsons*), English courts dealing with insanity defenses focused on a defendant's ability to distinguish right from wrong or good from evil. Although most American jurisdictions later adopted the *M'Naghten* "right-wrong" test, not all agreed on the meaning of the term "wrongfulness." In a famous 1915 New York case, *People v. Schmidt*, Judge Cardozo suggested that prior to *M'Naghten*, the meaning of "wrong" encompassed knowledge of what is legally wrong as well as what is morally wrong. The ALI standard, proposed in the Model Penal Code, gave jurisdictions the option of choosing either "criminality" or "wrongfulness" as a term for the concept which the insane defendant must "lack the substantial capacity to appreciate."

The Ninth Circuit has grappled with what wrongfulness means. They chose the term "wrongfulness" when adopting the ALI standard in *Wade v. United States* (1970). In *United States v. Sullivan* (1976), the Ninth Circuit made clear that a person who, due to a mental disorder, believed he was morally justified for an act he knew was criminal could still be considered insane. The Ninth Circuit also clarified that the belief was not limited to an actual delusion, as articulated by mental health professionals, but that a delusion could *not* simply be a belief by a defendant of moral justification, "without more" (i.e., without mental disorder).

In *United States v. Segna* (1977), the Ninth Circuit determined when a jury had to be given an explicit instruction about what was meant by "wrongfulness." Their decision contained a thoughtful analysis of three different meanings of the term. The defense argued that jurors should routinely be given an instruction explaining the broad "moral wrongfulness" definition as the standard for the Circuit. Such a routine use of the instruction may have served to broaden the standard of insanity and increase the number of defendants excused due to insanity. The Court of Appeals concluded that jurors had to be instructed on the broad "moral wrongfulness" definition of the term only when evidence presented at trial made the distinction between criminal and moral wrongfulness relevant.

In *United States v. Dubray* (1988), similar issues arose concerning the meaning of wrongfulness and jury instruction about wrongfulness. The United States Court of Appeals for the Eighth Circuit issued a holding similar to those given by the Ninth Circuit in *Sullivan* and *Segna*. We include this case because it broadens the application offered in these two earlier cases from the typically liberal Ninth Circuit to the routinely conservative heartland Eighth Circuit. *Dubray* was decided subsequent to passage of the Insanity Defense Reform Act era, whereas the earlier cases involved the ALI standard.

United States v. Sullivan

544 F.2d 1052 (1976)

Facts

Sullivan was charged with presenting false identification when purchasing several firearms. At a jury trial, experts for both the prosecution and defense agreed the defendant suffered from manic-depressive psychosis with grandiosity. The defense argued that Sullivan believed he was a retired, high-ranking military officer and was entitled to own a gun collection. The testimony of the defense expert raised the issue of the meaning of wrongfulness in the insanity standard. He testified that Sullivan understood that his behavior was wrong "intellectually" but not wrong "morally."

The Ninth Circuit in *Wade v. United States* had adopted the American Law Institute (ALI) Model Penal Code insanity standard with the use of the term "wrongfulness" in place of "criminality." Subsequently, in *United States v. McGraw*, they had interpreted the rule as, "a defendant lacks substantial capacity to appreciate the wrongfulness of his conduct if he knows his act to be criminal but commits it because of a delusion that it is morally justified." During Sullivan's trial, the court rejected two jury instructions proposed by the defense clarifying the term wrongfulness in line with *Wade* and *McGraw*, simply because there had been no evidence presented that the defendant had a delusion. Sullivan was convicted and appealed on the grounds that the trial court erred by refusing to adopt one of the proposed jury instructions.

Issue

Is the presence of a delusion a necessary element before a jury receives instructions about wrongfulness?

Holding

No, the jury should have been given one of the proposed clarifying instructions. The conviction was reversed and the case was remanded to the district court.

Analysis

The Ninth Circuit Court of Appeals concluded that the term "delusion," as articulated in *McGraw*, was intended to be a term of clarification, not limitation. It adds no additional element to be established for a defendant to be entitled to an instruction on the meaning of the insanity standard. The prosecution argued that without a delusion, as it might be defined by a psychiatrist, the insanity defense would be available to any offender who simply believed that his acts were morally justified. The Ninth Circuit agreed that a defendant who had a mistaken belief that he was morally justified "without more" did not lack the substantial capacity to appreciate the wrongfulness of his act but "simply chose not to do so." However, someone with a false belief that he was morally justified "resulting from a mental disease or defect" did lack the substantial capacity, irrespective of whether he could be correctly diagnosed medically as "delusional."

Edited Excerpts[1]

Opinion by Ely, Circuit Judge

Sullivan was convicted in a jury trial of having presented false identification in connection with several purchases of firearms. He defended his conduct on the ground that he was not legally sane at the time of the purchases. On appeal he contends that the trial court erred in refusing to adopt one of two jury instructions proposed by the defense, either of which would have clarified the concept of "wrongfulness" as it pertains to the insanity defense. (See *Wade* and *McGraw*.) We agree with the appellant for the reasons stated below and therefore reverse and remand.

During the course of the trial, expert witnesses for both the prosecution and the defense confirmed that Sullivan suffered from manic-depressive psychosis, a mental illness apparently characterized in some instances by a condition of extreme egocentricity, and manifested by displays of grandiosity. The defense submitted that Sullivan's illness reflected itself in his assumption of a role as a retired, high-ranking military officer and his insistence on having a gun collection, thereby leading to the offenses for which he was charged.

Although conceding Sullivan's mental illness, psychiatrists for the prosecution concluded that he was not "delusional" and did not lack substantial capacity, by virtue of his illness, either to appreciate the wrongfulness of his conduct or to conform his conduct to legal

---

[1] Readers are advised to quote only from the original published cases. See pages vi and vii.

requirements. Dr. Meyers, the sole expert witness testifying for the defense, agreed that Sullivan was not "delusional," at least "in the same sense as the schizophrenic," but nonetheless concluded that he lacked substantial capacity to appreciate the wrongfulness of his conduct and to conform his conduct to the requirements of law.

When expressing his expert opinion, Dr. Meyers at one point evinced confusion with respect to the proper legal connotation of "wrongfulness":

"The Court: Do you have an opinion whether the defendant did or did not lack substantial capacity to appreciate the wrongfulness of his conduct?"

"The Witness: May I ask a question, Your Honor?"

"The Court: Yes, sir."

"The Witness: In this respect, this refers only to intellectual, or does it refer also to moral capacity?"

"The Court: Well, that is the test the law applies, Doctor, and you have to take an understanding as you find it of that language."

"The Witness: Intellectually, I think he understood, morally, I do not think he did." [Cross-examination]

"The Court: Well, to put it another way, Doctor, would you say that his view was that although he knew and recognized that there was a law which said you couldn't do certain things and did have to do certain other things, that it was his view that the law did not apply to him?"

"The Witness: In his way of thinking, yes, in a way that's true."

"The prosecutor: Dr. Meyers, is that the basis then of your opinion that he lacks substantial capacity to appreciate the wrongfulness of his conduct?"

"The Witness: Yes."

Thus, Dr. Meyers' testimony obviously confronted the jury with conflicting concepts of "wrongfulness," one encompassing the intellectual ability to appreciate criminality, and the other contemplating capacity to appreciate moral wrongfulness. This conflict was aggravated by a portion of the prosecutor's closing argument:

"You also heard as to the appreciation of wrongfulness aspect, the testimony of Doctor Meyers. You heard Doctor Meyers say, 'Yes,' in his opinion, he felt the defendant did lack substantial capacity to appreciate the wrongfulness of his conduct. But recall later on in his testimony he stated that it was his opinion that the defendant did not lack, he did have substantial capacity to appreciate the criminality of his act. He thought that the defendant lacked the substantial capacity to appreciate the moral wrongfulness of his conduct, and remember, he stated, because of the fact that the defendant felt he was above the law."

In response, defense counsel exhorted: "I submit Ladies and Gentlemen, that in considering the test, was he as a result of mental disease or defect substantially unable to appreciate the wrongfulness of his conduct . . . that he may have understood that his act was criminal but he did not substantially appreciate that his act was immoral."

When the prosecutor objected to this statement, the court replied: "Well, I think the jury has come to the view already and certainly they should have that the law is going to come from this side of the bench. And that's the law you are going to have to apply. You may proceed."

Thus, the prosecutor's objection was not sustained, and whether the judge intended to do so or not, he implied to the jury that he would instruct them as to the legal definition of "wrongfulness" pertinent to evaluating Dr. Meyers' opinion and, ultimately, the culpability of the defendant. Moreover, the court's comments are subject to the interpretation that it was then intended that the jury would be instructed in line with the argument of the defense.

Subsequently, however, the court rejected two jury instructions tendered in the alternative by the defense designed to clarify the concept of "wrongfulness." The proposals, respectively, read as follows:

(1) For purposes of the insanity defense, wrongfulness means moral wrongfulness rather than criminal wrongfulness.

(2) You are instructed that the defendant lacked substantial capacity to appreciate the wrongfulness of his conduct, even if he knows his act to be criminal, but commits it because of a delusion that it was morally justified.

Essentially, both proposals quote statements made by this Court in *Wade* and in *McGraw*. The trial court refused to issue either of the above instructions on grounds that there was no evidence presented upon which to submit the factual issue to the jury that the defendant had suffered from a delusion that his activities were morally justified.

In *Wade* we held that, for purposes of the insanity defense, "wrongfulness" means moral wrongfulness rather than criminal wrongfulness. As we interpreted this rule in *McGraw*, "a defendant lacks substantial capacity to appreciate the wrongfulness of his conduct if he knows his act to be criminal but commits it because of a delusion that it is morally justified." Apparently, the court mistook our use of the word "delusion" as an attempt to restrict the types of mental illnesses which will support the issuance of a clarifying instruction as to the *Wade* definition of "wrongfulness." We seize this opportunity to disclaim any talismanic focus on the word "delusion." The word adds no additional element to those which must be established before an individual is entitled to any instruction on legal insanity; it is a word of clarification, not of limitation.

The prosecution urges that we construe "delusion" as a psychiatrist might define the term, that is, in terms of bizarre thought content associated with severe forms of mental illness; otherwise, so it is argued, the insanity defense will be available to those who commit criminal offenses because they simply "believe" their acts to be morally justified. We most assuredly agree that one who acts pursuant to a mistaken belief that he is morally justified, without more, does not legally lack substantial capacity to appreciate the moral wrongfulness of his act; he simply chooses not to do so. But someone who commits a criminal act under a false belief, the result of mental disease or defect, that such act is morally justified, does indeed lack substantial capacity to appreciate the wrongfulness of his conduct, irrespective of whether he can be correctly diagnosed, medically, as "delusional." The *Wade* test for legal insanity requires no more. There are doubtless many mental diseases or defects that can be even more severe than a condition described as "delusional."

Consequently, the Government stands in the position of conceding Sullivan's mental illness and his right to have the jury instructed on the test for insanity, yet contesting his right to an instruction clarifying the proper meaning of "wrongfulness," an operative word of that test in respect to which the jury had been exposed to confusing, if not diametrically opposing views. We held in *McGraw* that the trial court

> *"Delusion"* adds no additional element to those which must be established before an individual is entitled to any instruction on legal insanity; it is a word of clarification, not of limitation.

> We most assuredly agree that one who acts pursuant to a mistaken belief that he is morally justified, without more, does not legally lack substantial capacity to appreciate the moral wrongfulness of his act; he simply chooses not to do so.

> Someone who commits a criminal act under a false belief, the result of mental disease or defect, that such act is morally justified, does indeed lack substantial capacity to appreciate the wrongfulness of his conduct.

suffers the responsibility in this situation to instruct the jury that "wrongfulness" means moral wrongfulness rather than criminal wrongfulness. Accordingly, we conclude that the court erred by refusing to accept one of the aforementioned instructions submitted by the defense, particularly in light of the jury's probable expectation that a clarifying instruction would be forthcoming. We note in passing that either instruction would have been suitable in the present case, inasmuch as both accurately reiterate statements made by us in *Wade* and *McGraw*.

REVERSED and REMANDED.

United States v. Segna

555 F.2d 226 (1977)

Facts

Segna shot and killed an Indian policeman on the Navajo Reservation in Arizona. At trial, he pled insanity but was convicted of first-degree murder. Segna appealed, arguing prosecutorial misconduct in trial tactics and closing arguments, and judicial error in refusing to instruct the jury on the meaning of wrongfulness (see *Sullivan*) as it is used in the test of criminal responsibility.

At his trial, Segna had introduced testimony of several mental health expert witnesses and lay witnesses that he suffered from a delusion that he was a persecuted Indian. His expert witnesses offered the opinion that he was insane under the ALI standard used at that time in the Ninth Circuit. Having overcome the presumption of sanity, the prosecution had the burden of proving his sanity beyond a reasonable doubt. One psychiatrist testified Segna did not suffer from a mental illness and was sane at the time of the murder, but his opinion was compromised on cross-examination. In closing arguments, the prosecutor made an erroneous, misleading statement about the law which incorrectly shifted the burden of proof to the defendant. The judge also refused to give the jury an instruction explaining the meaning of wrongfulness.

On appeal, Segna argued the prosecution expert's testimony should be completely discredited as a matter of law, but the Ninth Circuit declined to do so. Segna also appealed that the prosecutor's statement in closing arguments constituted reversible error as did the judge's failure to give the instruction clarifying the insanity standard. The Ninth Circuit held the prosecutor's statements constituted "plain error" and reversed Segna's conviction, remanding the case to the trial court. To avoid an error in the trial on remand, the Court of Appeals also addressed the issue of the instruction on the meaning of wrongfulness.

Issue

When should a jury be given an instruction concerning the meaning of wrongfulness as it is used in the test of criminal responsibility?

Holding and Analysis

The Court of Appeals concluded that when properly requested, the District Court must instruct the jury on the meaning of wrongfulness when the issue is relevant. The issue is relevant when the record indicates the defendant realized his actions were illegal, but because of mental illness, believed those acts were morally justified. The Court of Appeals articulated three possible definitions of "wrong." The first was "contrary to the law." The second was "contrary to public morality," and the third was "contrary to one's own conscience." They explained that when they adopted the ALI standard (in *Wade*), they embraced the third definition as evidenced by their use of the word "wrong" rather than "criminal" in their formulation of the standard. The government had argued the position that a clarifying instruction should be given only in cases where an expert witness concluded that the defendant lacked the substantial capacity to appreciate the moral wrongfulness of his acts. The defense argued that juries should always be given a clarifying instruction because the term wrongfulness was always ambiguous. The Ninth Circuit rejected both positions, adopting the position that the instruction should be given when the evidence makes the clarification relevant.

Edited Excerpts[1]

Opinion by Wallace, Circuit Judge

Segna, a non-Indian, shot and killed an Indian policeman on the Navajo Indian Reservation in Arizona. After a trial where the only contested issue was Segna's legal sanity at the time of the offense he was convicted of first degree murder. Segna argues to us that the evidence was insufficient to prove his sanity beyond a reasonable doubt; that the district court erred in refusing to instruct the jury both on the meaning of "wrongfulness" as that word is used in the test of criminal responsibility and on the defendant's post-acquittal status; that prosecutorial misconduct in trial tactics and closing arguments requires a new trial; and that certain of the district court's evidentiary rulings were erroneous. We find the government's evidence of sanity sufficient to sustain the conviction, but because part of the prosecutor's unobjected-to closing argument constitutes plain error, we reverse and remand for a new trial.

Segna introduced substantial evidence that he was not legally responsible for the killing because of a mental disease or defect. This

---

[1] Readers are advised to quote only from the original published cases. See pages vi and vii.

evidence consisted of the testimony of three psychiatrists, one psychologist, and several lay witnesses and various exhibits including letters written by Segna before the killing. All of these expert witnesses agreed that Segna was suffering from a

> **All of these expert witnesses agreed that Segna was suffering from a fixed delusionary system, the central feature of which was Segna's belief that he was a persecuted Indian.**

fixed delusionary system, the central feature of which was Segna's belief that he was a persecuted Indian. Both the lay testimony and the non-testimonial evidence tended to substantiate this diagnosis. These experts also agreed that Segna, because of this mental disease, lacked substantial capacity at the time of the killing to conform his conduct to the requirements of the law or to appreciate the wrongfulness of his conduct (see *Wade*).

This evidence clearly destroyed the presumption of sanity and placed on the government the burden of establishing Segna's legal sanity beyond a reasonable doubt. In an effort to meet its burden, the government called several lay witnesses and one psychiatrist, Dr. Gorman. The lay witnesses testified that on occasion prior to and after the killing, Segna did not refer to himself as an Indian but as an Italian, his true ethnic derivation. Dr. Gorman disagreed with the experts called by Segna and opined that Segna was not legally insane under the *Wade* test at the time of the killing. In Gorman's view, Segna had an antisocial, psychopathic personality which did not constitute a mental disease or defect within the meaning of *Wade*.

During cross-examination of Gorman, the doctor's opinion was attacked in three ways. First, Segna's counsel established that the doctor's diagnosis was based on an incorrect view of the facts of Segna's prior life. Second, the doctor was required to modify substantially his definition of "antisocial, psychopathic personality" when counsel pointed out that the actual facts of Segna's life did not coincide with the symptoms which Dr. Gorman had originally stated were characteristic. Finally, Gorman was required to engage in rather farfetched speculation to account for Segna's pre-killing assertions that he was an Indian.

The jury resolved the evidentiary conflict against Segna. On appeal, he asks us to conclude that Gorman's testimony was completely discredited as a matter of law and that accordingly it cannot sustain a guilty verdict. We decline so to hold.

[*Interesting procedural issues are resolved in sustaining the trial court's holding.*]

Segna raises one issue on appeal which we believe should be addressed in an effort to avoid error in the trial on remand. Segna requested, but was refused, an instruction defining the term wrongfulness in the *Wade* test of legal insanity.[2] He proposed to define wrongfulness as meaning: "moral wrongfulness rather than criminal wrongfulness. In other words, if you find that the defendant, because of a mental disease or defect, lacked substantial capacity to appreciate the moral wrongfulness of his conduct even if he knows his conduct to be criminal but so commits it because of a delusion that he was morally justified then your verdict must be not guilty."

The district judge refused the instruction because he felt that the term moral added nothing and would only confuse the jury.

One of the classic debates in criminal law has centered on the meaning of the words wrong and wrongfulness as they are used in the various definitions of criminal responsibility. In this context, the word wrong has three possible definitions. First, the word may mean legally wrong, or "contrary to law." Thus a person is criminally responsible if he has substantial capacity to appreciate that his act violates the law. Second, the word may mean "contrary to public morality." Here a person is criminally responsible, regardless of his appreciation of his act's legal wrongfulness, if he is aware at the time of the offending act that society morally condemns such acts. Third, the word may mean "contrary to one's own conscience." Under this "subjective" approach, the accused is not criminally responsible for his offending act if, because of mental disease or defect, he believes that he is morally justified in his conduct—even though he may appreciate either that his act is criminal or that it is contrary to public morality.

In *Wade*, we adopted the third definition by choosing the alternate word wrongfulness[3] in the American Law Institute's test of legal insanity, rather than the Institute's initially accepted word criminality, and by then defining wrongfulness in subjective terms. In our view, use of the word wrongfulness in the test of legal insanity would "exclude from the criminally responsible category those who, knowing an act to be criminal, committed it because of a delusion that the act was morally justified" (*Wade*).

---

[2] A person is not responsible for criminal conduct if at the time of such conduct as a result of mental disease or defect he lacks substantial capacity either to appreciate the criminality (wrongfulness) of his conduct or to conform his conduct to the requirements of law (*Wade*).

[3] It is clear from the ALI debates leading to inclusion of the alternative word wrongfulness in the ALI test that the drafters intended that word to mean more than contrary to law. It is less clear, however, whether the drafters intended this expanded term to be measured objectively or subjectively, that is, whether they favored the second or the third definition of wrong. Nevertheless, the weight of the discussions points toward a preference for the third definition.

But one word can carry only a limited conceptual burden. Accordingly, in *McGraw*, we found it necessary to reverse and remand a case because the district court had refused to give a requested instruction elaborating on the meaning of the word wrongfulness. There, both sides had introduced expert testimony that because of mental illness McGraw believed that he was morally justified in committing the act, although the government's expert opined

> *In our view, use of the word wrongfulness in the test of legal insanity would "exclude from the criminally responsible category those who, knowing an act to be criminal, committed it because of a delusion that the act was morally justified."*

that McGraw did not lack the capacity to appreciate that society considered his conduct to be wrong. Likewise, in *Sullivan*, we reversed and remanded because the district court had refused a clarifying instruction on wrongfulness. As in *McGraw*, evidence arose during the course of the trial that Sullivan committed the criminal act under a false belief, resulting from a mental disease, that the act was morally justified.

The government argues that a clarifying, amplifying instruction is proper only when an expert witness concludes that the defendant lacks substantial capacity to appreciate the moral wrongfulness of his conduct. *Segna* suggests that the term wrongfulness is always ambiguous and that a clarifying instruction must be given on request. We reject both extremes and adhere to a more traditional rule that the district court must, when properly requested, instruct on the issue if the record contains evidentiary support for the defendant's theory that, although he realized the offending act was illegal, because of mental disease he possessed a false belief that the act was morally justified.

Reversed and remanded.

United States v. Dubray

854 F.2d 1099 (1988)

Facts

In March 1987, Pershing Dubray sexually assaulted a 60-year-old nun in her home. At trial, he presented an insanity defense. Testimony from the victim indicated that he spoke to the victim throughout the ordeal and suggested that he understood the wrongfulness of his conduct. A psychiatrist for the defense testified that Dubray had "the potential for a transient psychotic episode" which could have produced "a moral and cognitive break from reality." He was convicted of aggravated sexual assault, and he appealed on three issues.

Issues

First, does the presence of a "transient psychotic episode" constitute insanity? Second, was the court required to explain the distinction between criminal and moral wrongfulness to the jury? Third, did the government's expert witness violate the federal prohibition on ultimate opinion testimony when he refuted the defense psychiatrist's opinion that Dubray had a psychotic illness?

Holding

No, to all three questions.

Analysis

Regarding Dubray's first claim, the court clarified that the mere presence of a mental illness is insufficient to constitute an insanity defense. Rather, the mental illness must prevent the individual from appreciating the nature and quality or the wrongfulness of his act. Moreover, this case reinforced the existing burden and standard of proof.

Second, Dubray argued that the trial court should have instructed the jury regarding the distinction between criminal and moral wrongfulness. Citing *Sullivan*, the court noted that a delusional belief that one's actions are morally justified may establish an insanity defense, even when the defendant knows the conduct is illegal. Here, the court ruled that an instruction to the jury regarding criminal versus moral wrongfulness should occur only when evidence at the trial suggests that there is a meaningful distinction between the two.

Finally, the court rejected the argument that the prosecution expert addressed the ultimate issue. Although the court acknowledged that the prosecution expert's testimony had "definite implications" for Dubray's insanity defense, this is true for all expert testimony. The government's witness testified to the medical question of psychosis, not the legal question of sanity.

Edited Excerpts[1]

Opinion by Arnold, Circuit Judge

Pershing Dubray appeals from his conviction for aggravated sexual assault. Dubray admits that he committed rape on the Pine Ridge Indian Reservation on March 29, 1987. His only defense at trial was that he was insane at the time of the rape within the meaning of [federal statute]. On appeal, Dubray raises three grounds of error in his trial relating to his affirmative defense of insanity. We find no merit in these grounds, and so we affirm.

On the night of March 28, 1987, Dubray, a nineteen-year-old member of the Oglala Sioux tribe, had been out drinking with friends. In the early morning hours of March 29, he entered the mobile home of a 60-year-old Roman Catholic nun who lived on church property on the Pine Ridge reservation. For approximately four hours, Dubray struggled with the victim, beat her, pinned her to the bed, broke her wrist, threatened to kill her, and raped her.

The next day, police investigators arrested Dubray. After being advised of his rights, Dubray told the police that he had entered the victim's trailer, announcing "Lucifer is here," that he had fought with and raped the victim, and that he had later lost his memory until his arrest. Further investigation revealed that four years earlier, when Dubray was fifteen years old, he had been convicted of raping a 71-year-old nun at the same location under virtually identical circumstances.

> **Dubray entered the nun's trailer, announcing "Lucifer is here."**

At trial, the prosecution presented extensive testimony from the victim of the rape, who gave a detailed account of the attack. The nun testified that her attacker was lucid, speaking to her throughout the attack, and

---

[1] Readers are advised to quote only from the original published cases. See pages vi and vii.

that he appeared to know who she was and where they were. Each side presented psychiatric testimony on Dubray's sanity. Defendant's expert witness, Dr. Lord, testified that Dubray might have had the potential for a transient psychotic episode, which could have produced a moral and cognitive break from reality. The prosecution's expert, Dr. Kennelly, testified that nothing in the victim's account of her attacker suggested that Dubray was suffering from a transient psychosis, and that direct examination of Dubray did not reveal any evidence that he was psychotic at the time of the rape. The jury rejected Dubray's insanity defense, and found him guilty of aggravated sexual assault.

[*Some interesting procedural issues are resolved.*]

Dubray argues next that the trial court erred in refusing to submit his proposed insanity defense instruction to the jury. Dubray asked that the jury be instructed that "wrongfulness" implies moral, rather than criminal, wrongdoing, and proposed the verdict drawing this distinction discussed in *Segna*. Like the Ninth Circuit, our Court recognizes that a defendant's delusional belief that his criminal conduct is morally justified may

> **Dubray asked that the jury be instructed that "wrongfulness" implies moral, rather than criminal, wrongdoing.**

establish an insanity defense under federal law, even where the defendant knows that the conduct is illegal. See *United States v. Ming Sen Shiue.* The jury should be instructed on the distinction between moral and legal wrongfulness, however, only where evidence at trial suggests that this is a meaningful distinction in the circumstances of the case.

In this case, there is no evidence that Dubray knew that he was violating the law but nonetheless believed that he was acting morally. The

> **The jury should be instructed on the distinction between moral and legal wrongfulness only where evidence at trial suggests that this is a meaningful distinction in the circumstances of the case.**

unsuccessful defense case for insanity relied on psychiatric evidence which suggested a complete break with reality, rather than a mental state in which Dubray would have thought of rape as a morally necessary act proscribed by the law. Nothing in the trial record provides a basis on which the jury could believe that Dubray's understanding of moral wrongfulness somehow diverged from his understanding of the legal significance of rape. Because the moral/legal distinction was unnecessary to the jury's consideration of Dubray's defense, the trial court properly refused the defense's proposed instruction.

The conviction of Pershing Dubray is affirmed.

Summary

These cases highlight the imprecision that remains in some insanity language, and they make evident the often speculative nature of trying to determine what a person does or does not know. Not only is it difficult to determine what a person did or did not know, it is often unclear what knowledge is to be evaluated. It may be helpful to consider a statement from the *M'Naghten* panel in this regard: "If the question were to be put as to the knowledge of the accused solely and exclusively to the law of the land, it might tend to confound the jury, by inducing them to believe that an actual knowledge of the law of the land was essential in order to lead to a conviction; whereas the law is administered upon the principle that every one must be taken conclusively to know it, without proof that he does know it."

The most helpful part of a mental health expert's evaluation could be to consider the impediments in any "knowing" on the part of the defendant. What does it really mean to "know" that one's actions are wrong? Does this mean that one knows *why* an action is wrong? If someone knows it is *considered* wrong to commit an action, but believes that the act is nonetheless justified, does the person really *appreciate* that the action is wrong? We see very easily that the questions may have inherent limits on being answered definitively, even if we were able to assess *knowledge* to such levels of precision.

Section 6

What to Do With Insanity Acquittees?

Introduction to Section 6

Cases

   Lyles v. United States

   Jones v. United States

   Foucha v. Louisiana

Summary

Introduction to Section 6

In the case of Hadfield, who was found not guilty due to insanity for attempting to kill King George, England was confronted with the common problem of what to do with dangerous individuals who are not responsible for their actions. They passed new laws to deal with those individuals, and Hadfield remained in custody for the rest of his life. Balancing fair treatment for an accused who is not legally culpable with safety for the other members of society has remained a complex task. This chapter looks at three cases that have dealt with the disposition of not guilty by reason of insanity (NGRI) acquittees and the way that disposition should be considered at trial.

In *Lyles v. United States* (1957), the United States Court of Appeals for the District of Columbia Circuit addressed the issue of what a jury should be told about the disposition of a defendant who is found not guilty by reason of insanity. Although the fate of defendants found guilty or not guilty was common knowledge, the consequence of being found not guilty by reason of insanity was not. Reasoning that jurors might be influenced in their deliberations by a fear that the defendant would return to the community, the Court of Appeals addressed the issue of what information was appropriate for a jury when a defendant was asserting an insanity defense.

In *Jones v. United States* (1983), the United States Supreme Court addressed the issue of whether a defendant found not guilty by reason of insanity (in this case, for attempting to steal a jacket) could be held in an institution beyond the length of sentence he would have received if convicted of the offense. In its analysis, the Court made interesting assumptions about a defendant's dangerousness based on the NGRI finding. They distinguished this situation from that of a defendant committed to restore competency to stand trial (*Jackson v. Indiana*). They also distinguished the situation of an NGRI acquittee from that of a convicted offender, emphasizing that acquittees are committed for treatment and not for punishment. Using this reasoning they concluded that the length of a potential sentence to punish a culpable person was unrelated to the length of a civil commitment needed to treat the NGRI acquittee's mental disorder which made them a danger.

In *Foucha v. Louisiana* (1992), the United States Supreme Court again addressed the issue of an NGRI acquittee's commitment. In this case the Court was confronted with a state law that allowed for the continued confinement of a dangerous NGRI acquittee who was no longer mentally ill (and who may never have truly been mentally ill). They addressed the issues of due process and equal protection for persons found not guilty by reason of insanity. Although such individuals were not entitled to the same due process rights as civilly committed individuals from the community (under *Jones*), the Court held that an NGRI finding did not allow for indefinite commitment solely for dangerousness when an individual was no longer mentally ill.

Lyles v. United States

254 F.2d 275 (1957)

Facts

Archibald Lyles was indicted in 1954 for robbery, grand larceny, and unauthorized use of a motor vehicle. In February 1955, it was determined that he was not competent to stand trial, and he was committed to St. Elizabeths Hospital for treatment. In November 1955, he was declared competent and ordered to trial. At trial, he pleaded not guilty and relied on a defense of insanity. During instructions to the jury, the trial judge informed the jury that if Lyles were found not guilty by reason of insanity, he would be committed to St. Elizabeths until he was deemed safe to be released, and he would have no further consequences from the offense. He reminded the jurors that a doctor at St. Elizabeths had previously determined that Lyles had no mental disorder. The jury returned a verdict of guilty. He was sentenced and this appeal followed.

Issue

Although there were several issues on appeal, the issue of relevance here concerns the judge's instructions regarding the consequences of a verdict of not guilty by reason of insanity. In cases where the insanity defense is asserted, what, if anything, should the court instruct the jury about the consequences of a verdict of not guilty by reason of insanity?

Holding

The court should inform the jury that if the defendant is found not guilty by reason of insanity, he would be confined in a hospital until he had "recovered his sanity" and would not be a danger to himself or others. This instruction must be given unless the record reflects an affirmative waiver of the instruction on the part of the defendant.

Analysis

The appeals court reasoned that it was common knowledge that a verdict of guilty would lead to punishment, and a verdict of not guilty would mean the defendant goes free. On the other hand, they believed it was not common knowledge that a verdict of not guilty by reason of insanity "means neither freedom nor punishment." They believed the jury had a right to know the meaning of this verdict. The court also reasoned that a jury determining a defendant's mental state at the time of the offense (criminal responsibility) had no need to know about the defendant's mental state at the time of the trial (competency to stand trial), which was an issue solely for the judge. The jury also had no concern with the defendant's future mental state (when or whether the defendant would be released) or the related responsibilities of the hospital superintendent and the trial court. Although the appeals court believed the trial judge in Lyles' case used language in his instruction to the jury "not as precise as it might have been in stating the content of the statute," they did not find the error was sufficiently egregious to justify reversal. Lyles' conviction was affirmed.

Edited Excerpts[1]

Prettyman and Burger, Circuit Judges

Appellant was indicted in December 1954 for robbery, grand larceny, and unauthorized use of a motor vehicle. In a hearing conducted in February 1955 it was determined that he was not mentally competent to stand trial; accordingly he was committed to an institution to remain in custody until he was competent to be tried. Another hearing as to his competency was held in November 1955 and he was then judicially declared competent to be tried and was ordered to trial. On trial he pleaded not guilty and relied on a defense of insanity. The grand larceny charge was dismissed by the prosecution. The jury returned a verdict of guilty as to robbery and unauthorized use of a motor vehicle. He was duly sentenced and this appeal followed.

We consider [among several issues]: In cases where the defense of insanity is asserted what, if anything, should the court instruct the jury about the consequences of a verdict of not guilty by reason of insanity?

The judge told the jury: "If a defendant is found not guilty on the ground of insanity, it then becomes the duty of the Court to commit him to St. Elizabeths Hospital, and this the Court would do. The defendant then would remain at St. Elizabeths Hospital until he is cured and it is deemed safe to release him; and when that time arrives he will be released and will suffer no further consequences from this offense."

This point arises under the doctrine, well established and sound, that the jury has no concern with the consequences of a verdict, either in the

---

[1] Readers are advised to quote only from the original published cases. See pages vi and vii.

sentence, if any, or the nature or extent of it, or in probation. But we think that doctrine does not apply in the problem before us. The issue of insanity having been fairly raised, the jury may return one of three verdicts, guilty, not guilty, or not guilty by reason of insanity. Jurors, in common with people in general, are aware of the meanings of verdicts of guilty and not

> **But a verdict of not guilty by reason of insanity has no such commonly understood meaning. It means neither freedom nor punishment.**

guilty. It is common knowledge that a verdict of not guilty means that the prisoner goes free and that a verdict of guilty means that he is subject to such punishment as the court may impose. But a verdict of not guilty by reason of insanity has no such commonly understood meaning. As a matter of fact its meaning was not made clear in this jurisdiction until Congress enacted the statute of August 9, 1955. It means neither freedom nor punishment. It means the accused will be confined in a hospital for the mentally ill until the superintendent of such hospital certifies, and the court is satisfied, that such person has recovered his sanity and will not in the reasonable future be dangerous to himself or others. We think the jury has a right to know the meaning of this possible verdict as accurately as it knows by common knowledge the meaning of the other two possible verdicts.

We do not prescribe a form of instruction. We think a recitation of the statutory procedure in great detail, such as reading the entire section of the statute, would tend to increase confusion. We think that when the instruction is given the jury should simply be informed that a verdict of not guilty by reason of insanity means that the accused will be confined

> **We think that when the instruction is given the jury should simply be informed that a verdict of not guilty by reason of insanity means that the accused will be confined in a hospital for the mentally ill until he has recovered his sanity and will not in the reasonable future be dangerous to himself or to others.**

in a hospital for the mentally ill until the superintendent has certified, and the court is satisfied, that such person has recovered his sanity and will not in the reasonable future be dangerous to himself or to others, in which event and at which time the court shall order his release either unconditionally or under such conditions as the court may see fit.

Sometimes a defendant may not want such an instruction given. If that appears affirmatively on the record we would not regard failure to give it as grounds for reversal. Otherwise, whenever hereafter the defense of insanity is fairly raised, the trial judge shall instruct the jury as to the legal meaning of a verdict of not guilty by reason of insanity in accordance with the view expressed in this opinion.

The language used by the trial court in the present case is not as precise as it might have been in stating the content of the statute. But we think this failure is not error sufficient to require or justify reversal.

Having made to the jury the statement above quoted and discussed, the trial judge immediately said: "I think I should add that Dr. Cushard of St. Elizabeths Hospital testified, as you will recall, that on a prior occasion he found no mental disorder whatever in the defendant, and that the defendant was a man of average intelligence."

Dr. Cushard had so testified. The question is whether the trial judge erred in making the quoted remark at the time and in the context in which he made it. Clearly the trial judge could summarize and comment upon this part of the evidence, as he could upon all or any of the evidence, when he was summarizing the evidence in the case. Error is urged because he called attention to this evidence not in the course of his summation of evidence but in immediate connection with his statement to the jury that if acquitted by reason of insanity Lyles would be committed to a mental institution. The quoted remark is said to convey an emphatic inference that if so committed Lyles would shortly be released.

In a criminal case claims of insanity are possibly pertinent at three points of time, (1) the time of the offense, (2) the time of the trial, and (3) the time of possible release after acquittal by reason of insanity. [With respect to] potential release from commitment, the question is whether the accused has regained his sanity and whether he will in the reasonable future be dangerous to himself or others. That determination is confided by the statute in the superintendent of the hospital and the court. The function of each is a real responsibility.

This [consideration is] different from the question of mental responsibility for the alleged criminal act and from the question of mental competency to stand trial. It involves the possible danger attending the release of the accused. The jury upon the trial has no concern with the mental state of the accused at some future time, or with what the superintendent of the hospital may some day certify, or with what the court may thereafter find. These questions are in the future and cannot be determined as of the time of trial. They are by statute for the court and the superintendent, not for a jury—*a fortiori*[2] not for the jury in the box at the trial for the offense. The jury is entitled to know, as we have said, the legal significance of a verdict they are called upon to consider as part of their duty at the trial. They have no concern with a factual situation which may or may not develop in any one of many possible combinations of circumstances after their duties have been discharged and they are gone from the case. Evidence in respect to what the situation might be when in the future the problem of release from commitment arises is inadmissible at the trial. Evidence as to present mental disease may, as we have already twice said, be relevant and material to the problem of mental disease at the time of the offense, and it is admissible for that purpose. But such evidence is not admissible for the purpose of attempting to show the probable mental condition of the accused at some future time of possible release.

From the foregoing it necessarily follows that, if the judge submits to the jury the question of probable release of the accused at some future date, submits evidence to them upon that point, or comments to them respecting the speculative possibilities in that regard, he commits error.

In the case at bar the remark of the judge was a single sentence in the middle of a long charge. Moreover the court did not relate the remark of the doctor to the time of the trial or to any possible future time. The judge said that "on a prior occasion" the doctor found no mental disorder in the defendant; he did not identify the time of the prior occasion. No objection was made to the charge as given although prior notice of intention to object had been given. It seems to us that, in view of the nature of the remark, the fact that the judge did not emphasize it or impress it upon the jury unduly, the fact that he dated the opinion of the doctor as of an indefinite past time, the remark cannot be held to have affected substantial rights of the accused. We decline to reverse this case on this point.

The judgment of the District Court is Affirmed.

---

[2] *a fortiori.* With even better reason.

Jones v. United States

463 U.S. 354 (1983)

Facts

In September 1975, Michael Jones was arrested for petit larceny (attempted theft of a jacket), a misdemeanor, in the District of Columbia. He was committed to St. Elizabeths for a determination of his competency to stand trial. The evaluating psychologist reported he was competent to stand trial, suffered from schizophrenia, and his offense was a "product" of his mental disease. He subsequently pled and was found not guilty by reason of insanity. He was committed to St. Elizabeths as mentally ill and a danger to himself and others. At a second release hearing in February 1977, by which time he had been hospitalized more than a year, he demanded he be released unconditionally or recommitted under civil-commitment standards which would include a jury trial and proof of his mental illness and dangerousness by clear and convincing evidence. The Superior Court denied Jones's request. The District of Columbia Court of Appeals reversed, but then reheard the case *en banc*[1] and affirmed the judgment of the Superior Court. The U.S. Supreme Court then granted certiorari.

Issue

Must a defendant, who has been committed to a mental hospital following an acquittal by reason of insanity, be released because he has been hospitalized for a period longer than he would have served in prison if he had been convicted?

Holding

No.

Analysis

Jones argued that a finding of not guilty by reason of insanity did not afford a defendant the civil-commitment due process protections which the Court had established in *O'Connor v. Donaldson* and *Addington v. Texas*. He asserted that because he has been confined as long as he might

---

[1] *en banc.* With all members of the appellate court.

have been if convicted, he should be afforded these due process protections. The Court, however, held that a not guilty by reason of insanity finding was "sufficiently probative of mental illness and dangerousness to justify commitment" because it establishes: "(i) the defendant committed an act that constitutes a criminal offense, and (ii) he committed the act because of his mental illness." The Court concluded that a finding beyond a reasonable doubt that a person committed a criminal act "certainly indicates dangerousness." The Court distinguished this case from *Jackson v. Indiana*, because the purpose of the civil commitment was to protect the individual and society from his dangerousness, the treatment for which would not be related to the length of potential sentence he might have received if convicted.

Edited Excerpts[2]

Opinion: Justice Powell delivered the opinion of the Court.

The question presented is whether petitioner, who was committed to a mental hospital upon being acquitted of a criminal offense by reason of insanity, must be released because he has been hospitalized for a period longer than he might have served in prison had he been convicted. In the District of Columbia a criminal defendant may be acquitted by reason of insanity if his insanity is "affirmatively established by a preponderance of the evidence." If he successfully invokes the insanity defense, he is committed to a mental hospital. The statute provides several ways of obtaining release. Within 50 days of commitment the acquittee is entitled to a judicial hearing to determine his eligibility for release, at which he has the burden of proving by a preponderance of the evidence that he is no longer mentally ill or dangerous. If he fails to meet this burden at the 50-day hearing, the committed acquittee subsequently may be released, with court approval, upon certification of his recovery by the hospital chief of service. Alternatively, the acquittee is entitled to a judicial hearing every six months at which he may establish by a preponderance of the evidence that he is entitled to release.

Independent of its provision for the commitment of insanity acquittees, the District of Columbia also has adopted a civil-commitment procedure, under which an individual may be committed upon clear and convincing proof by the Government that he is mentally ill and likely to injure himself or others. The individual may demand a jury in the civil-commitment proceeding. Once committed, a patient may be released at any time upon certification of recovery by the hospital chief of service. Alternatively,

---

[2] Readers are advised to quote only from the original published cases. See pages vi and vii.

the patient is entitled after the first 90 days, and subsequently at 6-month intervals, to request a judicial hearing at which he may gain his release by proving by a preponderance of the evidence that he is no longer mentally ill or dangerous.

On September 19, 1975, petitioner was arrested for attempting to steal a jacket from a department store. The next day he was arraigned in the District of Columbia Superior Court on a charge of attempted petit larceny, a misdemeanor punishable by a maximum prison sentence of one year. The court ordered petitioner committed to St. Elizabeths, a public hospital for the mentally ill, for a determination of his competency to stand trial. On March 1, 1976, a hospital psychologist submitted a report to the court stating that petitioner was competent to stand trial, that petitioner suffered from "Schizophrenia, paranoid type," and that petitioner's alleged offense was "the product of his mental disease." The court ruled that petitioner was competent to stand trial. Petitioner subsequently decided to plead not guilty by reason of insanity. The Government did not contest the plea, and it entered into a stipulation of facts with petitioner. On March 12, 1976, the Superior Court found petitioner not guilty by reason of insanity and committed him to St. Elizabeths.

On May 25, 1976, the court held the 50-day hearing. A psychologist from St. Elizabeths testified on behalf of the Government that, in the opinion of the staff, petitioner continued to suffer from paranoid schizophrenia and that "because his illness is still quite active, he is still a danger to himself and to others." Petitioner's counsel conducted a brief cross-examination, and presented no evidence. The court then found that "the defendant-patient is mentally ill and as a result of his mental illness, at this time, he constitutes a danger to himself or others." Petitioner was returned to St. Elizabeths. Petitioner obtained new counsel and, following some procedural confusion, a second release hearing was held on February 22, 1977. By that date petitioner had been hospitalized for more than one year, the maximum period he could have spent in prison if he had been convicted. On that basis he demanded that he be released unconditionally or recommitted pursuant to civil-commitment standards, including a jury trial and proof by clear and convincing evidence of his mental illness and dangerousness. The Superior Court denied petitioner's request for a civil-commitment hearing, reaffirmed the findings made at the May 25, 1976 hearing, and continued petitioner's commitment to St. Elizabeths.

Petitioner appealed to the District of Columbia Court of Appeals. A panel of the court affirmed the Superior Court, but then granted rehearing and reversed. Finally, the court heard the case *en banc* and affirmed the judgment of the Superior Court. The Court of Appeals rejected the argument "that the length of the prison sentence petitioner might have received determines when he is entitled to release or civil commitment under D.C. Code." It then held that the various statutory differences between civil commitment and commitment of insanity acquittees were justified under the equal protection component of the Fifth Amendment.[3]

We granted certiorari and now affirm.

It is clear that "commitment for any purpose constitutes a significant deprivation of liberty that requires due process protection" (*Addington v. Texas*). Therefore, a State must have "a constitutionally adequate purpose for the confinement" (*O'Connor v. Donaldson*). Congress has determined that a criminal defendant found not guilty by reason of insanity in the District of Columbia should be committed indefinitely to a mental institution for treatment and the protection of society. Petitioner does not contest the Government's authority to commit a mentally ill and dangerous person indefinitely to a mental institution, but rather contends that "the petitioner's trial was not a constitutionally adequate hearing to justify an indefinite commitment."

Petitioner's argument rests principally on *Addington*, in which the Court held that the Due Process Clause requires the State in a civil-commitment proceeding to demonstrate by clear and convincing evidence that the individual is mentally ill and dangerous. Petitioner contends that these due process standards were not met in his case because the judgment of not guilty by reason of insanity did not constitute a finding of present mental illness and dangerousness and because it was established only by a preponderance of the evidence. Petitioner then concludes that the Government's only conceivably legitimate justification for automatic commitment is to ensure that insanity acquittees do not escape confinement entirely, and that this interest can justify commitment at most for a period equal to the maximum prison sentence the acquittee could have received if convicted. Because petitioner has been hospitalized for longer than the one year he might have served in prison, he asserts that he should be released unconditionally or recommitted under the District's civil-commitment procedures.

We turn first to the question whether the finding of insanity at the criminal trial is sufficiently probative of mental illness and dangerousness to justify commitment. A verdict of not guilty by reason of insanity establishes two facts: (i) the defendant committed an act that constitutes a criminal offense, and (ii) he committed the act because of mental illness. Congress has determined that these findings constitute an adequate basis

---

[3] See Appendix B (pp. 291-292).

for hospitalizing the acquittee as a dangerous and mentally ill person (expressing fear that "dangerous criminals, particularly psychopaths, may win acquittals of serious criminal charges on grounds of insanity" and yet "escape hospital commitment." "Where the accused has pleaded insanity as a defense to a crime, and the jury has found that the defendant was, in fact, insane at the time the crime was committed, it is just and reasonable in the Committee's opinion that the insanity, once established, should be presumed to continue and that the accused should automatically be confined for treatment until it can be shown that he has recovered"). We cannot say that it was unreasonable and therefore unconstitutional for Congress to make this determination.

The fact that a person has been found, beyond a reasonable doubt, to have committed a criminal act certainly indicates dangerousness. See *Lynch v. Overholser*. (The fact that the accused was found to have committed a criminal act is "strong evidence that his continued liberty could imperil 'the preservation of public peace' "). Indeed, this concrete evidence generally may be at least as persuasive as any predictions about dangerousness that might be made in a civil-commitment proceeding. We do not agree with petitioner's suggestion that the requisite dangerousness is not established by proof that a person committed a nonviolent crime against property. This Court never has held that "violence," however that term might be defined, is a prerequisite for a constitutional commitment.[4]

> *This Court never has held that "violence," however that term might be defined, is a prerequisite for a constitutional commitment.*

The judgment of the District of Columbia Court of Appeals is Affirmed.

> *To describe the theft of watches and jewelry as "nondangerous" is to confuse danger with violence.*

---

[4] See *Overholser v. O'Beirne*. ("To describe the theft of watches and jewelry as 'nondangerous' is to confuse danger with violence. Larceny is usually less violent than murder or assault, but in terms of public policy the purpose of the statute is the same as to both.") Thus, the "danger" may be to property rights as well as to persons. It also may be noted that crimes of theft frequently may result in violence from the efforts of the criminal to escape or the victim to protect property or the police to apprehend the fleeing criminal.

Dissent: Justice Brennan, with whom Justice Marshall and Justice Blackmun join, dissenting.

None of our precedents directly addresses the meaning of due process in the context of involuntary commitments of persons who have been acquitted by reason of insanity. Petitioner's argument rests primarily on two cases dealing with civil commitments: *O'Connor* and *Addington*. *O'Connor* held that a mentally ill individual has a "right to liberty" that a State may not abridge by confining him to a mental institution, even for the purpose of treating his illness, unless in addition to being mentally ill he is likely to harm himself or others if released. Then, in *Addington*, we carefully evaluated the standard of proof in civil commitment proceedings. We held that "due process requires the state to justify confinement by proof more substantial than a mere preponderance of the evidence," specifically "clear and convincing evidence."

The core of both cases is a balance of three factors: the governmental interest in isolating and treating those who may be mentally ill and dangerous; the difficulty of proving or disproving mental illness and dangerousness in court; and the massive intrusion on individual liberty that involuntary psychiatric hospitalization entails. Petitioner contends that the same balance must be struck in this case, and that the Government has no greater interest in committing him indefinitely than it has in ordinary civil commitment cases governed by the standards of *O'Connor* and *Addington*. While conceding that the Government may have legitimate reasons to commit insanity acquittees for some definite period without carrying the burden of proof prescribed in *Addington*,[5] he argues that he

---

[5] Petitioner does not dispute that the Government may commit him solely on the basis of his insanity acquittal for a definite period—as long as he could have been incarcerated had he been convicted on the criminal charges against him rather than acquitted by reason of insanity. The issue, therefore, is not whether due process forbids treating insanity acquittees differently from other candidates for commitment. Petitioner is willing to concede that they may be treated differently for some purposes, and for a limited period of time. The dispute before us, rather, concerns the question whether the differences between insanity acquittees and other candidates for civil commitment justify committing insanity acquittees indefinitely, without the Government ever having to meet the procedural requirements of *Addington*.

A number of our decisions have countenanced involuntary commitment without the full protections of *Addington* and *O'Connor*, but for the most part these have involved persons already in custody and strictly limited periods of psychiatric institutionalization. E.g., *Jackson v. Indiana* (acknowledging that the State's interest in determining whether an accused would become competent to stand trial in the foreseeable future justified commitment "for a reasonable period of time"); *McNeil v. Director, Patuxent Institution* (accepting the legitimacy of short-term commitment of a convicted criminal for psychiatric evaluation); *Humphrey v. Cady* (commitment of convicted sex offender, limited to duration of sentence); *Baxstrom v. Herold* (commitment of prison inmates who are determined to be mentally ill during their prison term). See also *Parham v. J. R. (burden* and standard of proof in short-term civil commitment).

cannot be confined indefinitely unless the Government accords him the minimum due process protections required for civil commitment.

The obvious difference between insanity acquittees and other candidates for civil commitment is that, at least in the District of Columbia, an acquittal by reason of insanity implies a determination beyond a reasonable doubt that the defendant in fact committed the criminal act with which he was charged. The Court holds that a finding of insanity at a criminal trial "is sufficiently probative of mental illness and dangerousness to justify commitment." First, it declares that "the fact that a person has been found, beyond a reasonable doubt, to have committed a criminal act certainly indicates dangerousness." Second, the Court decides that "it comports with common sense to conclude that someone whose mental illness was sufficient to lead him to commit a criminal act is likely to remain ill and in need of treatment." Despite their superficial appeal, these propositions cannot support the decision necessary to the Court's disposition of this case—that the Government may be excused from carrying the *Addington* burden of proof with respect to each of the *O'Connor* elements of mental illness and dangerousness in committing petitioner for an indefinite period.

Our precedents in other commitment contexts are inconsistent with the argument that the mere facts of past criminal behavior and mental illness justify indefinite commitment without the benefits of the minimum due process standards associated with civil commitment, most importantly proof of present mental illness and dangerousness by clear and convincing evidence. In *Addington* itself, the petitioner did not dispute that he had engaged in a wide variety of assaultive conduct that could have been the basis for criminal charges had the State chosen to prosecute him. Similarly, the petitioner in *Jackson v. Indiana* had been charged with two robberies, yet we required the State to follow its civil commitment procedures if it wished to commit him for more than a strictly limited period. As the Court indicates, these cases are perhaps distinguishable on the ground that there was never proof that a crime had been committed, although in *Addington* the petitioner's violent acts were before the jury. That objection, however, cannot be leveled at *Baxstrom v. Herold* or *Humphrey v. Cady*.

The petitioner in *Baxstrom* had been convicted of assault and sentenced to a term in prison, during which he was certified as insane by a prison physician. At the expiration of his criminal sentence, he was committed involuntarily to a state mental hospital under procedures substantially less protective than those used for civil commitment. We held that, once he had served his sentence, Baxstrom could not be treated differently from other candidates for civil commitment. The principal difference between this case and *Baxstrom* is petitioner's admission, intrinsic to an insanity plea in the District of Columbia at the time of his trial, that his crime was "the product" of his mental illness.

The Government's interests in committing petitioner are the same interests involved in *Addington, O'Connor, Baxstrom,* and *Humphrey*— isolation, protection, and treatment of a person who may, through no fault of his own, cause harm to others or to himself. Whenever involuntary commitment is a possibility, the Government has a strong interest in accurate, efficient commitment decisions. Nevertheless, *Addington* held both that the government's interest in accuracy was not impaired by a requirement that it bear the burden of persuasion by clear and convincing evidence, and that the individual's interests in liberty and autonomy required the government to bear at least that burden. An acquittal by reason of insanity of a single, nonviolent misdemeanor is not a constitutionally adequate substitute for the due process protections of *Addington* and *O'Connor*, i.e., proof by clear and convincing evidence of present mental illness or dangerousness, with the government bearing the burden of persuasion.

It is worth examining what is known about the possibility of predicting dangerousness from any set of facts. Although a substantial body of research suggests that a consistent pattern of violent behavior may, from a purely statistical standpoint, indicate a certain likelihood of further violence in the future, mere statistical validity is far from perfect for purposes of predicting which individuals will be dangerous. Commentators and researchers have long acknowledged that even the best attempts to identify dangerous individuals on the basis of specified facts have been inaccurate roughly two-thirds of the time, almost always on the side of over-prediction. On a clinical basis, mental health professionals can diagnose past or present mental condition with some confidence, but

> *Strong institutional biases lead [mental health professionals to overpredict] when they attempt to determine an individual's dangerousness, especially when the consequence of a finding of dangerousness is that an obviously mentally ill patient will remain within their control. (Brennan, dissenting)*

strong institutional biases lead them to err when they attempt to determine an individual's dangerousness, especially when the consequence of a finding of dangerousness is that an obviously mentally ill patient will remain within their control. Research is practically nonexistent on the relationship of nonviolent criminal behavior, such as petitioner's attempt to shoplift, to future dangerousness. We do not even know whether it is even statistically valid as a predictor of similar nonviolent behavior, much less of behavior posing more serious risks to self and others.

Even if an insanity acquittee remains mentally ill, so long as he has not repeated the same act since his offense the passage of time diminishes the likelihood that he will repeat it. Furthermore, the frequency of prior violent behavior is an important element in any attempt to predict future violence. Finally, it cannot be gainsaid that some crimes are more indicative of dangerousness than others. Subject to the limits of *O'Connor*, a State may consider nonviolent misdemeanors "dangerous," but there is room for doubt whether a single attempt to shoplift and a string of brutal murders are equally accurate and equally permanent predictors of dangerousness.

> **There is room for doubt whether a single attempt to shoplift and a string of brutal murders are equally accurate and equally permanent predictors of dangerousness. (Brennan, dissenting)**

Foucha v. Louisiana
504 U.S. 71 (1992)

Facts

Terry Foucha was charged in Louisiana with aggravated burglary and illegal discharge of a firearm. He was initially found incompetent to stand trial and treated. In 1984, he was found not guilty by reason of insanity. He was committed to the East Feliciana Forensic Facility. Under Louisiana law at that time, a defendant found not guilty by reason of insanity was committed to a psychiatric hospital until he proved he was no longer dangerous. In 1988, the superintendent of Feliciana recommended Foucha be released. The trial judge appointed a two-member sanity commission made up of the doctors who conducted the original pretrial evaluations. It was their opinion that Foucha had probably suffered from a drug-induced psychosis, a temporary condition, and had recovered. They said he showed no signs of a psychosis or neurosis but had an antisocial personality disorder, a condition that was not a mental disease and was not treatable. Foucha had been involved in several altercations at Feliciana, and the doctors concluded they could not certify "he would not constitute a menace to himself or others if released."

The Court ruled Foucha was a danger to himself and others and ordered him returned to the mental hospital. The Court of Appeal and Louisiana Supreme Court refused supervisory writs, stating: (a) Foucha had not proved he was not a danger, and (b) the Due Process and Equal Protection Clauses of the Constitution[1] were not violated by the statute which permitted the confinement of an insanity acquittee based on dangerousness alone. Foucha appealed to the United States Supreme Court, arguing that the Louisiana statute denied him due process and equal protection by committing him until he could prove he was not dangerous even though he was no longer mentally ill.

Issue

Does the continued commitment of a defendant who had been found not guilty by reason of insanity but is no longer mentally ill violate the Due Process and Equal Protection Clauses of the Fourteenth Amendment?[2]

[1] Clauses within the Fifth and Fourteenth Amendments; see Appendix B (pp. 291-292).
[2] See Appendix B (pp. 291-292).

Holding

Yes. The judgment of the Louisiana Supreme Court was reversed.

Analysis

Citing their previous decisions in *Addington v. Texas, Jackson v. Indiana, Jones v. United States*, and *O'Connor v. Donaldson*, the Supreme Court concluded that Foucha had not been afforded the same due process and protections given to other mentally ill civilly committed patients. They reasoned that a committed patient such as Foucha could not be distinguished from an inmate who committed a crime and comes to the end of his sentence. Both must have constitutionally adequate procedures. In *Jones* they had concluded that a not guilty by reason of insanity verdict showed that the defendant (a) had committed the crime, and (b) had done so due to mental illness; hence at the time of the verdict, even without a further showing by the state, it could be concluded he was still dangerous and mentally ill. But such an acquittee could only be held until he regained sanity or was no longer dangerous. Louisiana had not contended that Foucha was still mentally ill.

Louisiana had relied on *United States v. Salerno*, a decision upholding the confinement without bail of a pretrial defendant. The Court concluded that the confinement upheld in *Salerno* was narrowly drawn and time limited. The Louisiana statute allowed indefinite confinement with the state required to prove nothing. The doctor had testified only that he would not feel comfortable certifying Foucha would not be a danger. Furthermore, the Court reasoned that if the state was concerned about his violent criminal acts while at Feliciana, they should have prosecuted Foucha criminally. The Court warned that Louisiana's rationale would allow the indefinite commitment of an acquittee who was not mentally ill, based only on a personality disorder leading to dangerousness. They argued that the same could be true of any convicted criminal at the completion of a prison term, which would be "only a step away from substituting confinements for dangerousness for our present system, which incarcerates only those who are proved beyond reasonable doubt to have violated a criminal law" with only narrow exceptions and permissible confinements for mental illness.

Edited Excerpts[3]

Opinion: Justice White delivered the opinion of the Court, except as to Part III.

When a defendant in a criminal case pending in Louisiana is found not guilty by reason of insanity, he is committed to a psychiatric hospital

---

[3] Readers are advised to quote only from the original published cases. See pages vi and vii.

unless he proves that he is not dangerous. This is so whether or not he is then insane. After commitment, if the acquittee or the superintendent begins release proceedings, a review panel at the hospital makes a written report on the patient's mental condition and whether he can be released without danger to himself or others. If release is recommended, the court must hold a hearing to determine dangerousness; the acquittee has the burden of proving that he is not dangerous. If found to be dangerous, the acquittee may be returned to the mental institution whether or not he is then mentally ill. Petitioner contends that this scheme denies him due process and equal protection because it allows a person acquitted by reason of insanity to be committed to a mental institution until he is able to demonstrate that he is not dangerous to himself and others, even though he does not suffer from any mental illness.

Petitioner Terry Foucha was charged by Louisiana authorities with aggravated burglary and illegal discharge of a firearm. Two medical doctors were appointed to conduct a pretrial examination of Foucha. The doctors initially reported, and the trial court initially found, that Foucha lacked mental capacity to proceed, but four months later the trial court found Foucha competent to stand trial. The doctors reported that Foucha was unable to distinguish right from wrong and was insane at the time of the offense. On October 12, 1984, the trial court ruled that Foucha was not guilty by reason of insanity, finding that he "is unable to appreciate the usual, natural and probable consequences of his acts; that he is unable to distinguish right from wrong; that he is a menace to himself and others; and that he was insane at the time of the commission of the above crimes and that he is presently insane." He was committed to the East Feliciana Forensic Facility until such time as doctors recommend that he be released, and until further order of the court. In 1988, the superintendent of Feliciana recommended that Foucha be discharged or released. A three-member panel was convened at the institution to determine Foucha's current condition and whether he could be released or placed on probation without being a danger to others or himself. On March 21, 1988, the panel reported that there had been no evidence of mental illness since admission and recommended that Foucha be conditionally discharged.[4] The trial judge appointed a two-member sanity commission made up of the same two doctors who had conducted the pretrial examination. Their written report stated that Foucha "is presently in remission from mental illness but we cannot certify that he would not constitute a menace to himself or others if released." One of the doctors testified at a hearing that upon commitment Foucha probably suffered from a drug induced psychosis but that he had recovered from that temporary condition; that he evidenced no signs of

---

[4] Although the panel recited that it was charged with determining dangerousness, its report did not expressly make a finding in that regard.

psychosis or neurosis and was in "good shape" mentally; that he had, however, an antisocial personality, a condition that is not a mental disease and that is untreatable. The doctor also testified that Foucha had been involved in several altercations at Feliciana and that he, the doctor, would not "feel comfortable in certifying that Foucha would not be a danger to himself or to other people."

After it was stipulated that the other doctor, if he were present, would give essentially the same testimony, the court ruled that Foucha was dangerous to himself and others and ordered him returned to the mental institution. The Court of Appeal refused supervisory writs, and the State Supreme Court affirmed, holding that Foucha had not carried the burden placed upon him by statute to prove that he was not dangerous, that our decision in *Jones v. United States* did not require Foucha's release, and that neither the Due Process Clause nor the Equal Protection Clause was violated by the statutory provision permitting confinement of an insanity acquittee based on dangerousness alone.

Because the case presents an important issue and was decided by the court below in a manner arguably at odds with prior decisions of this Court, we granted certiorari.

Addington v. Texas held that to commit an individual to a mental institution in a civil proceeding, the State is required by the Due Process Clause to prove by clear and convincing evidence the two statutory preconditions to commitment: that the person sought to be committed is mentally ill and that he requires hospitalization for his own welfare and protection of others. Proof beyond a reasonable doubt was not required, but proof by preponderance of the evidence fell short of satisfying due process.[5]

When a person charged with having committed a crime is found not guilty by reason of insanity, however, a State may commit that person without satisfying the *Addington* burden with respect to mental illness

---

[5] Justice Thomas in dissent complains that Foucha should not be released based on psychiatric opinion that he is not mentally ill because such opinion is not sufficiently precise—because psychiatry is not an exact science and psychiatrists widely disagree on what constitutes a mental illness. That may be true, but such opinion is reliable enough to permit the courts to base civil commitments on clear and convincing medical evidence that a person is mentally ill and dangerous and to base release decisions on qualified testimony that the person is no longer mentally ill or dangerous. It is also reliable enough for the State not to punish a person who by a preponderance of the evidence is found to have been insane at the time he committed a criminal act, to say nothing of not trying a person who is at the time found incompetent to understand the proceedings. And more to the point, medical predictions of dangerousness seem to be reliable enough for Justice Thomas to permit the State to continue to hold Foucha in a mental institution, even where the psychiatrist would say no more than that he would hesitate to certify that Foucha would not be dangerous to himself or others.

and dangerousness (*Jones*). Such a verdict, we observed in *Jones*, "establishes two facts: (i) the defendant committed an act that constitutes a criminal offense, and (ii) he committed the act because of mental illness," an illness that the defendant adequately proved in this context by a preponderance of the evidence. From these two facts, it could be properly inferred that at the time of the verdict, the defendant was still mentally ill and dangerous and hence could be committed.

Justice Kennedy's assertion that we overrule the holding of *Jones* described in the above paragraph is fanciful at best. As that paragraph plainly shows, we do not question and fully accept that insanity acquittees may be initially held without complying with the procedures applicable to civil committees. As is evident from the ensuing paragraph of the text, we are also true to the further holding of *Jones* that both Justice Thomas and Justice Kennedy reject: that the period of time during which an insanity acquittee may be held in a mental institution is not measured by the length of a sentence that might have been imposed had he been convicted; rather, the acquittee may be held until he is either not mentally ill or not dangerous. Both Justices would permit the indefinite detention of the acquittee, although the State concedes that he is not mentally ill and although the doctors at the mental institution recommend his release, for no reason other than that a psychiatrist hesitates to certify that the acquittee would not be dangerous to himself or others.

Justice Kennedy asserts that we should not entertain the proposition that a verdict of not guilty by reason of insanity differs from a conviction. *Jones*, however, involved a case where the accused had been "found, beyond a reasonable doubt, to have committed a criminal act." We did not find this sufficient to negate any difference between a conviction and an insanity acquittal. Rather, we observed that a person convicted of crime may of course be punished. But "different considerations underlie commitment of an insanity acquittee. As he was not convicted, he may not be punished."

Justice Kennedy observes that proof beyond reasonable doubt of the commission of a criminal act permits a State to incarcerate and hold the offender on any reasonable basis. There is no doubt that the States have wide discretion in determining punishment for convicted offenders, but the Eighth Amendment[6] ensures that discretion is not unlimited. The Justice cites no authority, but surely would have if it existed, for the proposition that a defendant convicted of a crime and sentenced to a term of years may nevertheless be held indefinitely because of the likelihood that he will commit other crimes.

---

[6] See Appendix B (pp. 291-292).

We held, however, that "the committed acquittee is entitled to release when he has recovered his sanity or is no longer dangerous," that is, the acquittee may be held as long as he is both mentally ill and dangerous, but no longer. We relied on *O'Connor v. Donaldson*, which held as a matter of due process that it was unconstitutional for a State to continue to confine a harmless, mentally ill person. Even if the initial commitment was permissible, "it could not constitutionally continue after that basis no longer existed." In the summary of our holdings in our opinion we stated that "the Constitution permits the Government, on the basis of the insanity judgment, to confine him to a mental institution until such time as he has regained his sanity or is no longer a danger to himself or society."[7] The court below was in error in characterizing the above language from *Jones* as merely an interpretation of the pertinent statutory law in the District of Columbia and as having no constitutional significance. In this case, Louisiana does not contend that Foucha was mentally ill at the time of the trial court's hearing. Thus, the basis for holding Foucha in a psychiatric facility as an insanity acquittee has disappeared, and the State is no longer entitled to hold him on that basis (*O'Connor*).

The State, however, seeks to perpetuate Foucha's confinement at Feliciana on the basis of his antisocial personality which, as evidenced by his conduct at the facility, the court found rendered him a danger to himself or others. There are at least three difficulties with this position. First, even if his continued confinement were constitutionally permissible, keeping Foucha against his will in a mental institution is improper absent a determination in civil commitment proceedings of current mental illness and dangerousness. In *Vitek v. Jones*, we held that a convicted felon serving his sentence has a liberty interest, not extinguished by his confinement as a criminal, in not being transferred to a mental institution and hence classified as mentally ill without appropriate procedures to prove that he was mentally ill. "The loss of liberty produced by an involuntary commitment is more than a loss of freedom from confinement." Due process requires that the nature of commitment bear some reasonable relation to the purpose for which the individual is committed (*Jones*,

---

[7] Justice Thomas, dissenting, suggests that there was no issue of the standards for release before us in *Jones*. The issue in that case, however, was whether an insanity acquittee "must be released because he has been hospitalized for a period longer than he might have served in prison had he been convicted," and in the course of deciding that issue in the negative, we said that the detainee could be held until he was no longer mentally ill or no longer dangerous, regardless of how long a prison sentence might have been. We noted that Jones had not sought a release based on nonillness or nondangerousness, but as indicated in the text, we twice announced the outside limits on the detention of insanity acquittees. The Justice would "wish" away this aspect of *Jones*, but that case merely reflected the essence of our prior decisions.

Jackson v. Indiana). Here, according to the testimony given at the hearing in the trial court, Foucha is not suffering from a mental disease or illness. If he is to be held, he should not be held as a mentally ill person.

Second, if Foucha can no longer be held as an insanity acquittee in a mental hospital, he is entitled to constitutionally adequate procedures to establish the grounds for his confinement. *Jackson* indicates as much. There, a person under criminal charges was found incompetent to stand trial and was committed until he regained his sanity. It was later determined that nothing could be done to cure the detainee, who was a deaf mute. The state courts refused to order his release. We reversed, holding that the State was entitled to hold a person for being incompetent to stand trial only long enough to determine if he could be cured and become competent. If he was to be held longer, the State was required to afford the protections constitutionally required in a civil commitment proceeding. We noted, relying on *Baxstrom v. Herold*, that a convicted criminal who allegedly was mentally ill was entitled to release at the end of his term unless the State committed him in a civil proceeding. "There is no conceivable basis for distinguishing the commitment of a person who is nearing the end of a penal term from all other civil commitments" (*Jackson*, quoting *Baxstrom*).

Third, "the Due Process Clause contains a substantive component that bars certain arbitrary, wrongful government actions regardless of the fairness of the procedures used to implement them" (*Zinermon v. Burch*). Freedom from bodily restraint has always been at the core of the liberty protected by the Due Process Clause from arbitrary governmental action (*Youngberg v. Romeo*). "It is clear that commitment for any purpose constitutes a significant deprivation of liberty that requires due process protection" (*Jones*).

A State, pursuant to its police power, may of course imprison convicted criminals for the purposes of deterrence and retribution. But there are constitutional limitations on the conduct that a State may criminalize (*Robinson v. California*). Here, the State has no such punitive interest.

> **As Foucha was not convicted, he may not be punished.**

As Foucha was not convicted, he may not be punished. Here, Louisiana has by reason of his acquittal exempted Foucha from criminal responsibility.

The State may also confine a mentally ill person if it shows "by clear and convincing evidence that the individual is mentally ill and dangerous"

(*Jones*). Here, the State has not carried that burden; indeed, the State does not claim that Foucha is now mentally ill.

We have also held that in certain narrow circumstances persons who pose a danger to others or to the community may be subject to limited confinement and it is on these cases, particularly *United States v. Salerno*, that the State relies in this case.

Salerno, unlike this case, involved pretrial detention. We observed in *Salerno* that the "government's interest in preventing crime by arrestees is both legitimate and compelling," and that the statute involved there was a constitutional implementation of that interest. The statute carefully limited the circumstances under which detention could be sought to those involving the most serious of crimes (crimes of violence, offenses punishable by life imprisonment or death, serious drug offenses, or certain repeat offenders), and was narrowly focused on a particularly acute problem in which the government interests are overwhelming. In addition to first demonstrating probable cause, the Government was required, in a full-blown adversary hearing, to convince a neutral decision maker by clear and convincing evidence that no conditions of release can reasonably assure the safety of the community or any person, i.e., that the arrestee presents an identified and articulable threat to an individual or the community. Furthermore, the duration of confinement under the Bail Reform Act of 1984 was strictly limited. The arrestee was entitled to a prompt detention hearing and the maximum length of pretrial detention was limited by the "stringent time limitations of the Speedy Trial Act." If the arrestee were convicted, he would be confined as a criminal proved guilty; if he were acquitted, he would go free. Moreover, the Act required that detainees be housed, to the extent practicable, in a facility separate from persons awaiting or serving sentences or awaiting appeal.

Salerno does not save Louisiana's detention of insanity acquittees who are no longer mentally ill. Unlike the sharply focused scheme at issue in *Salerno*, the Louisiana scheme of confinement is not carefully limited. Under the state statute, Foucha is not now entitled to an adversary hearing at which the State must prove by clear and convincing evidence that he is demonstrably dangerous to the community. Indeed, the State need prove nothing to justify continued detention, for the statute places the burden on the detainee to prove that he is not dangerous. At the hearing which ended with Foucha's recommittal, no doctor or any other person testified positively that in his opinion Foucha would be a danger to the community, let alone gave the basis for such an opinion. There was only a description of Foucha's behavior at Feliciana and his antisocial personality, along with a refusal to certify that he would not be dangerous. When directly asked whether Foucha would be dangerous, Dr. Ritter said only, "I don't think I would feel comfortable in certifying that he would not be a danger to himself or to other people." This, under the Louisiana statute, was enough to defeat Foucha's interest in physical liberty. It is not enough to defeat Foucha's liberty interest under the Constitution in being freed from indefinite confinement in a mental facility.

Furthermore, if Foucha committed criminal acts while at Feliciana, such as assault, the State does not explain why its interest would not be vindicated by the ordinary criminal processes involving charge and conviction, the use of enhanced sentences for recidivists, and other permissible ways of dealing with patterns of criminal conduct. These are the normal means of dealing with persistent criminal conduct. Had they been employed against Foucha when he assaulted other inmates, there is little doubt that if then sane he could have been convicted and incarcerated in the usual way.

It was emphasized in *Salerno* that the detention we found constitutionally permissible was strictly limited in duration. Here, in contrast, the State asserts that because Foucha once committed a criminal act and now has an antisocial personality that sometimes leads to aggressive conduct, a disorder for which there is no effective treatment, he may be held indefinitely. This rationale would permit the State to hold indefinitely any other insanity acquittee not mentally ill who could be shown to have a personality disorder that may lead to criminal conduct.

> **This rationale would permit the State to hold indefinitely any other insanity acquittee not mentally ill who could be shown to have a personality disorder that may lead to criminal conduct.**

The same would be true of any convicted criminal, even though he has completed his prison term. It would also be only a step away from substituting confinements for dangerousness for our present system which, with only narrow exceptions and aside from permissible confinements for mental illness, incarcerates only those who are proved beyond reasonable doubt to have violated a criminal law.

"In our society liberty is the norm, and detention prior to trial or without trial is the carefully limited exception" (*Salerno*). The narrowly focused pretrial detention of arrestees permitted by the Bail Reform Act was found to be one of those carefully limited exceptions permitted by the Due Process Clause. We decline to take a similar view of a law like Louisiana's, which permits the indefinite detention of insanity acquittees who are not mentally ill but who do not prove they would not be dangerous to others.

Justice Thomas' dissent firmly embraces the view that the State may indefinitely hold an insanity acquittee who is found by a court to have been cured of his mental illness and who is unable to prove that he would not be dangerous. This would be so even though, as in this case, the court's finding of dangerousness is based solely on the detainee's antisocial personality that apparently has caused him to engage in altercations from time to time. Justice Thomas, however, does not challenge the holding of our cases that a convicted criminal may not be held as a mentally ill person without following the requirements for civil commitment, which would not permit further detention based on dangerousness alone. Yet it is surely strange to release sane but very likely dangerous persons who have committed a crime knowing precisely what they were doing but continue to hold indefinitely an insanity detainee who committed a criminal act at a time when, as found by a court, he did not know right from wrong. Justice Thomas' rationale for continuing to hold the insanity acquittee would surely justify treating the convicted felon in the same way, and if put to it, it appears that he would permit it. But as indicated in the text, this is not consistent with our present system of justice.

Justice Thomas relies heavily on the American Law Institute's (ALI) Model Penal Code and Commentary. However, the introductory passage that Justice Thomas quotes prefaces a more important passage that he omits. After explaining the rationale for the questionable provision, the Commentary states: "Constitutional doubts exist about the criterion of dangerousness. If a person committed civilly must be released when he is no longer suffering mental illness, it is questionable whether a person acquitted on grounds of mental disease or defect excluding responsibility can be kept in custody solely on the ground that he continues to be dangerous." Thus, while Justice Thomas argues that the Louisiana statute is not a relic of a bygone age, his principal support for this assertion is a 30-year-old provision of the Model Penal Code whose constitutionality has since been openly questioned by the ALI reporters themselves.

Similarly unpersuasive is Justice Thomas' claim regarding the number of States that allow confinement based on dangerousness alone. First, this assertion carries with it an obvious but unacknowledged corollary—the vast majority of States do not allow confinement based on dangerousness alone. Second, Justice Thomas' description of these state statutes also is importantly incomplete. Even as he argues that a scheme of confinement based on dangerousness alone is not a relic of a bygone age, Justice Thomas neglects to mention that two of the statutes he relies on have been amended, as Justice O'Connor notes. Nor does Justice Thomas acknowledge that at least two of the other statutes he lists as permitting confinement based on dangerousness alone have been given a contrary construction by highest state courts, which have found that the interpretation for which Justice Thomas cites them would be impermissible. Although provisions may on their face allow for confinement based on dangerousness alone, in virtually all actual cases the questions of dangerousness and continued mental disease are likely to be closely linked.

It should be apparent from what has been said earlier in this opinion that the Louisiana statute also discriminates against Foucha in violation of the Equal Protection Clause of the Fourteenth Amendment. *Jones* established that insanity acquittees may be treated differently in some respects from those persons subject to civil commitment, but Foucha, who is not now thought to be insane, can no longer be so classified. The State nonetheless insists on holding him indefinitely because he at one time committed a criminal act and does not now prove he is not dangerous. Louisiana law, however, does not provide for similar confinement for other classes of persons who have committed criminal acts and who cannot later prove they would not be dangerous. Criminals who have completed their prison terms, or are about to do so, are an obvious and large category of such persons. Many of them will likely suffer from the same sort of personality disorder that Foucha exhibits. However, state law does not allow for their continuing confinement based merely on dangerousness. Instead, the State controls the behavior of these similarly situated citizens by relying on other means, such as punishment, deterrence, and supervised release. Freedom from physical restraint being a fundamental right, the State must have a particularly convincing reason, which it has not put forward, for such discrimination against insanity acquittees who are no longer mentally ill.

Furthermore, in civil commitment proceedings the State must establish the grounds of insanity and dangerousness permitting confinement by clear and convincing evidence (*Addington*). Similarly, the State must establish insanity and dangerousness by clear and convincing evidence in order to confine an insane convict beyond his criminal sentence, when the basis for his original confinement no longer exists. See *Jackson* and *Baxstrom*. However, the State now claims that it may continue to confine Foucha, who is not now considered to be mentally ill, solely because he is deemed dangerous, but without assuming the burden of proving even this ground for confinement by clear and convincing evidence. The court below gave no convincing reason why the procedural safeguards against unwarranted confinement which are guaranteed to insane persons and those who have been convicted may be denied to a sane acquittee, and the State has done no better in this Court.

For the foregoing reasons the judgment of the Louisiana Supreme Court is reversed.

Justice O'Connor, concurring in part and concurring in the judgment.

Louisiana asserts that it may indefinitely confine Terry Foucha in a mental facility because, although not mentally ill, he might be dangerous to himself or to others if released. For the reasons given in Part II of the Court's opinion, this contention should be rejected. I write separately, however, to emphasize that the Court's opinion addresses only the specific statutory scheme before us, which broadly permits indefinite confinement of sane insanity acquittees in psychiatric facilities. This case does not require us to pass judgment on more narrowly drawn laws that provide for detention of insanity acquittees, or on statutes that provide for punishment of persons who commit crimes while mentally ill.

I do not understand the Court to hold that Louisiana may never confine dangerous insanity acquittees after they regain mental health. Under Louisiana law, defendants who carry the burden of proving insanity by a preponderance of the evidence will "escape punishment," but this affirmative defense becomes relevant only after the prosecution establishes beyond a reasonable doubt that the defendant committed criminal acts with the required level of criminal intent. Although insanity acquittees may not be incarcerated as criminals or penalized for asserting the insanity defense, this finding of criminal conduct sets them apart from ordinary citizens.

We noted in *Jones* that a judicial determination of criminal conduct provides "concrete evidence" of dangerousness. By contrast, "the only certain thing that can be said about the present state of knowledge and therapy regarding mental disease is that science has not reached finality of judgment" (quoting *Greenwood v. United States*). Louisiana evidently has determined that the inference of dangerousness drawn from a verdict of not guilty by reason of insanity continues even after a clinical finding of sanity, and that judgment merits judicial deference.

It might therefore be permissible for Louisiana to confine an insanity acquittee who has regained sanity if, unlike the situation in this case, the nature and duration of detention were tailored to reflect pressing public safety concerns related to the acquittee's continuing dangerousness. Although the dissenters apparently disagree, I think it clear that acquittees could not be confined as mental patients absent some medical justification for doing so; in such a case the necessary connection between the nature and purposes of confinement would be absent (see *Vitek v. Jones*, discussing infringements upon liberty unique to commitment to a mental hospital). Nor would it be permissible to treat all acquittees alike, without regard for their particular crimes. For example, the strong interest in liberty of a person acquitted by reason of insanity but later found sane might well outweigh the governmental interest in detention where the only evidence of dangerousness is that the acquittee committed a nonviolent or relatively minor crime. Equal protection principles may set additional limits on the confinement of sane but dangerous acquittees. Although I think it unnecessary to reach equal protection issues on the facts before us, the permissibility of holding an acquittee who is not mentally ill longer than a person convicted of the same crimes could be imprisoned is open to serious question.

The second point to be made about the Court's holding is that it places no new restriction on the States' freedom to determine whether, and to what extent, mental illness should excuse criminal behavior. The Court does not indicate that States must make the insanity defense available. It likewise casts no doubt on laws providing for prison terms after verdicts of "guilty but mentally ill." If a State concludes that mental illness is best considered in the context of criminal sentencing, the holding of this case erects no bar to implementing that judgment.

Finally, it should be noted that the great majority of States have adopted policies consistent with the Court's holding. Justice Thomas claims that 11 States have laws comparable to Louisiana's, but even this number overstates the case. Two of the States Justice Thomas mentions have already amended their laws to provide for the release of acquittees who do not suffer from mental illness but may be dangerous. Three others limit the maximum duration of criminal commitment to reflect the acquittee's specific crimes and hold acquittees in facilities appropriate to their mental condition. I do not understand the Court's opinion to render such laws necessarily invalid.

Today's holding follows directly from our precedents and leaves the States appropriate latitude to care for insanity acquittees in a way consistent with public welfare. Accordingly, I concur in Parts I and II of the Court's opinion and in the judgment of the Court.

Dissent: Justice Kennedy, with whom
The Chief Justice joins, dissenting.

As incarceration of persons is the most common and one of the most feared instruments of state oppression and state indifference, we ought to acknowledge at the outset that freedom from this restraint is essential to the basic definition of liberty in the Fifth[8] and Fourteenth Amendments of the Constitution. I agree with the Court's reaffirmation of this first premise. But I submit with all respect that the majority errs in its failure to recognize that the conditions for incarceration imposed by the State in this case are in accord with legitimate and traditional state interests, vindicated after full and fair procedures. The error results from the majority's primary reliance on cases, such as *O'Connor* and *Addington*, which define the due process limits for involuntary civil commitment. The majority relies on these civil cases while overruling without mention one of the holdings of our most recent and significant precedent from the criminal context, *Jones*.

This is a criminal case. It began one day when petitioner, brandishing a .357 revolver, entered the home of a married couple, intending to steal. He chased them out of their home and fired on police officers who confronted him as he fled. Petitioner was apprehended and charged with aggravated burglary and the illegal use of a weapon. There is no question that petitioner committed the criminal acts charged. Petitioner's response was to deny criminal responsibility based on his mental illness when he committed the acts. He contended his mental illness prevented him from distinguishing between right and wrong with regard to the conduct in question.

Mental illness may bear upon criminal responsibility, as a general rule, in either of two ways: First, it may preclude the formation of *mens rea*, if the disturbance is so profound that it prevents the defendant from forming the requisite intent as defined by state law; second, it may support an affirmative plea of legal insanity. Depending on the content of state law, the first possibility may implicate the State's initial burden, under *In re Winship*, to prove every element of the offense beyond a reasonable doubt, while the second possibility does not.

The State's burden is unaffected by an adjudication without trial, such as occurred here, because state law requires the trial court to determine, before accepting the plea, that there is a factual basis for it. There is no dispute that the trial court complied with state law and made the requisite findings. Compliance with the standard of proof beyond a reasonable doubt is the defining, central feature in criminal adjudication, unique to

---

[8] See Appendix B (pp. 291-292).

the criminal law (*Addington*). Its effect is at once both symbolic and practical, as a statement of values about respect and confidence in the criminal law and an apportionment of risk in favor of the accused. We have often subjected to heightened due process scrutiny, with regard to both purpose and duration, deprivations of physical liberty imposed before a judgment is rendered under this standard. The same heightened due process scrutiny does not obtain, though, once the State has met its burden of proof and obtained an adjudication. It is well settled that upon compliance with *In re Winship*, the State may incarcerate on any reasonable basis.

As Justice Thomas observes in his dissent, the majority errs by attaching "talismanic significance" to the fact that petitioner has been adjudicated "not guilty by reason of insanity." A verdict of not guilty by reason of insanity is neither equivalent nor comparable to a verdict of not guilty standing alone. We would not allow a State to evade its burden of proof by replacing its criminal law with a civil system in which there is no presumption of innocence and the defendant has the burden of proof. Nor should we entertain the proposition that this case differs from a conviction of guilty because petitioner has been adjudged "not guilty by reason of insanity," rather than "guilty but insane." Petitioner has suggested no grounds on which to distinguish the liberty interests involved or procedural protections afforded as a consequence of the State's ultimate choice of nomenclature. The due process implications ought not to vary under these circumstances. This is a criminal case in which the State has complied with the rigorous demands of *In re Winship*.

The majority's failure to recognize the criminal character of these proceedings and its concomitant standards of proof leads it to conflate the standards for civil and criminal commitment in a manner not permitted by our precedents. *O'Connor* and *Addington* define the due process limits of involuntary civil commitment. Together they stand for the proposition that in civil proceedings the Due Process Clause requires the State to prove both insanity and dangerousness by clear and convincing evidence. Their precedential value in the civil context is beyond question. But it is an error to apply these precedents, as the majority does today, to criminal proceedings. By treating this criminal case as a civil one, the majority overrules a principal holding in *Jones*.

In *Jones* we considered the system of criminal commitment enacted by Congress for the District of Columbia. Congress provided for acquittal by reason of insanity only after the Government had shown, beyond a reasonable doubt, that the defendant had committed the crimes charged. In cases of acquittal by reason of insanity, District law provided for automatic commitment followed by periodic hearings, where the insanity acquittee was given the opportunity to prove that he was no longer insane or dangerous. Petitioner in *Jones* contended that *Addington* and *O'Connor* applied to criminal proceedings as well as civil, requiring the Government to prove insanity and dangerousness by clear and convincing evidence before commitment. We rejected that contention. In *Jones* we distinguished criminal from civil commitment, holding that the Due Process Clause permits automatic incarceration after a criminal adjudication and without further process. The majority today in effect overrules that holding. It holds that "keeping Foucha against his will in a mental institution is improper absent a determination in civil commitment proceedings of current mental illness and dangerousness." Our holding in *Jones* was clear and to the contrary. We should not so disregard controlling precedent.

Our respect for the Court's opinion in *Jones* should be informed by the recognition that its distinction between civil and criminal commitment is both sound and consistent with long-established precedent. First, as described above, the procedural protections afforded in a criminal commitment surpass those in a civil commitment; indeed, these procedural protections are the most stringent known to our law. Second, proof of criminal conduct in accordance with *In re Winship* eliminates the risk of incarceration for mere idiosyncratic behavior, because a criminal act by definition is not within a range of conduct that is generally acceptable (*Jones*). The criminal law defines a discrete category of conduct for which society has reserved its greatest opprobrium and strictest sanctions; past or future dangerousness, as ascertained or predicted in civil proceedings, is different in kind. Third, the State presents distinct rationales for these differing forms of commitment: In the civil context, the State acts in large part on the basis of its *parens patriae* power to protect and provide for an ill individual, while in the criminal context, the State acts to ensure the public safety.

The majority's opinion is troubling at a further level, because it fails to recognize or account for profound differences between clinical insanity and state-law definitions of criminal insanity. It is by now well established that insanity as defined by the criminal law has no direct analog in medicine or science. The divergence between law and psychiatry is caused in part

> *It is by now well established that insanity as defined by the criminal law has no direct analog in medicine or science. (Kennedy, dissenting)*

by the legal fiction represented by the words "insanity" or "insane," which are a kind of lawyer's catchall and have no clinical meaning. Consistent with the general rule that the definition of both crimes and defenses is a matter of state law, the States are free to recognize and define the insanity defense as they see fit. "Nothing could be less fruitful than for this Court to be impelled into defining some sort of insanity test in constitutional terms" (*Powell v. Texas*).

As provided by Louisiana law, and consistent with both federal criminal law and the law of a majority of the States, petitioner was found not guilty by reason of insanity under the traditional *M'Naghten* test. Louisiana law provides a traditional statement of this test: "If the circumstances indicate that because of a mental disease or mental defect the offender was incapable of distinguishing between right and wrong with reference to the conduct in question, the offender shall be exempt from criminal responsibility."

Because the *M'Naghten* test for insanity turns on a finding of criminal irresponsibility at the time of the offense, it is quite wrong to place reliance on the fact, as the majority does, that Louisiana does not contend that petitioner is now insane. This circumstance should come as no surprise, since petitioner was competent at the time of his plea, and indeed could not have entered a plea otherwise (*Drope v. Missouri*). Present sanity would have relevance if petitioner had been committed as a consequence of civil proceedings, in which dangerous conduct in the past was used to predict similar conduct in the future. It has no relevance here, however. Petitioner has not been confined based on predictions about future behavior but rather for past criminal conduct. Unlike civil commitment proceedings, which attempt to divine the future from the past, in a criminal trial whose outcome turns on *M'Naghten*, findings of past insanity and past criminal conduct possess intrinsic and ultimate significance.

The system here described is not employed in all jurisdictions. Some have supplemented the traditional *M'Naghten* test with the so-called "irresistible impulse" test; others have adopted a test proposed as part of the Model Penal Code; and still others have abolished the defense altogether. Since it is well accepted that the States may define their own crimes and defenses, the point would not warrant further mention, but for the fact that the majority loses sight of it. In describing our decision in *Jones*, the majority relies on our statement that a verdict of not guilty by reason of insanity establishes that the defendant "committed the act because of mental illness." That was an accurate statement in *Jones* but not here. The defendant in *Jones* was acquitted under the *Durham* test for insanity, which excludes from punishment criminal conduct that is the product of a mental disease or defect. In a *Durham* jurisdiction, it would be fair to say, as the Court did in *Jones*, that a defendant acquitted by reason of insanity "committed the act because of mental illness." The same cannot be said here, where insanity under *M'Naghten* proves only that the defendant could not have distinguished between right and wrong. It is no small irony that the aspect of *Jones* on which the majority places greatest reliance, and indeed cites as an example of its adherence to *Jones*, has no bearing on the Louisiana statute at issue here.

The establishment of a criminal act and of insanity under the *M'Naghten* regime provides a legitimate basis for confinement. Although Louisiana has chosen not to punish insanity acquittees, the State has not surrendered its interest in incapacitative incarceration. Incapacitation for the protection of society is not an unusual ground for incarceration, and insanity acquittees are a special class of offenders proved dangerous beyond their own ability to comprehend. The wisdom of incarceration under these circumstances is demonstrated by its high level of acceptance. Every State provides for discretionary or mandatory incarceration of insanity acquittees.

It remains to be seen whether the majority, by questioning the legitimacy of incapacitative incarceration, puts in doubt the confinement of persons other than insanity acquittees. Parole release provisions often place the burden of proof on the prisoner to prove his lack of dangerousness. To use a familiar example, under the federal parole system in place until the enactment of the Sentencing Guidelines, an inmate could not be released on parole unless he established that his release would not jeopardize the public welfare. This requirement reflected the incapacitative aspect of the use of imprisonment which has the effect of denying the opportunity for future criminality, at least for a time. It is difficult for me to reconcile the rationale of incapacitative incarceration, which underlies these regimes, with the opinion of the majority, which discounts its legitimacy.

I also have difficulty with the majority's emphasis on the conditions of petitioner's confinement. In line with Justice O'Connor's concurring opinion, the majority emphasizes the fact that petitioner has been confined in a mental institution, suggesting that his incarceration might not be unconstitutional if undertaken elsewhere. The majority offers no authority for its suggestion, while Justice O'Connor relies on a reading of *Vitek*, which was rejected by the Court in *Jones*. The petitioner did not rely on this argument at any point in the proceedings, and we have not the authority to make the assumption, as a matter of law, that the conditions of petitioner's confinement are in any way infirm. Ours is not a case, as in

Vitek, where the State has stigmatized petitioner by placing him in a mental institution when he should have been placed elsewhere. *Jones* is explicit on this point: "A criminal defendant who successfully raises the insanity defense necessarily is stigmatized by the verdict itself, and thus the commitment causes little additional harm in this respect." Nor is this a case, as in *Washington v. Harper*, in which petitioner has suffered some further deprivation of liberty to which independent due process protections might attach. Both the fact and conditions of confinement here are attributable to petitioner's criminal conduct and subsequent decision to plead insanity. To the extent the majority relies on the conditions of petitioner's confinement, its decision is without authority, and most of its opinion is nothing more than confusing dicta.

I submit that today's decision is unwarranted and unwise. Petitioner has been incarcerated for less than one-third the statutory maximum for the offenses proved by the State. In light of these facts, the majority's repeated reference to "indefinite detention," with apparent reference to the potential duration of confinement, and not its lack of a fixed end point, has no bearing on this case. It is also significant to observe that this is not a case in which the incarcerated subject has demonstrated his nondangerousness. Within the two months before his release hearing, petitioner had been sent to a maximum security section of the Feliciana Forensic Facility because of altercations with another patient. Further, there is evidence in the record which suggests that petitioner's initial claim of insanity may have been feigned. The medical panel that reviewed petitioner's request for release stated that there is no evidence of mental illness, and indeed that there was never any evidence of mental illness or disease since admission. In sum, it would be difficult to conceive of a less compelling situation for the imposition of sweeping new constitutional commands such as the majority imposes today.

Because the majority conflates the standards for civil and criminal commitment, treating this criminal case as though it were civil, it upsets a careful balance relied upon by the States, not only in determining the conditions for continuing confinement, but also in defining the defenses permitted for mental incapacity at the time of the crime in question. In my view, having adopted a traditional and well-accepted test for determining criminal insanity, and having complied with the rigorous demands of *In re Winship*, the State possesses the constitutional authority to incarcerate petitioner for the protection of society. I submit my respectful dissent.

Justice Thomas, with whom The Chief Justice and Justice Scalia join, dissenting.

The Louisiana statutory scheme the Court strikes down today is not some quirky relic of a bygone age, but a codification of the current provisions of the American Law Institute's Model Penal Code. Invalidating this quite reasonable scheme is bad enough; even worse is the Court's failure to explain precisely what is wrong with it. In parts of its opinion, the Court suggests that the scheme is unconstitutional because it provides for the continued confinement of insanity acquittees who, although still dangerous, have "recovered" their sanity.

The Court errs, in large part, because it fails to examine in detail the challenged statutory scheme and its application in this case. Under Louisiana law, a verdict of "not guilty by reason of insanity" differs significantly from a verdict of "not guilty." A simple verdict of not guilty following a trial means that the State has failed to prove all of the elements of the charged crime beyond a reasonable doubt. A verdict of not guilty by reason of insanity, in contrast, means that the defendant committed the crime, but established that he was "incapable of distinguishing between right and wrong" with respect to his criminal conduct. Insanity, in other words, is an affirmative defense that does not negate the State's proof, but merely "exempts the defendant from criminal responsibility."

After adjudicating a defendant not guilty by reason of insanity, a trial court must hold a hearing on the issue of dangerousness. The law specifies that "if the court determines that the defendant cannot be released without a danger to others or to himself, it shall order him committed to a mental institution." Dangerous to others means the condition of a person whose behavior or significant threats support a reasonable expectation that there is a substantial risk that he will inflict physical harm upon another person in the near future.

After holding the requisite hearings, the trial court in this case ordered Foucha committed to the Feliciana Forensic Facility. After his commitment, Foucha was entitled, upon request, to another hearing six months later and at yearly intervals after that. In addition, Louisiana law provides that a release hearing must be held upon recommendation by the superintendent of a mental institution. In early 1988, Feliciana's superintendent recommended that Foucha be released, and a three-doctor panel met to review the case. The panel concluded that there is no evidence of mental illness. In fact, the panel stated that there was never any evidence of mental illness or disease since admission. Although the panel did not discuss whether Foucha was dangerous, it recommended to the trial court that he be conditionally released.

As a result of these recommendations, the trial court scheduled a hearing to determine whether Foucha should be released. Foucha had the burden at this hearing to prove that he could be released without danger to others or to himself. The court appointed two experts (the same doctors who had examined Foucha at the time of his original commitment) to evaluate his dangerousness. These doctors concluded that Foucha "is presently in remission from mental illness," but said that they could not "certify that he would not constitute a menace to himself or to others if released." On November 29, 1988, the trial court held the hearing, at which Foucha was represented by counsel. The court concluded that Foucha is a danger to others, and ordered that he be returned to Feliciana.

The Court today concludes that Louisiana has denied Foucha both procedural and substantive due process. In my view, each of these conclusions is wrong. I shall discuss them in turn.

What the Court styles a "procedural" due process analysis is in reality an equal protection analysis. The Court first asserts (contrary to state law) that Foucha cannot be held as an insanity acquittee once he "becomes" sane. That being the case, he is entitled to the same treatment as civil committees. "If Foucha can no longer be held as an insanity acquittee," the Court says, "he is entitled to constitutionally adequate procedures [those afforded in civil commitment proceedings] to establish the grounds for his confinement." This, of course, is an equal protection argument (there being no rational distinction between A and B, the State must treat them the same); the Court does not even pretend to examine the fairness of the release procedures the State has provided.

I cannot agree with the Court's conclusion because I believe that there is a real and legitimate distinction between insanity acquittees and civil committees that justifies procedural disparities. Unlike civil committees, who have not been found to have harmed society, insanity acquittees have been found in a judicial proceeding to have committed a criminal act. The distinction between civil committees and insanity acquittees, after all, turns not on considerations of present sanity, but instead on the fact that the latter have "already unhappily manifested the reality of antisocial conduct" (*Dixon v. Jacobs*). "The prior antisocial conduct of an insanity acquittee justifies treating such a person differently from ones otherwise civilly committed for purposes of deciding whether the patient should be released" (*Powell v. Florida*). While a State may renounce a punitive interest by offering an insanity defense, it does not follow that, once the acquittee's sanity is "restored," the State is required to ignore his criminal act, and to renounce all interest in protecting society from him.

Furthermore, the Federal Constitution does not require a State to "ignore the danger of 'calculated abuse of the insanity defense.' " A State that decides to offer its criminal defendants an insanity defense, which the defendant himself is given the choice of invoking, is surely allowed to attach to that defense certain consequences that prevent abuse. In effect, the defendant, by raising the defense of insanity—and he alone can raise it—postpones a determination of his present mental health and acknowledges the right of the state, upon accepting his plea, to detain him for diagnosis, care, and custody in a mental institution until certain specified conditions are met. A State may reasonably decide that the integrity of an insanity-acquittal scheme requires the continued commitment of insanity acquittees who remain dangerous. Surely, the citizenry would not long tolerate the insanity defense if a serial killer who convinces a jury that he is not guilty by reason of insanity is returned to the streets immediately after trial by convincing a different factfinder that he is not in fact insane.

> **Surely, the citizenry would not long tolerate the insanity defense if a serial killer who convinces a jury that he is not guilty by reason of insanity is returned to the streets immediately after trial by convincing a different factfinder that he is not in fact insane. (Thomas, dissenting)**

As the American Law Institute has explained: "It seemed preferable to the Institute to make dangerousness the criterion for continued custody, rather than to provide that the committed person may be discharged or released when restored to sanity as defined by the mental hygiene laws. Although his mental disease may have greatly improved, an insanity acquittee may still be dangerous because of factors in his personality and background other than mental disease. Also, such a standard provides a means for the control of the occasional defendant who may be quite dangerous but who successfully feigned mental disease to gain an acquittal." That this is a reasonable legislative judgment is underscored by the fact that it has been made by no fewer than 11 state legislatures, in addition to Louisiana's, which expressly provide that insanity acquittees shall not be released as long as they are dangerous, regardless of sanity.[9]

---

[9] The Court and the concurrence dispute this list of statutes. [They] note that two of the States have enacted new laws, not yet effective, modifying their current absolute prohibitions on the release of dangerous insanity acquittees; that courts in two other States have apparently held that mental illness is a prerequisite to confinement; and that three of the States place caps of some sort on the duration of the confinement of insanity acquittees. Those criticisms miss my point. I cite the 11 state statutes above only to show that the legislative judgments underlying Louisiana's scheme are far from unique or freakish, and that there is no well-established practice in our society, either past or present, of automatically releasing sane but dangerous insanity acquittees.

The Court suggests an alternative "procedural" due process theory that is, if anything, even less persuasive than its principal theory. "Keeping Foucha against his will in a mental institution is improper absent a determination in civil commitment proceedings of current mental illness and dangerousness." The Court cites *Vitek v. Jones* as support. There are two problems with this theory. First, it is illogical: Louisiana cannot possibly extend Foucha's incarceration by adding the procedures afforded to civil committees, since it is impossible to civilly commit someone who is not presently mentally ill. Second, the theory is not supported by *Vitek*. Stigmatization (our concern in *Vitek*) is simply not a relevant consideration where insanity acquittees are involved. As we explained in *Jones*: "A criminal defendant who successfully raises the insanity defense necessarily is stigmatized by the verdict itself, and thus the commitment causes little additional harm in this respect." It is implausible, in my view, that a person who chooses to plead not guilty by reason of insanity and then spends several years in a mental institution becomes unconstitutionally stigmatized by continued confinement in the institution after "regaining" sanity.

The Court next concludes that Louisiana's statutory scheme must fall because it violates Foucha's substantive due process rights. I disagree. Until today, I had thought that the analytical framework for evaluating substantive due process claims was relatively straightforward. Certain substantive rights we have recognized as "fundamental"; legislation trenching upon these is subjected to "strict scrutiny," and generally will be invalidated unless the State demonstrates a compelling interest and narrow tailoring. Such searching judicial review of state legislation, however, is the exception, not the rule, in our democratic and federal system; we have consistently emphasized that "the Court has no license to invalidate legislation which it thinks merely arbitrary or unreasonable" (*Regents of University of Michigan v. Ewing*).

I fully agree with the Court, and with Justice Kennedy, that freedom from involuntary confinement is at the heart of the "liberty" protected by the Due Process Clause. But a liberty interest *per se* is not the same thing as a fundamental right. Whatever the exact scope of the fundamental right to "freedom from bodily restraint" recognized by our cases,[10] it certainly

---

[10]The Court cites only *Youngberg v. Romeo*, in support of its assertion that "freedom from bodily restraint has always been at the core of the liberty protected by the Due Process Clause from arbitrary governmental action." What "freedom from bodily restraint" meant in that case, however, is completely different from what the Court uses the phrase to mean here. *Youngberg* involved the substantive due process rights of an institutionalized, mentally retarded patient who had been restrained by shackles placed on his arms for portions of each day. What the Court meant by "freedom from bodily restraint," then, was quite literally freedom not to be physically strapped to a bed. That case in no way established the broad "freedom from bodily restraint"—apparently meaning freedom from all involuntary confinement—that the Court discusses today.

cannot be defined at the exceedingly great level of generality the Court suggests today. There is simply no basis in our society's history or in the precedents of this Court to support the existence of a sweeping, general fundamental right to "freedom from bodily restraint" applicable to all persons in all contexts. If convicted prisoners could claim such a right, for example, we would subject all prison sentences to strict scrutiny. This we have consistently refused to do.

The critical question here, then, is whether insanity acquittees have a fundamental right to "freedom from bodily restraint" that triggers strict scrutiny of their confinement. Neither Foucha nor the Court provides any evidence that our society has ever recognized any such right. To the contrary, historical evidence shows that many States have long provided for the continued institutionalization of insanity acquittees who remain dangerous.

Moreover, this Court has never applied strict scrutiny to the substance of state laws involving involuntary confinement of the mentally ill, much less to laws involving the confinement of insanity acquittees. To the contrary, until today we have subjected the substance of such laws only to very deferential review. Thus, in *Jackson*, we held that Indiana's provisions for the indefinite institutionalization of incompetent defendants violated substantive due process because they did not bear any "reasonable" relation to the purpose for which the defendant was committed. Similarly, in *O'Connor*, we held that the confinement of a nondangerous mentally ill person was unconstitutional not because the State failed to show a compelling interest and narrow tailoring, but because the State had no legitimate interest whatsoever to justify such confinement.

Similarly, in *Jones*, we held (in addition to the procedural due process holdings described above) that there was no substantive due process bar to holding an insanity acquittee beyond the period for which he could have been incarcerated if convicted. We began by explaining the standard for our analysis: "The Due Process Clause 'requires that the nature and duration of commitment bear some reasonable relation to the purpose for which the individual is committed.' " We then held that "in light of the congressional purposes underlying commitment of insanity acquittees," which we identified as treatment of the insanity acquittee's mental illness and protection of the acquittee and society, "petitioner clearly errs in contending that an acquittee's hypothetical maximum sentence provides the constitutional limit for his commitment." Given that the commitment law was reasonably related to Congress' purposes, this Court had no basis for invalidating it as a matter of substantive due process.

It is simply wrong for the Court to assert today that we "held" in *Jones* that "the committed acquittee is entitled to release when he has recovered his sanity or is no longer dangerous." We specifically noted in *Jones* that no issue regarding the standards for the release of insanity acquittees was before us. The question we were answering in the part of *Jones* from which the Court quotes was whether it is permissible to hold an insanity acquittee for a period longer than he could have been incarcerated if convicted, not whether it is permissible to hold him once he becomes "sane." As noted above, our substantive due process analysis in Jones was straightforward: Did the means chosen by Congress (commitment of insanity acquittees until they have recovered their sanity or are no longer dangerous) reasonably fit Congress' ends (treatment of the acquittee's mental illness and protection of society from his dangerousness)?

In its arguments before this Court, Louisiana chose to place primary reliance on our decision in *Salerno*, in which we upheld provisions of the Bail Reform Act of 1984 that allowed limited pretrial detention of criminal suspects. That case, as the Court notes, is readily distinguishable. Insanity acquittees, in sharp and obvious contrast to pretrial detainees, have had their day in court. Although they have not been convicted of crimes, neither have they been exonerated, as they would have been upon a determination of "not guilty." Insanity acquittees thus stand in a fundamentally different position from persons who have not been adjudicated to have committed criminal acts. That is what distinguishes this case (and what distinguished *Jones*) from *Salerno* and *Jackson*. In *Jackson*, as in *Salerno*, the State had not proved beyond a reasonable doubt that the accused had committed criminal acts or otherwise was dangerous. The Court disregards this critical distinction, and apparently deems applicable the same scrutiny to pretrial detainees as to persons determined in a judicial proceeding to have committed a criminal act.

If the Court indeed means to suggest that all restrictions on "freedom from bodily restraint" are subject to strict scrutiny, it has (at a minimum) wrought a revolution in the treatment of the mentally ill. Civil commitment as we know it would almost certainly be unconstitutional; only in the rarest of circumstances will a State be able to show a "compelling interest," and one that can be served in no other way, in involuntarily institutionalizing a person. All procedures involving the confinement of insanity acquittees and civil committees would require revamping to meet strict scrutiny. Thus, to take one obvious example, the automatic commitment of insanity acquittees that we expressly upheld in *Jones* would be clearly unconstitutional, since it is inconceivable that such commitment of persons who may well presently be sane and nondangerous could survive strict scrutiny. (In *Jones*, of course, we applied no such scrutiny; we upheld the practice not because it was justified by a compelling interest, but because it was based on reasonable legislative inferences about continuing insanity and dangerousness.)

As explained above, the Court's opinion is profoundly ambiguous on the central question in this case: Must the State of Louisiana release Terry Foucha now that he has "regained" his sanity? In other words, is the defect in Louisiana's statutory scheme that it provides for the confinement of insanity acquittees who have recovered their sanity, or instead that it allows the State to confine sane insanity acquittees (1) indefinitely (2) in a mental facility? To the extent the Court suggests the former, I have already explained why it is wrong. I turn now to the latter possibility, which also is mistaken.

To begin with, I think it is somewhat misleading to describe Louisiana's scheme as providing for the "indefinite" commitment of insanity acquittees. As explained above, insanity acquittees are entitled to a release hearing every year at their request, and at any time at the request of a facility superintendent. Like the District of Columbia statute at issue in *Jones*, then, Louisiana's statute provides for "indefinite" commitment only to the extent that an acquittee is unable to satisfy the substantive standards for release. If the Constitution did not require a cap on the acquittee's confinement in *Jones*, why does it require one here?

Furthermore, any concerns about "indefinite" commitment here are entirely hypothetical and speculative. Foucha has been confined for eight years. Had he been convicted of the crimes with which he was charged, he could have been incarcerated for 32 years. Thus, I find quite odd Justice O'Connor's suggestion that this case might be different had Louisiana, like the State of Washington, limited confinement to the period for which a defendant might have been imprisoned if convicted. Foucha, of course, would be in precisely the same position today—and for the next 24 years— had the Louisiana statute included such a cap. Thus, the Court apparently finds fault with the Louisiana statute not because it has been applied to Foucha in an unconstitutional manner, but because the Court can imagine it being applied to someone else in an unconstitutional manner.

Finally, I see no basis for holding that the Due Process Clause *per se* prohibits a State from continuing to confine in a "mental institution"— the federal constitutional definition of which remains unclear—an insanity acquittee who has recovered his sanity. As noted above, many States have long provided for the continued detention of insanity acquittees who remain dangerous. Neither Foucha nor the Court present any evidence that these States have traditionally transferred such persons from mental institutions to other detention facilities. Therefore, there is simply no basis for this Court to recognize a "fundamental right" for a sane insanity acquittee to be transferred out of a mental facility. Removing sane insanity acquittees from mental institutions may make eminent sense as a policy matter, but the Due Process Clause does not require the States to conform to the policy preferences of federal judges. I have no idea what facilities the Court or Justice O'Connor believe the Due Process Clause mandates for the confinement of sane-but-dangerous insanity acquittees. Presumably prisons will not do, since imprisonment is generally regarded as "punishment." May a State designate a wing of a mental institution or prison for sane insanity acquittees? May a State mix them with other detainees? Neither the Constitution nor our society's traditions provide any answer to these questions.

I respectfully dissent.

Summary

We learn in Howell's report of the *Hadfield* case that, after acquittal, Hadfield was sent to an asylum where he remained until his death. It was clear to the court (and affirmed by his attorney, Lord Erskine) that Hadfield was too dangerous to be released. There may have been a meaningful difference at that time between asylums and prisons, and sending him to an asylum was likely a form of compassion. It would not be too difficult to imagine circumstances in which prison may now be more livable than state hospitals, but it is reasonable to expect that we can effectively treat most mental disorders in relatively little time as compared to Hadfield's time. The fact that most persons with mental disorders can currently be rapidly and effectively treated presents problems for those who wish to see insanity acquittees "locked away forever." Whether Foucha was truly mentally ill or whether he successfully feigned insanity, the only basis for holding him after acquittal was if he persisted in presenting a risk to others because of a mental disorder. Whether he was inherently dangerous solely because of personality traits was not an issue for determination in his release. And, as noted in *Jones*, the length of commitment may exceed the period for which an individual may have been sentenced if the result had been conviction.

At the time of their acquittal, persons claiming insanity have just proven that they were mentally ill to the extent that they could not appreciate what they were doing or could not control their behavior, and as a consequence, engaged in actions which would otherwise be considered criminal. It is reasonable to require that such persons be committed until there is a decision that they are no longer dangerous due to a mental disorder. It is common for insanity acquittees to receive a conditional commitment upon acquittal to determine if extended commitment is necessary. For individuals who have successfully demonstrated that they were mentally disordered at the time of the crime, it is likely that they will have received effective treatment subsequent to their arrest, perhaps only to ensure they are competent to proceed. Persons who were mentally ill to the extent that they were insane may have received sufficient treatment by the time of their acquittal to make a commitment unnecessary.

Such considerations are paramount in the context of civil commitment and release, but *Lyles* clarifies that jurors need not concern themselves with prognosis. Jurors should know that an insanity acquittal will lead to hospitalization, but the length of such confinement is immaterial to their charge.

Section 7

Prosecuting the Mentally Ill

Introduction to Section 7

Cases

   Whalem v. United States

   Marble v. United States

   United States v. Edwards

Summary

Introduction to Section 7

    This section addresses two substantial issues that arise in the trials of defendants who pursue an insanity defense or who, though obviously eligible for such a defense, choose not to pursue it. The Sixth Amendment[1] of the United States Constitution enumerates fair trial rights afforded a defendant in a criminal trial, which includes a right to present one's own defense. This right sometimes conflicts with the intent to punish only the guilty, for example, when a mentally ill defendant who probably was not guilty by reason of insanity chooses not to raise an insanity defense at the time of trial.

    In *Whalem v. United States* (1965), the United States Court of Appeals for the District of Columbia Circuit addressed this issue. Whalem, who had a history of mental disorder prior to his offense, chose not to raise an insanity defense at trial for robbery and attempted rape. An appeal of his conviction by the Circuit Court raised issues of whether a competent defendant had a right to refuse to plead insanity and whether the court had an obligation to raise the issue on its own motion. The Circuit Court reasoned that responsibility was a major foundation for the structure of criminal law and that insanity rules were society's codification of moral judgment regarding criminal responsibility. They concluded that a judge must have the discretion to raise an insanity defense over the defendant's objection to uphold this structural foundation of law.

    In the years following *Whalem*, the United States Supreme Court issued two decisions, *North Carolina v. Alford* and *Faretta v. California*, which gave great deference to a defendant's Sixth Amendment rights to choose his own best defense, even when the outcome might be in conflict with

---

[1] See Appendix B (pp. 291-292).

more abstract notions of justice. Following those holdings, the D.C. Circuit Court of Appeals again addressed the issue of a competent defendant's right to refuse an insanity defense in *Marble v. United States* (1991). In *Marble*, the Court of Appeals noted the weight granted to a defendant's own decisions by the U.S. Supreme Court in *Alford* and *Faretta*. They also noted that insanity had been made an affirmative defense by the Insanity Defense Reform Act (IDRA) in the interim and that Congress had intended to restrict insanity defenses to the most severe cases. Based on these principles, they overturned *Whalem* to give competent defendants the right to accept responsibility, even when the facts may suggest that they were not criminally responsible.

Finally, in *United States v. Edwards* (1987), the United States Court of Appeals for the Eleventh Circuit dealt with another old issue made new by the IDRA, the testimony of experts. The use of medical experts occurred at least as early as the trial of *Hadfield*. The issue of what experts could testify to was among the questions posed by the House of Lords to the English judiciary in *M'Naghten*. In the U.S. Courts, the problem of expert testimony "invading the province of the jury" became especially acute with the "product" test employed by the D.C. Circuit. Even after the D.C. Circuit abandoned that test in favor of the ALI standard, the trial of John Hinckley was seen as an unseemly "battle of experts." Congress then revised the Federal Rules of Evidence as part of the IDRA to exclude testimony by experts on the "ultimate issues," intent or insanity in criminal trials. In *Edwards*, the Eleventh Circuit interpreted the meaning of that limitation as applied to the facts of an actual trial. They concluded that Congress had never intended to limit the flow of diagnostic or clinical information and had intended for experts to testify fully regarding a defendant's "diagnosis, mental state, and motivation" at the time of the offense in order to provide juries with the information they needed to decide the "ultimate issue" of criminal responsibility.

Whalem v. United States

346 F.2d 812 (1965)

Facts

Whalem was convicted of robbery and attempted rape. At the time of the crimes, he was on convalescent leave from St. Elizabeths Hospital where he had been civilly committed in 1956. Due to his commitment history, the prosecution requested a competency evaluation, which took place at St. Elizabeths. The hospital submitted a report holding that although he had experienced a schizophrenic reaction, catatonic type, he was competent and his alleged crimes were not a product of his mental disease. At defense request, a second evaluation was conducted at D.C. General Hospital. They concluded that he was competent to stand trial and suffered from a passive aggressive character disorder and a low IQ, which did not constitute a mental disease or defect. The case went to trial, and the defendant and his counsel chose not to raise the issue of insanity. After conviction, the defendant appealed to a three-judge panel on the basis of evidentiary issues and a jury instruction regarding the evidence. The full Court ordered a rehearing *en banc*[1] and raised two other issues concerning whether a competency hearing should have been held and whether the trial judge should have raised the insanity issue *sua sponte*.[2]

Issue

(a) Does a competent defendant have a right to refuse to plead insanity even when there are facts supporting the defense? (b) If so, does the trial judge err by not raising the issue of insanity *sua sponte* and instructing the jury thereon?

Holding

(a) The defendant may refuse to raise the insanity defense. (b) A trial judge must have the discretion to impose an unwanted insanity defense in the pursuit of justice. In this case, the evidence did not necessitate

---

[1] *en banc.* With all members of the appellate court.
[2] *sua sponte.* Upon the court's own initiative.

injecting the insanity defense, which the defendant and his counsel chose not to raise. There was no error and the conviction was affirmed.

Analysis

The Court recognized that the concept of responsibility is a major foundation for the structure of criminal law. The legal definition of insanity is the "codification of the moral judgment of society as respects a man's criminal responsibility." Insane defendants are "blameless in the eyes of society" and not subject to punishment. In order to uphold this structural foundation, a trial judge must refuse to allow the conviction "of an obviously mentally irresponsible defendant." If there is sufficient question about the defendant's responsibility (see *Davis v. United States*), the judge must have the discretion to raise the issue and impose the unwanted defense on the defendant and the additional burden of proof on the prosecution.

Edited Excerpts[3]

Opinion by Bastian

When this case was first argued to a division of three judges, appellant, convicted of robbery and attempt to commit rape, questioned the sufficiency of the evidence of his identification, the jury instructions which he alleges failed to properly emphasize evidence favorable to his case, and introduction into evidence of clothing taken from him after his arrest. Before an opinion was issued by the division the full Court *sua sponte* ordered a rehearing *en banc*. At the rehearing *en banc* two other issues were raised, namely (1) whether there was sufficient evidence in the record pertaining to appellant's lack of sanity to raise the issue of insanity even though appellant himself refused to do so, and whether in view of such evidence the trial judge erred by not raising the insanity issue *sua sponte* and instructing the jury thereon, despite appellant's wishes to the contrary; and (2) whether the trial judge erred in proceeding to trial without holding a hearing to determine appellant's competency to stand trial, which hearing, appellant now urges, was required notwithstanding his lack of objection to two hospital reports that he was competent.

At the time of the crimes in question appellant was on convalescent leave from St. Elizabeths Hospital, to which he had been civilly committed in 1956. After his arrest for the crimes in question, the Government, reciting appellant's prior commitment, successfully moved for a mental

[3] Readers are advised to quote only from the original published cases. See pages vi and vii.

examination and appellant was committed to St. Elizabeths pursuant to D.C. Code. The hospital superintendent subsequently informed the court that in his opinion appellant was "mentally competent to understand the nature of the charges pending against him and to assist properly in the preparation of his defense." The court was also informed by the superintendent that appellant was, both then (at the time of the report in March 1963) and at the time of the crime, suffering from a mental disease, diagnosed as schizophrenic reaction, catatonic type (in remission), but that the crimes were not products of this disease. Appellant's counsel then moved for a further mental examination and appellant was sent to D.C. General Hospital which reported that appellant was "mentally competent as to be able to understand the proceeding against him and to be able to properly assist in the preparation of his defense." In addition, the D.C. General report noted that although appellant manifested a passive aggressive character disorder and a low I.Q., his condition did not constitute a mental disease or defect. After receipt of these reports neither the Government nor the defense objected to the hospitals' certifications nor did they request a hearing. The case proceeded to trial without a hearing on the issue of appellant's competency. At trial no issue of insanity was raised by defense counsel, who was acting under instructions given him by appellant as well as counsel's own judgment that the issue of insanity should be left out of the case.

The question is whether or not a competent defendant may refuse to plead insanity even though there may be facts available to support that defense; and if so, whether the trial judge commits error by not raising the issue of insanity *sua sponte* and instructing the jury thereon (assuming, of course, that the trial judge knows of the facts which could support an insanity plea).

In our view, a defendant may not keep the issue of insanity out of the case altogether. He may, if he wishes, refuse to raise the issue of insanity, but he may not, in a proper case, prevent the court

> **He may, if he wishes, refuse to raise the issue of insanity, but he may not, in a proper case, prevent the court from injecting it.**

from injecting it. We as much as held this in *Overholser v. Lynch*, and that aspect of our holding was not disturbed by the Supreme Court. However, in the event of acquittal by reason of insanity following a defendant's affirmative refusal to rely on this ground, the automatic commitment procedures would not apply (*Lynch v. Overholser*).

One of the major foundations for the structure of the criminal law is the concept of responsibility, and the law is clear that one whose acts would otherwise be criminal has committed no crime at all if because of incapacity due to age or mental condition he is not responsible for those acts. If he does not know what he is doing or cannot control his conduct or his acts are the product of a mental disease or defect, he is morally blameless and not criminally responsible. The judgment of society and the law in this respect is tested in any given case by an inquiry into the sanity of the accused. In other words, the legal definition of insanity in a criminal case is a codification of the moral judgment of society as respects a man's criminal responsibility; and if a man is insane in the eyes of the law, he is blameless in the eyes of society and is not subject to punishment in the criminal courts.

In the courtroom confrontations between the individual and society the trial judge must uphold this structural foundation by refusing to allow the conviction of an obviously mentally irresponsible defendant, and when there is sufficient question as to a defendant's mental responsibility at the time of the crime, that issue must become part of the case. Just as the judge must insist that the *corpus delicti* be proved before a defendant who has confessed may be convicted, so too must the judge forestall the conviction of one who in the eyes of the law is not mentally responsible for his otherwise criminal acts. We believe then that, in the pursuit of justice, a trial judge must have the discretion to impose an unwanted defense on a defendant and the consequent additional burden of proof on the Government prosecutor. So, our query is whether in this case there was a combination of factors which required the trial judge to inject the insanity issue for, if such factors existed, his failure to do so is an abuse of discretion and constitutes error.

In the instant case, both hospital reports available to the trial judge negated a defense of insanity (the one indicating no mental disease or defect, the other indicating lack of productivity). There was testimony by appellant on cross-examination that he had previously been committed to St. Elizabeths, but the details were not brought out since the Government was trying to show only that appellant was familiar with the hospital grounds where the attack took place. At the time of this testimony, the trial judge, in a bench conference, quite properly advised defense counsel that if there was an insanity issue to be raised it should be raised. Near the end of the trial, defense counsel informed the court that both he and his client agreed that the insanity issue should not be raised. There was, of course, no request by appellant for any insanity instructions and none were given. Under these circumstances we conclude that the trial judge did not abuse his discretion by not injecting the issue of insanity into the case. Accordingly, there being no error, the convictions are affirmed.

Marble v. United States

940 F.2d 1543 (1991)

Facts

The defendant committed a somewhat odd bank robbery in Washington, DC. He resisted, over the urging of his appointed counsel, to pleading not guilty by reason of insanity. The attorney raised the possibility that the court should impose an insanity defense, and the judge appointed an *amicus*[1] counsel to make the case for such an imposition. A competency evaluation was conducted, and Marble, who was then effectively treated, was found competent to stand trial. A bifurcated trial was conducted, and Marble was found guilty by a jury. He indicated he did not want to plead insanity because he preferred a definite sentence to an indefinite civil commitment. The court refused to impose the insanity defense, but ordered the *amicus* counsel to appeal the refusal.

Issue

Did the trial court abuse its discretion by failing to impose an insanity defense on a competent defendant?

Holding

No. A district court must allow a competent defendant to accept responsibility for a crime committed when he may have been suffering from a mental disease.

Analysis

In previous cases, *Whalem v. United States* and *United States v. Robertson*, the District of Columbia Circuit Court of Appeals had become the only federal court of appeals to impose a duty on a district court to raise an insanity defense. Few other courts had even considered the issue. The court had based those much earlier decisions on a principle that an insane defendant was "blameless in the eyes of society and is not subject to punishment in the criminal courts" and the premise that the insanity defense was "not strictly an affirmative defense and can be raised by

---

[1] *amicus.* A friend of the court; in this context, someone who participates in the argument of a case even though not one of the litigants.

either the court or the prosecution." Since that time, the United States Supreme Court in *North Carolina v. Alford* rejected the view that the law authorized a conviction only where guilt was shown. They held that the trial court had the discretion to accept a defendant's strategic plea of guilty while he simultaneously claimed his innocence. In *Faretta v. California*, the Supreme Court held that the Sixth Amendment guaranteed a defendant the right to waive counsel and make his own defense. Finally, the Insanity Defense Reform Act (IDRA) of 1984 made the insanity defense an affirmative defense and required a "severe" mental disorder. Based on the IDRA's "clear policy" to hold responsible "all but the most patently insane offenders" and the Supreme Court's deference (in *Faretta* and *Alford*) to a defendant's "strategic decisions," the Circuit Court of Appeals held that *Whalem* and its progeny were overruled, and a district court must allow a competent defendant to accept responsibility for a crime he committed when he may have been suffering from a mental disease.

Edited Excerpts[2]

Opinion by Ginsburg, Circuit Judge

Ronald Marble appeals his conviction for bank robbery on the ground that the district court abused its discretion by failing to impose the insanity defense over Marble's competent objection, or alternatively that the court did not conduct a sufficient hearing to determine the propriety of imposing the defense. Because we find that the district court acted within its discretion, we affirm.

One day in 1988, Ronald Marble walked into the Signet Bank branch office at 2000 M Street in Washington, DC, and approached a customer representative with the declared intention of opening an account. Perhaps because he gave two different names to the bank officer, he met with no success on that mission. Marble then ambled over to the nearest in a row of six tellers and handed her a note, scrawled on a piece of paper bag, that said, "This is a holdup. Put the money in the bag." After the first teller had emptied her cash drawer, Marble told her to pass the bag to the next teller in line; in this way, all six tellers contributed to the two bulging bags of cash that constituted Marble's unlawful withdrawal. Bags in hand, Marble delivered the simple valediction, "Peace," and walked out of the bank.

The police were summoned. A bystander told them that Marble had gone thataway; looking around the indicated corner, an officer saw Marble

---

[2] Readers are advised to quote only from the original published cases. See pages vi and vii.

walking down the street with an overflowing bag of currency in each hand, oblivious to the banknotes spilling onto the ground. The officer arrested Marble; a search produced, in addition to the bank's cash, an eight-inch steak knife wrapped in a paper towel.

> *An officer saw Marble walking down the street with an overflowing bag of currency in each hand, oblivious to the banknotes spilling onto the ground.*

Not surprisingly, when Marble was indicted and tried for bank robbery, his appointed counsel urged him to plead not guilty by reason of insanity. Marble resisted, thinking (for bizarre reasons not relevant here) that a jury would find him innocent. Again not surprisingly, Marble's competence to stand trial was drawn into question. His appointed attorney also raised the possibility that the court should impose an insanity defense, and the district court appointed *amicus* counsel to make the case for *sua sponte*[3] imposition of the insanity defense.

Following a hearing at which medical experts testified, the court found Marble competent to stand trial. Marble's lucidity, it seems, varies according to the consistency with which he takes his prescribed medication. He had been remiss for several months before the robbery, but was regularly and adequately medicated by the time of trial. Because Marble's preferences and intentions respecting the insanity defense were unclear, however, the district court bifurcated the trial, thus postponing until the case was resolved on the merits both consideration of Marble's choice not to plead insanity and the question of his competence to make that choice.

After the jury had convicted Marble of bank robbery, the district court determined that Marble was competent to waive the insanity defense. Marble indicated that he did not want to plead insanity because he would rather receive

> *Marble indicated that he did not want to plead insanity because he would rather receive a definite sentence to an institution for the criminally insane than face an indefinite civil commitment.*

a definite sentence to an institution for the criminally insane than face an indefinite civil commitment. The court, remarking that Marble stated his choice "in a very clear-eyed, straight up way," declined to impose the insanity defense against the defendant's will. Instead the district court

---

[3] *sua sponte.* Upon the court's own initiative.

ordered *amicus* counsel to appeal the court's refusal to impose the defense, and so the case comes here.

This circuit allows, and in theory may sometimes require, the district court to impose the defense of insanity over the objection of a defendant who is competent at the time of trial. Marble contends that the district court in this case abused its discretion by failing to impose that defense, or at the least by failing to conduct a more comprehensive hearing on the question whether to impose it.

In *Whalem v. United States*, the leading case in the field, this court explained the rationale for requiring the district court to raise the issue of insanity on its own motion: "If a man is insane in the eyes of the law, he is blameless in the eyes of society and is not subject to punishment in the criminal courts. The trial judge must uphold this structural foundation by refusing to allow the conviction of an obviously mentally irresponsible defendant, and when there is sufficient question as to a defendant's mental responsibility at the time of the crime, that issue must become part of the case." The court continued, "In the pursuit of justice, a trial judge must have the discretion to impose an unwanted defense on a defendant and the consequent additional burden of proof on the Government prosecutor." The district court might abuse that discretion by failing to impose the defense where "a combination of factors requires the trial judge to inject the insanity issue."

Early cases applying *Whalem* emphasized the discretionary nature of the court's decision whether to impose the insanity defense. Although in the 25 years since *Whalem* we have never reversed a district court's exercise of that discretion, we did once warn that "a defendant who has a substantial insanity defense may decide to waive that defense, but if the trial court failed to raise the defense *sua sponte*, then the defendant has a ground for appellate reversal on the basis of *Whalem*" (*United States v. Wright*).

In *United States v. Robertson*, the court laid down specific procedures to be followed by the district court when a defendant declines to raise the insanity defense although there is "sufficient question" of mental responsibility to go to the jury. We required the district court to "insure that he hear evidence supporting as well as opposing the imposition of an insanity defense," and suggested that "the appointment and participation of *amicus* counsel may well be the only way to elicit such evidence." Although the district court "is of course not bound to adopt in whole or in part the views of any expert," the trial judge was directed to "conduct on the record a thorough exploration of the differing views of the experts and in addition set forth in reasonable detail the reasons for his own ultimate determination."

No other federal court of appeals has imposed a duty upon the district court to raise the insanity defense; indeed, only a few have even considered the issue. Members of this court have long recognized the "troubling questions" raised by the imposition of the insanity defense over the objection of a defendant who is competent to stand trial. Developments in the law required us to revisit those troubling questions; further development since then prompts us yet again to reconsider the rationale for the rule of *Whalem*.

The Supreme Court has held that the Constitution permits a trial court to accept a defendant's guilty plea although the defendant simultaneously protests his innocence of the crime charged (*North Carolina v. Alford*). The Court rejected the view that our law only authorizes a conviction where guilt is shown. A trial court has discretion to refuse a defendant's guilty plea, or to accept it and thereby to honor his strategic choice to acquiesce in a determinate criminal penalty. The Court has also held that the Sixth Amendment[4] guarantees a defendant the right to conduct his own defense (*Faretta v. California*). In so doing the Court reaffirmed the "nearly universal conviction that forcing a lawyer upon an unwilling defendant is contrary to his basic right to defend himself if he truly wants to do so." The Court explained that "the Sixth Amendment does not provide merely that a defense shall be made for the accused; it grants to the accused personally the right to make his defense."

The *Whalem* line of cases is in substantial tension with both *Alford* and *Faretta* insofar as it precludes a district court from simply deferring to the choice of a competent defendant not to plead insanity, and may at times require the court to override that choice. *Alford* stands clearly for the proposition that a court may defer to a defendant's strategic choice to accept criminal responsibility even if his actual culpability is neither proven nor admitted. This seriously undermines the *Whalem* rationale that the law does not countenance the punishment of a person whose crime has been proved beyond a reasonable doubt but whose mental responsibility (although not denied) is objectively in doubt.

Furthermore, to impose a particular defense upon an accused, in essence to force him to affirm that he is insane, makes not only appointed counsel but the defendant himself "an organ of the State. Unless the accused has acquiesced, the defense presented is not the defense guaranteed him by the Constitution, for, in a very real sense, it is not his defense" (*Faretta*).

---

[4] See Appendix B (pp. 291-292).

Nonetheless, this court refused to modify the rule of *Whalem* in light of *Alford* and *Faretta*, because "neither case involved an insanity plea." Echoing *Whalem*, we maintained that the issue of a defendant's sanity calls into question "the very capacity of our legal system to assign blame" (*Wright*).

After we had adhered to *Whalem* in *Wright*, the Insanity Defense Reform Act of 1984 made insanity an affirmative defense in the federal courts. In both *Whalem* and *Wright*, however, the court had expressed and to a significant degree rested upon the view that insanity is fundamentally different from other defensive pleas—a view that was more compelling when the Government was required to prove beyond a reasonable doubt the defendant's mental responsibility for his crimes. In holding that a defendant "may not, in a proper case, prevent the court from injecting the issue of insanity," the *Whalem* court had relied solely upon *Overholser v. Lynch*. In *Lynch* we reversed a district court's grant of habeas corpus relief in a case in which the trial court had (1) refused to allow the competent defendant, assisted by counsel, to plead guilty, (2) admitted testimony of the defendant's mental condition at the time of the offense, over his objection, and (3) ultimately found the defendant not guilty by reason of insanity.

This court approved the trial court's handling of the case, saying that: "The cases establish almost a positive duty on the part of a trial judge not to impose a criminal sentence on a mentally ill person. The decision to plead guilty and forgo an insanity defense was one which the defendant and his counsel did not have an absolute right to make." Our conclusion rested squarely upon the premise that "insanity is not strictly an affirmative defense and can be raised by either the court or the prosecution," and upon

> **Convicting the competent mentally ill criminal is no longer "wrong" in the judgment of the Congress—nor, we infer, of the public it represents.**

the moral judgment that "imprisonment was wrong in the case of a mentally ill person." The IDRA stripped away those underpinnings of *Lynch*, and hence of the only authority supporting *Whalem*. As an affirmative defense, the insanity issue no longer "imposes an additional burden of proof on the Government prosecutor" (*Whalem*). Convicting the competent mentally ill criminal is no longer "wrong" in the judgment of the Congress—nor, we infer, of the public it represents. Instead of excusing the competent mentally ill from criminal liability, the Congress has now provided standards to govern their confinement and treatment, so that "imprisonment of a mentally ill person" is not the only alternative to acquittal by reason of insanity. The defense of insanity is available only to a person able to prove by clear and convincing evidence his inability to appreciate the nature and quality or the wrongfulness of his acts, and that such inability resulted from a "severe" mental disorder.

Now that the Congress has undercut both the technical and the policy bases for *Lynch* and *Whalem*, the reasoning in *Wright* cannot stand; we can no longer distinguish the decision not to plead insanity from other aspects of a defendant's right, established in *Faretta*, to direct his own defense. Moreover, unlike *Faretta*, the *Whalem* line of cases does not rest upon a constitutional ground, cf. *Leland v. Oregon*. The IDRA reflects a more authoritative social judgment, and one that squarely contradicts the judicial predilections underlying *Whalem*. Thus we are constrained to conclude that the *Whalem* line of cases has become a "victim of the shifting sands" of statute and case law. Guided by the clear policy of the IDRA to hold criminally responsible all but the most patently insane offenders, and the Supreme Court's deference, expressed in *Faretta* and *Alford*, to a competent defendant's strategic decisions, we hold that a district court must allow a competent defendant to accept responsibility for a crime committed when he may have been suffering from a mental disease. Insofar as they hold to the contrary, *Whalem* and its progeny are overruled.

The ultimate effect of the *Whalem-Robertson* doctrine has perhaps been slight: this court has never reversed a district court's exercise of the discretion it allows on the question whether to impose an insanity defense. As this case illustrates, however, *Whalem* may require the district court to explore complex, delicate, and disputed issues of fact—a diversion that can no longer be justified in light of the repudiation, by the Congress and the Supreme Court, of the premises underlying that effort.

When a defendant can make no clear choice for or against raising the defense, and the evidence suggests that the defense is viable, it might then be appropriate for the court to exercise its discretion to instruct the jury *sua sponte*. We need not, however, speculate about what to do when the defendant cannot make a choice. It is sufficient for the present case, and we hold, that a district court must honor the choice of a competent defendant not to raise the insanity defense.

> **The district court in this case was under no duty to impose the insanity defense over Marble's competent objection.**

Because the district court in this case was under no duty to impose the insanity defense over Marble's competent objection, it did not abuse its discretion, and the judgment is affirmed.

United States v. Edwards

819 F.2d 262 (1987)

Facts

Roland Edwards pled not guilty by reason of insanity for a bank robbery in Naples, Florida. Dr. Vilasuso testified for the defense, stating that Edwards was "off the wall" and probably suffered from manic-depressive illness. Dr. Jaslow, testifying for the prosecution in rebuttal, stated that Edwards's actions were reasonably well controlled and goal directed, and he was not in "an active manic state" at the time of the robbery. He explained that Edwards was experiencing financial problems with the IRS at the time of the robbery. He was asked if Edwards's feelings were understandable, given his problems. A defense objection to the question was overruled. Dr. Jaslow replied that Edwards's feelings were quite understandable in the circumstances. The jury found Edwards guilty, and he appealed, claiming that the District Court erred in allowing Dr. Jaslow's response to that question.

Issue

Did the testimony of the government witness violate Rule 704(b) (part of the Insanity Defense Reform Act) of the Federal Rules of Evidence, by expressing an opinion concerning the ultimate issue?

Holding

No.

Analysis

The Court, citing the congressional record concerning the Insanity Defense Reform Act, stated that Congress did not intend "to limit the flow of diagnostic and clinical information." They held that Dr. Jaslow's testimony offered no conclusions about Edwards but simply "that people who are not insane can nevertheless become frantic over a financial crisis." They also cited, as would later the Eighth Circuit Court of Appeals (see *United States v. Dubray*), Congress's intent: "Psychiatrists, of course, must be permitted to testify fully about the defendant's diagnosis, mental state and motivation (in clinical and commonsense terms) at the time of the alleged act so as to permit the jury or judge to reach the ultimate conclusion about which they and only they are expert."

Edited Excerpts[1]

Opinion by Vance

Roland Edwards was charged with unarmed bank robbery. He pleaded not guilty by reason of insanity. After a two day trial, a jury returned a verdict of guilty. Edwards appeals, claiming that the district court allowed improper psychiatric testimony. He argues that the district court erred in permitting a government witness to give opinion testimony in violation of Federal Rules of Evidence 704(b), [which] provides:

"No expert witness testifying with respect to the mental state or condition of a defendant in a criminal case may state an opinion or inference as to whether the defendant did or did not have the mental state or condition constituting an element of the crime charged or of a defense

> **Ultimate issues are matters for the trier of fact alone.**

thereto. Such ultimate issues are matters for the trier of fact alone."

We affirm.

On April 30, 1984, Edwards entered a bank in Naples, Florida and handed a teller a note demanding that she place all "twenties, fifties, and hundreds" in a bank bag. The note was handwritten and legible. Edwards told the teller that he had worked in a bank, "knew what he was doing," and warned her "not to do anything." Edwards carried a vinyl zipper bag which contained a bulky L-shaped object. Throughout the robbery, he kept his right hand inside the bag, handling the object in such a way that the teller thought it was a gun. Edwards left the bank with $2,040. He sprinted to a pick-up truck and sped away.

A bystander thought he saw the name "Edwards Construction" on the side of the getaway vehicle. Shortly after the robbery, sheriff's deputies located Edwards' ex-wife. She contacted Edwards using a beeper that he carried. Edwards returned her call, and at his ex-wife's urging, Edwards admitted that he had "robbed a bank."

At trial Edwards did not contest his role in the bank robbery, but argued that he was insane at the time that he committed the offense. Edwards' ex-wife and an old friend testified that they believed Edwards to be incapable of criminal activity. The crux of the defense case, however,

---

[1] Readers are advised to quote only from the original published cases. See pages vi and vii.

was the testimony of Doctor Adolfo Vilasuso, a board-certified psychiatrist. Doctor Vilasuso examined Edwards approximately six times during October 1985, and continued seeing Edwards once or twice a week up to the date of trial in February 1986. Doctor Vilasuso noted that Edwards had endured a difficult past and stated that he thought Edwards was "off the wall." Doctor Vilasuso testified that he had a "very, very strong suspicion" that Edwards suffered from "manic-depressive" illness during April 1984. The government countered with the rebuttal testimony of Doctor Albert Jaslow, another psychiatrist. Doctor Jaslow concluded from Edwards' description of events that Edwards was not in "an active manic state" at the time of the robbery because Edwards' actions were reasonably well controlled and goal directed.

The testimony at issue concerns Doctor Jaslow's analysis of Edwards' frustration with his financial problems at the time of the robbery:

Q (by Prosecutor): What sort of things were going on that would have depressed him?

A (by Doctor Jaslow): His inability to come to grips with his financial problems; inability to handle the relationship with the I.R.S., who were after him and who were not permitting him to, according to him, of course, to settle down sufficiently so he could gain enough monies to take care of the financial problems and so on. These were bothering him tremendously, of course.

Q: Were these feelings understandable, in your opinion?

Defense Counsel: Objection. It's improper. That's not a proper question for a doctor.

The Court: Overruled.

A: Under the circumstances of the responsibilities, the problems that he had, it was quite understandable. He would be disturbed; it was quite understandable he would be upset. It's quite understandable he would be frantically trying to find ways to modify his situation so he could get on with his life.

Edwards contends that the trial court erred in allowing this testimony because it contained a psychiatrist's opinion concerning his sanity, the ultimate issue at trial. We disagree.

"In resolving the complex issue of criminal responsibility, it is of critical importance that the defendant's entire relevant symptomatology be brought before the jury and explained" (*Gordon v. United States*). It has long been the position of our court that this is the only way a jury may become sufficiently informed so as to make a determination of a defendant's legal sanity. This was also the attitude of Congress when it passed Rule 704(b): "Psychiatrists, of course, must be permitted to testify fully about the defendant's diagnosis, mental state and motivation (in clinical and commonsense terms) at the time of the alleged act so as to permit the jury or judge to reach the ultimate conclusion about which they and only they are expert."

> **Psychiatrists must be permitted to testify fully about the defendant's diagnosis, mental state and motivation at the time of the alleged act.**

Congress did not enact Rule 704(b) so as to limit the flow of diagnostic and clinical information. Every actual fact concerning the defendant's mental condition is still as admissible after the enactment of Rule 704(b) as it was before. Rather, the Rule "changes the style of question and answer that can be used to establish both the offense and the defense thereto." The prohibition is directed at a narrowly and precisely defined evil: When, however, "ultimate issue" questions are formulated by the law and put to the expert witness who must then say "yea" or "nay," then the expert witness is

> **[The expert] no longer addresses medical concepts but instead must infer or intuit what is in fact unspeakable, namely, the probable relationship between medical concepts and legal or moral constructs such as free will.**

required to make a leap in logic. He no longer addresses himself to medical concepts but instead must infer or intuit what is in fact unspeakable, namely, the probable relationship between medical concepts and legal or moral constructs such as free will. These impermissible leaps in logic made by expert witnesses confuse the jury.

Accordingly, Rule 704(b) forbids only "conclusions as to the ultimate legal issue to be found by the trier of fact." The ultimate legal issue at Edwards' trial was whether Edwards "lacked substantial capacity either to appreciate the wrongfulness of his conduct or to conform his conduct to the requirements of law." In fact, the challenged statements offer no conclusions at all about Edwards. Doctor Jaslow was simply observing that people who are not insane can nevertheless become frantic over a financial crisis.

The prosecution placed Doctor Jaslow on the stand to dispute Doctor Vilasuso's diagnosis. Using a common sense generalization, Doctor Jaslow explained why the defendant's behavior—his frantic efforts to pay bills, his manifestations of energy, his lack of sleep, and his feelings of depression—did not necessarily indicate an active manic state. We think that the doctor played exactly the kind of role which Congress contemplated for the expert witness: It is clear that the psychiatrist's first obligation and expertise in the courtroom is to "do psychiatry," i.e., to present medical information and opinion about the defendant's mental state and motivation and to explain in detail the reason for his medical-psychiatric conclusions.

We conclude that the district court committed no error in permitting this testimony.

Affirmed.

Summary

A number of cases (*Whalem, Frendak v. United States, Marble, Alford*, and *Faretta*) are well worth reading together to gain an appreciation of how the courts construe defendants potentially making unwise decisions about their defense. We recall from *Pike* a reference to old English law that a person could not attempt to void a contract on his own testimony that he was insane when he made the contract. The argument was that "if he were insane, he would not know it." We should not be surprised when defendants are reluctant to claim that they have a mental disorder, even when it might exculpate them. *Frendak*, in particular, carefully analyzes the pros and cons to the defendant of an insanity defense. Within the federal jurisdictions, the Insanity Defense Reform Act (IDRA) resolved the problems faced in *Whalem* and *Frendak*; the IDRA took away the opportunity of the judge to interject an insanity defense over the objection of a competent defendant: in federal jurisdictions, the insanity defense is an affirmative defense—it has to be initiated by the defendant.

The Federal Rules of Evidence (FRE) limit the testimony by experts regarding ultimate issues only in the case of criminal responsibility. In every other area of expertise, the FRE allows experts to give an opinion regarding ultimate issues. There are many good reasons to resist giving ultimate opinions even where allowed, and *Edwards* provides a process for providing meaningful testimony without taking on the role of decision maker. Consistent with *McDonald*, mental health experts serve best when they speak to the issues about which they have specialized knowledge. Within the domain of insanity evaluations, mental health experts contribute useful information when they speak about a defendant's "diagnosis, mental state, and motivation" at the time of the offense. Any jurisdiction then has sufficient information to apply whichever of the various standards regarding insanity it deems appropriate.

Appendices

Appendix A: Legal Citations

Appendix B: Relevant Clauses and
Amendments of the
United States
Constitution

Appendix A

Legal Citations

Addington v. Texas, 441 U.S. 418 (1979)

Ake v. Oklahoma, 470 U.S. 68 (1985)

Baxstrom v. Herold, 383 U.S. 107 (1966)

Blocker v. United States, 288 F.2d 853 (1961)

Carter v. United States, 252 F.2d 608 (1957)

Clark v. Arizona, 548 U.S. ___ (2006)

Davis v. United States, 160 U.S. 469 (1895)

Dixon v. Jacobs, 427 F.2d 589 (1970)

Drope v. Missouri, 420 U.S. 302 (1975)

Durham v. United States, 214 F.2d 862 (1954)

Faretta v. California, 422 U.S. 806 (1975)

Finger v. Nevada, 27 P.3d 66 (2001)

Foucha v. Louisiana, 504 U.S. 71 (1992)

Frendak v. United States, 408 A.2d 364 (1979)

Gordon v. United States, 404 U.S. 828 (1971)

Greenwood v. United States, 350 U.S. 366 (1956)

Holloway v. United States, 148 F.2d 665 (1945)

Hopps v. People, 31 Ill. 385

Humphrey v. Cady, 405 U.S. 504 (1972)

In re Rosenfield, 157 F.Supp. 18 (1957)

In re Winship, 397 U.S. 358 (1970)

Jackson v. Indiana, 406 U.S. 715 (1972)

Jones v. United States, 463 U.S. 354 (1983)

Leland v. Oregon, 343 U.S. 790 (1952)

Lyles v. United States, 254 F.2d 275 (1957)

Lynch v. Overholser, 369 U.S. 705 (1962)

Marble v. United States, 940 F.2d 1543 (1991)

McDonald v. United States, 312 F.2d 874 (1962)

McNeil v. Director, Patuxent Institution, 407 U.S. 245 (1972)

Morissette v. United States, 342 U.S. 246 (1952)

North Carolina v. Alford, 400 U.S. 25 (1970)

O'Connor v. Donaldson, 422 U.S. 563 (1975)

Overholser v. Lynch, 288 F.2d 388 (1961)

Overholser v. O'Beirne, 302 F.2d 852 (1961)

Parham v. J. R., 442 U.S. 584 (1979)

Parsons v. State, 2 So. 854 (1886)

Patterson v. New York, 432 U.S. 197 (1977)

Penry v. Lynaugh, 492 U.S. 302 (1989)

People v. Schmidt, 110 N.E. 945 (1915)

Powell v. Florida, 579 F.2d 324 (1978)

Powell v. Texas, 392 U.S. 514 (1968)

Queen v. M'Naghten, 10 Clark & F.200, 2 Eng. Rep. 718 (H.L. 1843)

Regents of University of Michigan v. Ewing, 474 U.S. 214 (1985)

Rex v. Arnold, 16 How.St.Tr. 695 (1724)

Rex v. Hadfield, 27 How.St.Tr. 1282 (1800)

Robinson v. California, 370 U.S. 660 (1962)

Sauer v. United States, 241 F.2d 640 (1957)

Smith v. United States, 36 F.2d 548 (1929)

State v. Felter, 25 Iowa 67

State v. Herrera, 895 P.2d 359 (Utah 1995)

State v. Korell, 690 P.2d 992 (Montana 1984)

State v. Lewis, 22 P. 241 (1889)

State v. Mott, 931 P.2d 1046 (1997)

State v. Pike, 49 N.H. 399 (1870)

State v. Searcy, 798 P.2d 914 (Idaho 1990)

Tatum v. United States, 190 F.2d 612 (1951)

Taylor v. United States, 7 App.D.C. 27 (1895)

United States v. Brawner, 471 F.2d 969 (1972)

United States v. Currens, 290 F.2d 751 (1961)

United States v. Dubray, 854 F.2d 1099 (1988)

United States v. Edwards, 819 F.2d 262 (1987)

United States v. Guiteau, 10 F. 161 (1882)

United States v. Lee, 15 D.C. (4 Mackey), 489 (1886)

United States v. McGraw, 515 F.2d 758 (1975)

United States v. Ming Sen Shiue, 650 F.2d 919 (1981)

United States v. Robertson, 507 F.2d 1148 (1974)

United States v. Salerno, 481 U.S. 739 (1987)

United States v. Segna, 555 F.2d 226 (1977)

United States v. Sullivan, 544 F.2d 1052 (1976)

United States v. Wright, 627 F.2d 1300 (1980)

Vitek v. Jones, 445 U.S. 480 (1980)

Wade v. United States, 426 F.2d 64 (1970)

Washington v. Harper, 494 U.S. 210 (1990)

Washington v. United States, 390 F.2d 444 (1967)

Whalem v. United States, 346 F.2d 812 (1965)

Williams v. United States, 312 F.2d 862 (1962)

Youngberg v. Romeo, 457 U.S. 307 (1982)

Zinermon v. Burch, 494 U.S. 113 (1990)

Appendix B

Relevant Clauses and Amendments of the United States Constitution

Amendment V. No person shall be held to answer for a capital, or otherwise infamous crime, unless on a presentment or indictment of a Grand Jury, except in cases arising in the land or naval forces, or in the Militia, when in actual service in time of War or public danger; nor shall any person be subject for the same offence to be twice put in jeopardy of life or limb; nor shall be compelled in any criminal case to be a witness against himself, nor be deprived of life, liberty, or property, without due process of law; nor shall private property be taken for public use, without just compensation.

Amendment VI. In all criminal prosecutions, the accused shall enjoy the right to a speedy and public trial, by an impartial jury of the State and district wherein the crime shall have been committed, which district shall have been previously ascertained by law, and to be informed of the nature and cause of the accusation; to be confronted with the witnesses against him; to have compulsory process for obtaining witnesses in his favor, and to have the Assistance of Counsel for his defense.

Amendment VIII. Excessive bail shall not be required, nor excessive fines imposed, nor cruel and unusual punishments inflicted.

Amendment XIV. *(Section 1).* All persons born or naturalized in the United States, and subject to the jurisdiction thereof, are citizens of the United States and of the State wherein they reside. No State shall make or enforce

any law which shall abridge the privileges or
immunities of citizens of the United States; nor shall
any State deprive any person of life, liberty, or
property, without due process of law; nor deny to
any person within its jurisdiction the equal protection
of the laws.

If You Found This Book Useful . . .

You might want to know more about our other titles.

If you would like to receive our latest catalog, please return this form:

Name: _____
(Please Print)

Address: _____

Address: _____

City/State/Zip: _____
This is ☐ home ☐ office

Telephone: (_____) _____

E-mail: _____

Fax: (_____) _____

I am a:

☐ Psychologist
☐ Psychiatrist
☐ Attorney
☐ Clinical Social Worker

☐ Mental Health Counselor
☐ Marriage and Family Therapist
☐ Not in Mental Health Field
☐ Other: _____

◆   ◆   ◆

Professional Resource Press
P.O. Box 15560
Sarasota, FL 34277-1560

Telephone: 800-443-3364
FAX: 941-343-9201
E-mail: orders@prpress.com
Website: http://www.prpress.com

ECR/3/07

Add A Colleague To Our Mailing List . . .

If you would like us to send our latest catalog to one of your colleagues, please return this form:

Name: _____
(Please Print)

Address: _____

Address: _____

City/State/Zip: _____
This is ❐ home ❐ office

Telephone: (_____)_____

E-mail: _____

Fax: (_____) _____

This person is a:

❐ Psychologist   ❐ Mental Health Counselor
❐ Psychiatrist   ❐ Marriage and Family Therapist
❐ Attorney   ❐ Not in Mental Health Field
❐ Clinical Social Worker   ❐ Other: _____

Name of person completing this form: _____

◆   ◆   ◆

Professional Resource Press
P.O. Box 15560
Sarasota, FL 34277-1560

Telephone: 800-443-3364
FAX: 941-343-9201
E-mail: orders@prpress.com
Website: http://www.prpress.com